LAW AND THE REGULATORS

Law and the Regulators

TONY PROSSER

CLARENDON PRESS · OXFORD
1997

Oxford University Press, Great Clarendon Street, Oxford OX2 6DP
Oxford New York
Athens Auckland Bangkok Bogota Bombay
Buenos Aires Calcutta Cape Town Dar es Salaam
Delhi Florence Hong Kong Istanbul Karachi
Kuala Lumpur Madras Madrid Melbourne
Mexico City Nairobi Paris Singapore
Taipei Tokyo Toronto Warsaw
and associated companies in
Berlin Ibadan

Oxford is a trade mark of Oxford University Press

Published in the United States
by Oxford University Press Inc., New York

British Library Cataloguing in Publication Data
Data available

Library of Congress Cataloging in Publication Data
Data available
ISBN 0–19–876391–3

1 3 5 7 9 10 8 6 4 2

Typeset by Hope Services (Abingdon) Ltd.
Printed in Great Britain
on acid-free paper by
Biddles Ltd., Guildford and King's Lynn

Preface

This book aims to contribute to the ever-growing debate about regulation in the United Kingdom, a debate largely stimulated by the creation of the new regulatory offices as part of the privatization of public utilities, but which has much older roots. It is written from the viewpoint of a public lawyer, and so it is not surprising that the central theme will be that of regulatory legitimacy; in a democracy, how can regulators justify exercising power with no direct democratic mandate? I hope to suggest that both substantive and procedural justifications can be found for this in any democracy, and moreover that they permit regulators to take decisions based on a variety of different rationales, including social rationales. They need not, and should not, confine themselves to attempting to mimic the outcomes likely to be produced by an efficiently operating market, though creating the conditions in which markets can operate is rightly one of their most important functions. Nor will regulation wither away; in important respects it has become more far-reaching and complex, and this will not necessarily change with the growth of competition in some previously regulated markets. These themes are developed through examining the law and practical operation of the five new utility regulators in telecommunications, gas, water, electricity, and rail and drawing on that of older regulators in aviation and broadcasting; I also suggest that overseas experience from the United States and Continental Europe has been unjustly neglected as source of regulatory lessons. I have tried to cover developments up to the end of 1996.

Inevitably there are areas of regulatory operation which have had to be given briefer treatment in this book than they merit. Thus there is little discussion of the role of the regulators in handling grievances or in determining individual disputes; the former has been well covered as part of an overall examination of grievance handling in the United Kingdom recently,[1] whilst the latter will merit separate treatment elsewhere. Rather the focus is on larger policy issues, such as price-setting which, though in form a dispute

[1] See Birkinshaw, P., *Grievances, Remedies and the State* (2nd edn., Sweet & Maxwell, London, 1995).

between the regulator and the regulated company, can have much wider implications for consumers, employees, and the economy as a whole; indeed, one of the procedural inadequacies of the legal requirements for some aspects of price control is to misrepresent the dispute as one between regulator and company only. Even in discussing these wider issues, I have not covered in detail techniques of self-regulation as they would merit separate treatment, as would the general operation of the competition authorities. Rather, my focus has been specifically on the major issues of regulation of utilities and related industries, and broader issues of regulation must await analysis elsewhere.

I have reason to be grateful to a large number of institutions and individuals who have assisted in writing this book. The most important was John Boyle who worked as research assistant with me for a year; his aid in gathering materials and discussing the economic issues involved was quite invaluable. I am also most grateful to the Faculty of Law and Financial Studies at the University of Glasgow for allowing me funds received for improving our research performance to employ him and for travel. Secondly, I must thank Professor Sabino Cassese at the Centro di Diritto Amministrativo at the University of Rome 'La Sapienza' for offering me a visiting fellowship there for a month in April–May 1996. I have used some Italian materials in Chapter 10, but the visit was most valuable in giving me the space to think through my ideas at a time when the book was taking shape. I would also like to thank the Society of Public Teachers of Law Academic Purposes Fund for assisting in funding a visit to the USA in the summer of 1996 to undertake interviewing.

A number of regulatory staff have been most helpful in agreeing to be interviewed, though of course the book does not necessarily reflect their views. I would like to mention particularly Christine Farnish at OFTEL, David Barnes at OFGAS, David Hauser at OFFER, and Roy Wardle at OFWAT. In the USA I was most generously helped by Louis Ceddia and Jean Lowe at the New York Public Service Commission, by Gary Siegel, Mark Nadel, and John Morabito in the Federal Communications Commission, and by Nettie Hoge and Eugene Coyle at Toward Utility Rate Normalization (TURN) in San Francisco; in Italy I was also granted a most useful interview with Avv. Giovanni Gentile, Direttore Centrale of the Direzione Affari Legali at ENEL. I am also grateful to John Turner for help with selecting relevant material from the United States and Stefaan Verhulst for comments on the broadcasting material. Finally, I thank Charlotte Villiers for all types of support and tolerance during the preparation of the work.

Table of Contents

Abbreviations

CAA	Civil Aviation Authority
DGFT	Director General of Fair Trading
FCC	Federal Communications Commission
ICSTIS	Independent Committee for the Supervision of Standards of Telephone Information Services
MMC	Monopolies and Mergers Commission
OFFER	Office of Electricity Regulation
OFGAS	Office of Gas Supply
OFWAT	Office of Water Services
OFT	Office of Fair Trading
OFTEL	Office of Telecommunications
ORR	Office of the Rail Regulator
REC	Regional Electricity Company

Table of Cases

Table of Statutes

European Community Legislation

1

What Should the Regulators Be Doing?

The concept of regulation has become central to debates about the running of industry in the United Kingdom in a way which would have been inconceivable only a few years ago. Until the 1980s regulation was little discussed, and in particular hardly any concern existed with designing institutions to undertake this task. Public ownership, it was assumed, was the main way of making key industries reflect the 'public interest' and of curbing their monopoly powers, and this left little room for explicitly working out the principles underlying the exercise of public power and how this exercise could be made accountable.

All this has changed, especially since the privatization of the utilities from 1984. This is, of course, in some ways paradoxical. These years have been characterized as those of the 'rolling back of the state', the passing of enterprises to the impersonal hand of the market rather than to public institutions reflecting some form of non-market principles. Yet in practice far more controversy has taken place over the role of regulators than was ever the case at the time of nationalization. This is only an apparent paradox, however; there are good reasons why these issues came out into the open after privatization. Distancing of the enterprises from government has brought the debate into the open and has required clearer consideration of why particular regulatory approaches have been adopted, and of accountability; we now have a real regulatory debate in the United Kingdom for the first time for many years.

Why the Regulation Debate?

It would be a mistake to suppose that discrete institutions for the regulation of private enterprise first arrived in the United Kingdom during the 1980s. Even in the sectors to be described in this book, the Civil Aviation Authority has a much longer history, as have the predecessors to the Independent Television Commission (the

Independent Television Authority and the Independent Broadcasting Authority). Transport was also a sector characterized by
regulatory institutions such as the Traffic Commissioners and the
Transport Tribunal, and more information on all these institutions
will be given in Chapter 2.

Nevertheless, after the Second World War nationalization
became the characteristic British means for importing public interest elements into the running of key industries. It is this which goes
a long way to explain the lack of debate about regulatory principles before the 1980s. On the one hand, there was never a single
clear rationale for the sort of regulation represented by public ownership, or indeed for what public ownership was to achieve.[1]
Indeed, once can trace a fundamental divide between the different
views on the purpose of nationalization. From the political left the
pre-eminent opinion was that the purpose of nationalization was to
permit the 'public control' of enterprises, and so would be characterized by the pursuit of policies which had social rather than economic justification. To quote a document from as late as 1986:

[a]s a criterion for how society's labour and resources should be used for
the benefit of the mass of the people, private profit is worse than useless.
. . . The common concept of efficiency does not make sense because it fails
to take account of the full economic and social effects of companies'
actions.[2]

This is to be contrasted with the view which appeared in the
Reports of the Select Committee on Nationalised Industries and in
a series of White Papers that the role of nationalization was to
increase economic efficiency through the employment of techniques
such as marginal cost pricing and appraisal of investment through
discounted cash flow; the industries were to be testbeds of economic, rather than social or political, principle.[3]

The key point for our purposes is, however, that the structures
adopted for nationalization never required a clear and public resolution of the conflict between different rationales for public ownership. The notoriously vague objectives given the industries, the lack
of any public forum for their analysis, and the continuing confu-

---

[1] See generally Prosser, T., *Nationalised Industries and Public Control* (Blackwell,
Oxford, 1986), esp. ch. 2.
[2] Campaign for Labour Party Democracy, *The Case for Public Ownership*
(Labour Party, London, 1986), 9, 17.
[3] See Prosser, n. 1 above, ch. 3.

sion of responsibilities between ministers and enterprises meant that any such conflict could be fudged; the sort of long-term vision which could have resulted in such a resolution was precisely what was lacking in policy towards the nationalized industries.[4]

This is what privatization changed. The separation of the enterprises from government and the creation of regulators operating at arm's length from ministers operated precisely to force the problems of regulatory rationale out into the open. The process was not, in fact peculiar to the United Kingdom and has been described neatly by the European Commission in proposals for the definition of universal service in the liberalization of telecommunications markets:

As long as telecommunications services were provided under direct State authority and as long as the [operating company], in dealing with users, benefited from certain legal immunities under national law, a definition in general terms, even though imprecise, of the notion of universal service could appear to have been sufficient.

As the traditional operators become increasingly independent and once the market is opened on the basis of free competition to new operators, it is necessary to determine the principles according to which the cost of universal service obligations can be shared amongst market participants. A clearer definition of universal service principles is vital to this process.[5]

This, then, is the explanation of the late development of the debate on regulation in the United Kingdom; the structures adopted for nationalization had never required a resolution of the problems of conflicting regulatory rationales, but privatization and the creation of new regulators flushed this question out into the open. Thus the problems debated are not necessarily due to deficiencies of the new regulators but may merely have been brought into the open for the first time.

This is not to say, however, that on privatization a satisfactory resolution of the problems was reached. What has occurred is that the debate over regulation has failed to address fundamental questions of why regulation takes place and what basic principles should be used by regulators; too often regulation has been seen as

---

[4] For the definitive, and damning, statement of the confusion see National Economic Development Office, *A Study of UK Nationalised Industries* (HMSO, London, 1976).

[5] EC Commission, *Developing Universal Service for Telecommunications in a Competitive Environment*, COM(93)159 final, 1993.

merely a political fight between regulators, consumers, regulated companies, and their shareholders. As we shall see, there are elements of the British arrangements which encourage the failure to engage in deeper analysis of regulation, but what this book will attempt to do is to examine, from the viewpoint of a lawyer interested in political economy, the principles which have been created or have emerged as the basis for regulatory interventions and the institutions and procedures through which they have been implemented in practice.

What is Regulation?

Defining regulation is by no means a simple matter. One recent commentator has pointed to at least five meanings of the term; another has pointed to important distinctions between usage in Europe and in the United States.[6] Definitions include, at the most general level, the act of controlling, directing, or governing according to a rule, principle, or system. This includes any conscious ordering of activity, and so has always been of fundamental importance in the United Kingdom (and indeed, in any social group). At the most specific extreme, regulation refers to the legal rules and other measures which express such command and control arrangements, contrasted with other forms of law such as criminal and contract law; given the relatively limited use of law in most areas of UK regulation this has not become an important British usage so far. It is thus already apparent that the definition of regulation is by no means a simple business, especially given the different levels of generality at which the term is used. Nevertheless, whilst not attempting the rigour of a formal definition, it is possible to extract a core conception which dominates most usage of the term in the current debates. This takes elements from usages between the extremes described above and consists of public interventions which affect the operation of markets through command and control, though one should be aware of the fact that command and control may be delegated through use of 'self-regulation'. The usage seems to correspond to the definitions used by many economists; a useful example which is broadly representative of the

---

[6] Daintith, T., *Encyclopedia of Comparative Law: vol XVII, Law, State and Economy* (Mohr, Tübingen, forthcoming), paras. 1–7: Majone, G., *Deregulation or Re-regulation* (Pinter, London, 1990), 7–8.

definitions in standard economics texts is that '[i]n its widest conception [regulation] is state intervention in the economic decisions of companies.'[7] This usage is also close to the sense used in popular debate and by the industries; to take one striking example, the Chairman's address at the Annual General Meeting of British Telecom in 1992 included the following:

Regrettably, the trend in regulation in the UK—and not just telecommunications—appears to be towards greater intervention in management, without a clearly expressed vision or set of long-term objectives.

   Regulators can be tempted to embark on a course of social engineering, or to tinker with operational matters in response to short-term political and media pressures. Paradoxically, there is a real danger that regulated privatised businesses may be subject to more state interference than they were as nationalised industries.[8]

The key point which must be emphasized about this core usage is that it contrasts the economic, or the working of markets, with the political, or regulation; the latter is seen as 'social engineering' based on non-economic goals and thus subject to suspicion as potentially arbitrary.

   This may be the core usage, but one of the main arguments of this book will be that, despite its importance in the literature and in debate, this usage is seriously inadequate as an account of what regulators do (or should do). Its inadequacy stems partly from the fact that it sees regulation as an external political constraint on markets, yet this is misleading for at least two reasons. Regulation is necessary for efficiency maximization through providing surrogates for market forces where natural monopoly elements exist in a business; a major role of the regulators has also been to *create* and to police markets where they would not arise or continue spontaneously. It will be appropriate to state now a major theme of this book which will be used to structure the following sectoral chapters. The regulation being considered involves three quite different tasks. The first is that of *regulating monopoly*, mimicking the effect of market forces through implementing controls on prices and on quality of service. The second is *regulation for competition*; creating the conditions for competition to exist and policing it to ensure that

[7] Foster, C. D., *Privatization, Public Ownership and the Regulation of Natural Monopoly* (Blackwell, Oxford, 1992), 186.
   [8] Quoted in Veljanovski, C., *The Future of Industry Regulation in the UK* (European Policy Forum, London, 1993), 23.

it continues to exist. Examples are fixing the conditions for the interconnection of competing but interdependent systems, scrutiny of trading practices, and, in a different sense, examining proposed takeovers and mergers. Thirdly, there is *social regulation* where the rationale is not primarily economic but is linked to notions of public service. Examples include ensuring the provision of universal service and some environmental regulation. Failure to separate adequately these different types of regulation has caused much confusion in current regulatory debate and, in particular, has led to an assumption that some types of regulation, especially social regulation, are illegitimate, or that, with the decline of natural monopoly, regulation can be replaced with self-regulating competition.

It should now be eminently clear that any attempt to provide an all-embracing definition of regulation at the outset would be unhelpful, both because of the variety of competing definitions at different levels of generality and the under-inclusive nature of those most commonly used. A more productive approach will be to examine the rationales or purposes of various forms of regulation, and especially to note the tensions between them as these are of considerable practical importance. The discussion will begin with a brief assessment of the types of rationales underlying recent development of regulatory institutions in the United Kingdom before discussing in more general and abstract terms possible regulatory rationales.

Regulatory Rationales and UK Utility Privatization

In discussion and analysis of regulatory issues the United Kingdom has long lagged far behind other nations in which regulation achieved a high profile much earlier, notably the United States. This was particularly so in matters of the legal techniques for regulation and for rendering regulation more accountable.[9] Thus it is all the more surprising that the British Government chose not to use this experience in designing regulatory institutions for the privatized utilities. At the time of the first privatization of a public utility, British Telecom, institutional design was uninfluenced by US experience (except perhaps through perceptions of regulation there as a model to be avoided at all costs); in the next utility

[9] See Graham, C., and Prosser, T., *Privatizing Public Enterprises* (Clarendon Press, Oxford, 1991), chs. 6–7, and Ch. 10 below.

privatization, that of British Gas, the Government effectively rejected recommendations from the Energy Select Committee that it study in depth the merits of the US system so as to provide lessons for the United Kingdom.[10]

The nearest thing to a statement of regulatory rationales on privatization was the first of the two reports which the Government commissioned from Professor Littlechild (later appointed Director General of Electricity Supply), that concerning regulation of the profitability of British Telecom.[11] This was the main source for the adoption of the price control formulae based on changes in the retail price index and efficiency gains by the utilities. According to the report, the primary purpose of regulation is to protect consumers; inefficiency, high costs, excess profits and high wages are only of significance in so far as they lead to higher consumer prices.[12] In this sense regulation is a second best as '[c]ompetition is indisputably the most effective means—perhaps ultimately the *only* effective means—of protecting consumers against market power. Regulation is essentially a means of preventing the worst excesses of monopoly; it is not a substitute for competition. It is a means of 'holding the fort' until competition arrives.'[13] It is thus clear that, at least for Littlechild, the rationale for regulation was an economic one rather than one of social engineering (consumer satisfaction being after all the ultimate goal of economic efficiency); it also anticipates the hypothesis which will be demonstrated later to the effect that much of the regulators' work has been to develop and police competitive markets rather than to restrict their operation, although the metaphor of 'holding the fort' suggests that this was envisaged as a temporary rather than a permanent phenomenon. Professor Littlechild also produced a second report on regulating the privatized water authorities.[14] This also stressed regulating monopoly in view of the limited opportunities for competition in the market for water services; here regulation was likely to be permanent rather than temporary, as in telecommunications. This second report placed greater stress on the importance of quality standards, of the opportunities for 'yardstick competition'

---

[10] Further details will be given in Ch. 2 below.
[11] Littlechild, S., *Regulation of British Telecommunications' Profitability* (Department of Trade and Industry, London, 1984).
[12] *Ibid.* para. 4.6.   [13] *Ibid.* para. 4.11.
[14] Littlechild, S., *Economic Regulation of Privatized Water Authorities* (Department of the Environment, London, 1986).

comparing the performance of each company, and of the role of the capital markets in securing efficient management of the industry.

Important as the two Littlechild Reports were as the closest thing we have to a statement of the rationale for UK utilities regulation, they are of very limited usefulness as a statement of regulatory philosophy for the privatized utilities. First, as we shall see in a moment, the legal duties imposed on the regulators depart in important ways from this economics-based model which underlay the report. Secondly, the report seriously underestimated the complexity of the regulatory task. The image of 'holding the fort' until the arrival of competition suggests a conception of regulation as an essentially temporary phenomenon; yet in practice it is well established as a permanent feature of the landscape of public utilities. Indeed, as privatization has succeeded privatization regulatory arrangements have become increasingly complicated and demanding. Secondly, the stress is very much on regulating monopoly; although regulation for competition is acknowledged in the telecommunications report, the assumption is that growing competition will itself make regulation unnecessary; nor is there any real acceptance of the potential role of social regulation, public subsidy being preferred instead.[15] Thirdly, even as regards price control of monopoly, the reports envisage a more static and mechanical model of price control than that which has occurred in practice. The most important product of the reports was the adoption of the RPI–X model of price control by which selected prices were to be limited by reference to the rate of inflation minus a sum representing feasible efficiency gains. A major rationale for the adoption of this formula was the avoidance of the discretionary judgements characteristic of US regulation based on assessing an acceptable rate of return; the report envisaged that the figure set be revised only each five years or thereabouts, and that it would have the advantage that the regulator 'does not have to make any judgements or calculations with respect to capital, allocation of costs, rates of return, future movements of costs and demand, desirable performance, etc.'.[16] Yet, as we shall see, in practice renegotiation of the price control figure has had to be more frequent and has

---

[15] *Ibid.* paras. 4.14, 14.7–8.
[16] *Ibid.* paras. 13.14, 13.20.

involved precisely the sort of judgements which it was hoped the formula would make unnecessary.

In this matter of price control review, as well as in other aspects of the regulation of public utilities, the Littlechild Reports offer virtually no guidance on the principles which regulators should use in approaching their tasks. In fact, what has occurred is that this has been left to the regulators themselves on the basis of personalized decisions determining the practical resolution of problems. Indeed, given the lack of a clearer rationale the regulatory system has inevitably assumed what is probably its most criticized characteristic in the post-privatization United Kingdom; highly personalized regulation. In almost every case where new regulatory arrangements have been created on privatization, powers have been vested in an individual director-general assisted by an office but with legal responsibility vested in him or her alone; a model based on the Director General of Fair Trading. This contrasts with both the earlier regulatory arrangements such as those in civil aviation and in broadcasting, and the regulatory commissions of the United States; a further contrast is that the legal controls over the regulators are far more restricted, both on procedure and substance, than is the case across the Atlantic. This personalized system of regulation reflects the traditionally highly personalized traditions of government in the United Kingdom where, as Kenneth Dyson has put it, '[t]he hitching of monarchical prerogatives on to parliamentarianism, combined with ministerial responsibility, meant that governments became personified in the "over-life-size" role of ministers.'[17] However, the regulators are not, of course, subject even to the semblance of responsibility to Parliament which attaches to ministers. The assumption with the new regulators seems to be that appointing an acceptable personality as regulator will ensure the right result. The Government may have been fortunate in that it has appointed individuals of high quality, and personalized regulation may have had advantages in facilitating a strong and single-minded approach in each sector from the outset, but this highly personalized nature of regulation hardly encourages the development of consistent regulatory philosophies across sectors or through time.

No adequate statement of regulatory rationales has thus emerged for regulation in the United Kingdom. In a moment we shall

---

[17] Dyson, K., *The State Tradition in Western Europe* (Martin Robertson, Oxford, 1980), 40–1.

examine the degree to which the legal provisions applying to the regulators provide further guidance towards such rationales. First, however, it is important to stress that neither the creation of regulatory institutions nor the activity of regulation exists in a vacuum. A number of different rationales for regulation have already been identified in other times and other nations, and it is necessary to examine and classify them before dealing in more detail with UK experience.

Why Regulation?

It is important for me to clarify at the outset the central concern of this section, which will also be fundamental to the book as a whole. It is *not* to analyse the motives which account for the introduction of regulation by politicians and bureaucrats. The debate between the public interest and public choice schools is of course a current and influential one, if often appearing remarkably sterile.[18] However, as we shall see later, the motives for regulating, as well as being irreducibly mixed, do not necessary spell out the rationales to be employed by regulators, for these have to be gathered from the interpretation of materials which do not necessarily reflect legislators' motives; for otherwise it would be impossible to handle the unforeseen, and it is the unforeseen that dominates the current work of the utilities regulators.[19] In this section I shall point to the range of possible rationales available from various accounts of regulation in terms of function rather than motives; this will then be followed by an analysis of legal provisions to decide how the possible regulatory rationales have been limited through norms applying to regulators in the United Kingdom.[20]

The starting point for an analysis of regulatory rationales is to make clear that they may arise from two different types of argument which I will characterize (with admitted over-simplification)

---

[18] For summaries of what is now a very extensive literature see Foster, n. 7 above, ch. 11 and Ogus, A., *Regulation: Legal Form and Economic Theory* (Clarendon Press, Oxford, 1994), ch. 4.

[19] Cf. Sunstein, C., *After the Rights Revolution: Reconceiving the Regulatory State* (Harvard, Cambridge, Mass., 1990), 47–8, 127–37.

[20] For comprehensive accounts of different regulatory rationales see e.g. Breyer, S., *Regulation and its Reform* (Harvard, Cambridge, Mass., 1982), pp. 15–35; Ogus, n. 18 above, ch. 3; Sunstein, n. 19 above, chs. 1–2.

as economic and social.[21] By economic arguments I mean those in which the aim is the maximization of economic efficiency. The justification for such regulation is first the existence of monopoly power; where it is not possible to introduce effective competition, or to introduce it immediately, regulation can act as a surrogate for the market forces which are unable to operate and so increase allocative efficiency.[22] This has obvious application to the privatized utilities in the United Kingdom which do retain considerable monopoly elements in their markets, especially those for domestic consumers; as we have seen the first, and initially dominant, type of regulation applying to them was concerned precisely to regulate monopoly through mimicking competition by means of price and quality controls. Moreover, this rationale can also be used to support the second type of regulation, regulation for competition, through seeking to limit the conditions in which monopoly power can arise and so distort allocative efficiency.

Indeed, Sir Christopher Foster has argued in what is the best account of British regulation to emerge so far, that *the* task of the utility regulators is to apply economic criteria with the goal of increasing efficiency in the sense of Pareto efficiency with its goal of a state of the economy in which no reallocation of resources could make anyone better off without making someone else worse off.[23] This approach retains an important role for the regulator (although regulation is a second best to competition), for in the case of natural monopolies profit maximization by the firm does not correspond to efficiency maximization.[24] However, through providing a clear criterion for the exercise of the regulator's powers, efficiency maximization provides a means by which the regulator's decisions can be non-arbitrary; the technical expertise of the economic regulator becomes his or her source of legitimacy. By contrast, social considerations are to be left to government with its democratic mandate; for the regulator to mix the two 'inevitably leads to an incoherence where it becomes progressively harder for a regulator to defend what he is doing without contradiction'.[25]

---

[21] Cf. Ogus, n. 18 above.

[22] For summaries see Breyer, n. 20 above, 15–19 and Ogus, n. 18 above, 30–3.

[23] For a simple introduction to the concept of Pareto efficiency see e.g. Sloman, J., *Economics* (2nd edn., Harvester Wheatsheaf, Hemel Hempstead, 1994), sec. 11.1.

[24] Foster, n. 7 above, esp. ch. 9.   [25] *Ibid.* 7.

Much of this book will examine whether this view can be an adequate guide for the utility regulators and the implications will be further assessed in later chapters. It should also be noted here that other economic rationales for regulation exist. The most familiar is the correction of spillover costs, or externalities, where the unregulated price of an item does not reflect the true cost to society of producing that item; this is part of a larger category of public goods characterized by degrees of market failure.[26] In this case also the justification is that regulation effects an allocation of resources which better avoids economic waste. The classic example is of course that of pollution costs, which would otherwise not be fully reflected in the costs of the production process but be borne by the public and so not properly transmitted as signals to producers; the alternative of private bargaining between polluters and victims which could otherwise reallocate costs may be less effective than regulation because of the transaction costs involved. Though the externalities rationale for regulation has played a major role in the literature and has been an important practical justification for regulation in areas such as the environment and health and safety, it will play a lesser role in this book than the regulation of natural monopoly because of the nature of the enterprises around which the regulation being examined here is centred. In one case, that of water and sewerage, environmental issues have played a major role, but fully to discuss environmental regulation would require a separate book. This does not exhaust the range of economic arguments for regulation; another example is that of correcting lack of sufficient information to permit consumers to make rationale choices within competitive markets.[27] This is of course one of the major justifications of regulation of the market for financial services in which there are very clear incentives for the suppression of information; in this sense this rationale is allied to the prevention of fraud but is also important in broader consumer protection. It plays a role in the work of the regulators examined in this book, for example in the issuing of quality standards and publication of performance against them. A further controversial question has been that of the access to information by the regulators themselves.

The rationales for regulation listed here as economics-based do not form an exhaustive list of such rationales, but should give some

---

[26] For summaries see Breyer, n. 20 above, 23–6; Ogus, n. 18 above, 33–8.

[27] Again, see Breyer, n. 20 above, 26–8 and Ogus, n. 18 above, 38–41.

flavour of the most important ones. It should be noted that these rationales need not have a theoretical base derived from exclusively economic reasoning; for example the arguments based on economic efficiency can also be justified by wider, rights-based, non-utilitarian arguments. One example would be Dworkin's concept of a right to equal respect and concern, which may both justify the employment of economic efficiency-based arguments on the basis that markets treat people as equals by requiring them to take responsibility for the true costs of their actions, and yet justify regulatory interventions in other circumstances.[28] This brings us to other rationales for regulation which have their foundation not in economic but in social reasoning.

There is a large number of such non-economic reasons for regulation.[29] Some involve large matters of governmental policy, some are designed more particularly to benefit consumers. The former category contains an extremely varied range of obligations, including, for example, the requirement which existed for a number of years after privatization that electricity generation from nuclear and renewable sources be funded by a levy on all consumers,[30] and the powers given the minister to require coal stocks to be maintained at power stations, both of which are at least in part based on the need for diversity of energy sources and for the power to resist industrial action. The latter category, of consumer-oriented social regulation, would seem to overlap with the economic rationales described above, but the crucial distinction to be made is that its basis, rather than being to assist in a more efficient allocation of resources to consumers, is basically a distributive one, based on a desire to avoid an undesirable distribution of wealth or opportunity.[31] To illustrate the difference between economic and social rationales for regulation, a distinction can be made between rules prohibiting undue preference or discrimination in pricing or the provision of services, and those designed to support a universal service to all categories of consumers regardless of cost differences. The former are justified by a desire to avoid unfair competition and

---

[28] Dworkin, R., *Law's Empire* (Fontana, London, 1986), ch. 8, and his *A Matter of Principle* (Harvard, Cambridge, Mass., 1985), chs. 11–12; cf. Stewart, R., 'Regulation in a Liberal State: The Role of Non-Commodity Values' (1983) 92 *Yale Law Journal* 1537–90 at 1572.

[29] Breyer, n. 20 above, 32–5; Ogus, n. 18 above, 46–54; Stewart, n. 28 above.

[30] See Foster, n. 7 above, 303.

[31] Ogus, n. 18 above, 48–51; Stewart, n. 28 above, 1566–76.

allocative efficiency by preventing pricing at below cost.[32] Universal service provisions are however justified by the need to provide access to public services for all groups regardless of their place in the distribution of incomes; as the European Commission put it at an early stage of preparations for liberalization of telecommunications services, universal service is:

the basic voice telephony offering which must be generally provided, on the basis of a uniform charge not directly linked in every case to the actual costs incurred, to all customers reasonably requesting it. Universal service obligations imposed by national legislation or authorization regimes generally oblige market participants to provide a certain basic service to customers whom they may otherwise have insufficient economic incentive to serve.[33]

The universal service obligation will be considered in depth in discussion of the obligations of the privatized utilities below; it is of particular importance given the justification often advanced for nationalization that it permits exactly such a universal service in services necessary for participation in social life; much opposition to privatization, especially in Continental Europe, has been based precisely on the claim that it calls into question universal service. There are also other types of social obligation which will be examined in this book. An obvious one, of enormous practical importance, is that of the regulation of independent television. In this case the Independent Television Commission has, as well as some powers of economic regulation, much more important powers and duties designed for the maintenance of the standards of public service broadcasting; for example, limits on violence, advertising time, and programme content. In addition, the Commission has the task of maintaining a type of diversity in broadcasting which a market-based system selling audiences to advertisers cannot deliver; a form of right to diversity. This is difficult to justify by efficiency-based economic arguments, and there are no problems here of natural monopoly (at least since the development of cable and satellite delivery); rather the aim is an egalitarian one of providing access to viewing for as large a range of social groups as possible. This encouragement of diversity can in itself be seen as a form of uni-

---

[32] Foster, n. 7 above, 198–9, 292–4.   [33] EC Commission, n. 5 above, 4.

versal service by maximizing the range of tastes and interests catered for.[34]

It will at times be difficult to separate the economics-based rationales for regulation from those based on social reasoning. Thus environmental protection provisions can be seen as both correcting the maldistribution of resources caused by externalities and implementing social rights to a clean environment; similarly regulatory controls designed to prevent the premature exhaustion of limited natural resources can be seen as correcting the absence of a proper pricing system for such resources or as protecting the rights of future generations. Nevertheless, a distinction can be made based on the differing underlying justifications for the rationales referred to above. Thus economic regulation has the ultimate justification of maximizing allocative efficiency, and any concern it may have with the distribution of resources is as a means of achieving that goal. Social regulation does not have such a justification but may be rights-based; the rights it recognizes are not necessarily derived from utilitarianism and are not limited to rights tradable in the market-place. Thus this form of regulation includes in its justifications distributive concerns designed to permit as wide a range of social groups as possible to participate in the services provided in a given society.[35] This is too narrow to encompass *all* social regulation, for example that relating to the environment, but is of key importance for the regulation of utilities and for the other regulatory institutions to be described in this book. This raises the question of how the rights and other interests forming the basis of social regulation can be identified in practice. In Chapter 10 below it will be suggested that this has taken place in some other jurisdictions through the concept of *service public* or *servizio pubblico* and that this concept can provide a jurisprudential source for their further development.

Identifying Regulatory Rationales: Statutes and Licences

It will be recalled that a distinguished economic commentator on regulation of the privatized utilities suggests that there is a clear distinction between economic and social rationales for regulation, in that the former provide a means by which the regulator's decisions

---

[34] Stewart, n. 28 above, 1568.   [35] Stewart, n. 28 above, 1566, 1568.

can be non-arbitrary; the technical expertise of the regulator in economics becomes his source of legitimacy. By contrast, social considerations should be left to government with its democratic
mandate.[36] The implication is, it seems, that one can separate out
economic efficiency from other goals in terms of the existence of
right answers to questions. Thus the economic reasoning employed
is seen as non-arbitrary and permitting of rational answers, while
social disputes are essentially arbitrary because the answers depend
on value judgements on which reasonable people disagree. At best,
governmental decisions on such social matters can reflect the aggregate of preferences of an electorate; at worst, they reflect the unde-
mocratic activities of lobbyists for special interest groups or the
budget and bureau maximization of politicians and bureaucrats
behaving as public choice theory would suggest. The argument is
thus that if regulators depart from economic criteria they will
become lost in a quagmire of subjective values in which they have
no justification for exercising their choices.[37]

Yet this argument assumes that regulators operate in a legal
vacuum; that their exercise of power is up to their own ranking of
values rather than being constrained by legislative instruments.
What needs to be established to support it is either that the legislative instruments provide no coherent guidance for their decisions,
or that the guidance provided confirms that their central objective
is the maximization of economic efficiency. In this section I shall
examine in general outline the legislative duties which apply to the
regulators to assess whether either of these views can be supported.
Most of the discussion will concern the regulators of the recently
privatized utilities as it is here that the interrelationship between
efficiency maximization and social goals can be illustrated most
clearly. One caveat made earlier must be repeated; my examination
is not aimed at establishing the intention of Parliament, still less of
the Government, in imposing regulatory duties at the time of privatization. Such collective intent is usually impossible to establish,
and legislative intention as the sole basis for interpretation in these
circumstances is jurisprudentially indefensible.[38] Rather, I shall
attempt to see whether the legislative provisions themselves provide
the basis of a coherent structure of principle for regulatory deci-

[36] Foster, n. 7 above, ch. 9.
[37] Cf. Stewart, n. 28 above, at 1537 and Sunstein, n. 19 above, at 73.
[38] Dworkin (1986), n. 28 above, ch. 9.

sions; I will then supplement what emerges with discussion of the relevant common law and the emerging principles of the law of the European Community. This analysis of legal principles is made more important by the fact that, as we shall see in Chapter 2, judicial review of the regulators' decisions may be more important in the future, and this will require more sophisticated analysis of what the legal principles require and permit than has so far been undertaken. It will be recalled that three types of regulation were identified earlier; regulating monopoly, regulation for competition, and social regulation, and these categories may be used to classify the various principles involved.

The relevant sources are the privatization statutes and the related licences (also called authorizations and appointments) issued by the minister; they will be analysed in more detail in later chapters, so here only a brief overview will be given. To start with the first of the utilities to be privatized, British Telecom, the Telecommunications Act 1984 imposes two primary duties on the regulator (and on the minister). The first is to ensure that, so far as is practicable, telecommunications services are provided throughout the United Kingdom which satisfy all reasonable demands, including in particular emergency services, public call-box services, directory inquiries, maritime services, and services in rural areas.[39] This might be seen as merely a statement of the principle that telecommunications companies are to meet demand as indicated through the market place. However, it is striking that services in relation to which costs are likely to be particularly high are specified as those which nevertheless have to be provided; this suggests that the concept of reasonable demands is used in a broad social sense indicating the principle of a universal right of access to telecommunications services. This view is reinforced by the licence under which British Telecom operates, which necessitates the provision of a service to anyone who requires it unless the regulator is satisfied that demand can be met by other means. Importantly, this provision prevails over that prohibiting undue preference, i.e. prices not related to costs.[40] The other primary statutory duty is to ensure that providers of telecommunications services are able to finance them, a provision of the utmost importance for price control, as we

---

[39] S. 3(1)(a).
[40] Department of Trade and Industry, *Licence Granted to British Telecommunications* (HMSO, London, 1984), conds. 1 and 17 as amended.

shall see in later chapters.[41] What is most striking is that the maintenance and promotion of effective competition and the promotion
of the interests of consumers and users are only secondary duties
expressly made subject to the primary duties; they are not overriding regulatory goals.[42] Thus the legislative mandate for telecommunications regulation would appear to place highest priority on
social regulation and regulating monopoly; regulation for competition has only a secondary role.

A broadly similar pattern was followed in the case of the other
statutes. Gas was somewhat different, in view of the fact that the
principle of universal service cannot be adopted in full due to the
prohibitive cost of laying pipes in rural areas, and the original
statute included a duty to secure that all reasonable demands are
met but only 'so far as it is economical to do so'.[43] Nevertheless,
the Act imposed a duty on a public gas supplier to supply gas to
premises within twenty-five yards of a main, and the authorization
contains detailed conditions aimed at limiting disconnections.[44]
Fundamental changes have been made, however, by the Gas Act
1995 as part of the preparations for liberalization of the domestic
market. These include adding a primary duty to secure effective
competition and replacing the duty to supply in the statute with a
duty limited to connection by a public gas transporter; nevertheless,
as we shall see, important social obligations have been retained.[45]
As regards the water industry in England and Wales, the Water
Industry Act 1991 imposes primary duties of ensuring that the functions of water and sewage undertakers are properly carried out in
every area of England and Wales together with the financing duty,
here specifying the securing of a reasonable return on capital. The
secondary duties include the protection of the interests of consumers, especially in rural areas, and of pensioners, and merely
facilitating competition; there are also general environmental and
recreational duties.[46] In the case of electricity the primary duties
include a duty to promote competition, although even here we find
the protection of the interests of consumers in rural areas on pric-

---

[41] Telecommunications Act 1984, s. 3(1)(b).
[42] *Ibid.* s. 3(2).   [43] Gas Act 1986, s. 4(1)(a).
[44] Gas Act 1986, s. 10; Department of Energy, *Authorization Granted to the British Gas Corporation* (HMSO, London, 1986), cond. 12A as amended.
[45] Gas Act 1995, s. 1, and Sched. 3, para. 4, effective from 1 Mar. 1996.
[46] Water Industry Act 1991, ss. 2(4), 3–5; for environmental regulation see the Water Resources Act 1991 and the Environment Act 1995.

ing matters, and of the disabled and pensioners on quality matters amongst the secondary duties; there is also a unique primary duty applying only to the North of Scotland requiring the regulator to ensure that there is no distinction between tariffs for urban and rural areas.[47]

In all four of the main utility regulation statutes, then, there is no suggestion that the maximization of economic efficiency is to be the overriding regulatory goal; indeed, the concept of universal service looms large in these duties, as does regulating monopoly; regulation for competition only seriously emerges later with the electricity and the 1995 gas legislation. In other post-privatization regulatory regimes it is clear also that maximization of allocative efficiency is not the overriding aim; thus in the case of the railways, the duties imposed on the regulator include the protection of the interests of users of rail services and the promotion of the use of the railway network, though this latter provision is qualified by 'to the greatest extent that he considers economically practicable'.[48] The legislation also contains highly complex provisions for the limitation and regulation of the withdrawal of passenger services, the equivalent of the provisions in licences referred to above aimed at limiting disconnection of services.[49] The model closest to the maximization of allocative efficiency goal is that applying to the privatized airports, which is of course consonant with the role of the airports as suppliers of services which are not normally regarded as essential in the way in which one might regard energy, water, or even the telephone, and with the fact that the main users are airlines rather than individuals, and so better able to look after their own interests.[50]

To these examples must be added that referred to earlier of regulation which is most clearly concerned with non-economic goals; that designed to protect public-service broadcasting against threats to its survival. Thus the duties applying to the Independent Television Commission include, for example, requirements to avoid the inclusion in programmes of material which offends against good taste or decency, and Channel 3 licensees have to include

[47] Electricity Act 1989, s. 3(4)–(5), 3(2)(a); Industry Department for Scotland, *Scottish Hydro-Electric plc: Generation, Transmission and Public Electricity Supply Licence* (HMSO, London, 1989), Pt. V, cond. 4(4).
[48] Railways Act 1993, s. 4(1).   [49] Railways Act 1993, ss. 37–50.
[50] Airports Act 1986, s. 39(2).

regional, religious, and children's programmes. The principle of diversity of output is also fundamental to the public-service concept contained in the legislation.[51] In addition, the bidding processes for Channel 3 licences, though in principle decided by the award to the highest cash bidder, in fact involved a substantial 'quality threshold' which had to be met by bidders; as a result, half the licences were awarded to other than the highest cash bidder, as we shall see in Chapter 9.

My contention that the legislative mandates of the regulators contain a number of different rationales, including social regulation, may appear surprising for two reasons. The first is the common view that the financing duties mean that the interests of shareholders is given a clear priority over other interests, including consumers; thus according to one account of regulation from a social policy perspective,

the model of regulation constructed in Britain gives clear and unambiguous priority—in statute at least—to the interests of utility company shareholders . . . [t]he regulators' duties with respect to the protection of consumers are secondary and subject to the fulfilment of primary duties such as those cited above [i.e. the financing duties of the privatized utilities].[52]

This argument is reinforced by the provisions forbidding 'undue discrimination' or 'undue preference' in the utility licences; for example, that of British Telecom provides that '[t]he Licensee shall not (whether in respect of the charges or other terms and conditions applied or otherwise) show undue preference to, or exercise undue discrimination against, particular persons or persons of any class or description (including, in particular, persons in rural areas)'.[53] It is thus suggested that it would be unlawful for regulators to attempt to implement social or redistributive goals; according to the same author, such a statutory requirement has 'the effect of circumscribing the scope for regulatory intervention aimed at assisting groups of consumers who experience specific problems in accessing, or maintaining access to, utility services and it effectively forecloses the option of pursuing equity objectives as a part of regulatory

---

[51] Broadcasting Act 1990, ss. 6, 16.
[52] Ernst, J., *Whose Utility? The Social Impact of Public Utility Privatization and Regulation in Britain* (Open University Press, Buckingham, 1994), 60.
[53] Department of Trade and Industry, n. 40 above, cond. 17.

policy-making'.[54] There are a number of reasons, however, for believing that the real position is much more complex, and that regulators have more room for manœuvre in the choice of social goals than this view would suggest.

First, if the financing duty is an overriding goal, it is hard to envisage the reasons for including other duties which contradict it; for example, in telecommunications the inclusion of socially advantageous but potentially unremunerative services such as emergency services and the provision of services in rural areas as part of the primary duties and promoting the interests of consumers, particularly those of pensionable age, in the secondary duties. A single overriding duty to prioritize the interests of shareholders would in every case override the contradictory secondary duties, and so make them redundant. This makes it imperative that the first primary duty, that of ensuring that services are provided which satisfy all reasonable demands, is also subjected to analysis. The provision could be interpreted in two possible ways. First it could mean that demand is to be met in the market place, and so be seen as mandating a form of allocative efficiency. On this interpretation, the role of the regulator is simply to see that the provision of services is responsive to signals transmitted by the market; reasonable demand simply means the offer of a market price for supply. The prohibition on undue preference could be seen as reinforcing this. However, it is difficult to see this interpretation as compatible with the rest of the primary duty, which, in the case of telecommunications for example, emphasizes the duty to ensure the provision of services such as public call-box services and services in rural areas; all of these are precisely those which were assumed to be *least* likely to be provided under that market model. It is also incompatible with the duty to supply; that in electricity has been noted in recent case law as not involving any discretion whether the company supplies or not; 'save in certain narrowly defined circumstances, if a consumer requests the supply of electricity, the supplier is obliged to supply'.[55] This is not consistent with the supplier being an ordinary company free to maximize shareholder return, nor with the existence of a primary regulatory duty of facilitating such maximization. This approach also appeared in a decision of the Court

---

[54] Ernst, n. 52 above, 61.
[55] *Norweb plc* v. *Dixon* [1995] 3 All ER 952 at 959; see the Electricity Act 1989, ss. 16–17.

of Appeal refusing to lift an interim injunction preventing British Telecom from withdrawing service in accordance with the terms of its contract; as the Master of the Rolls put it:

[i]t is therefore correct, speaking very generally, to regard BT as a privatised company, no longer a monopoly, but still a very dominant supplier closely regulated to ensure that it operates in the interests of the public and not simply in the interests of its shareholders should those be in conflict. . . . BT should not be permitted to exercise a potentially disastrous power of termination without demonstrable reason or cause for doing so.[56]

Finally, the BT and other licences contain a number of other obligations incompatible with the notion of a single overriding duty to maximize shareholder return; these include the requirement to provide special telephones for the hearing impaired and other facilities for blind and disabled people.[57]

The second objection to the analysis made here is closely related to the first. It is that the regulators, when attempting to benefit particular groups of consumers on social grounds, are directly in breach of the prohibitions on undue discrimination or undue preference.[58] It is suggested that these provisions require cost-reflectiveness in tariffs, and examples are given of decisions by the telecommunications and gas regulators pursuing policies which contradict this and so are apparently *ultra vires*. It is also suggested that it would be more effective and transparent for government to implement redistributive goals through the tax and benefit systems. As regards the legal issue, it is my contention here that the social duties are more far-reaching than this analysis suggests; for example, the licence under which British Telecom operates enforces provision of a service to anyone who requires it unless the regulator is satisfied that demand can be met by other means, a provision which is expressed to prevail over the prohibition of undue preference.[59] It could also be noted that the prohibition on undue discrimination existed under nationalization also, yet extensive cross-subsidization

---

[56] *Timeload Ltd* v. *British Telecommunications Plc* [1995] EMLR 459 (CA); see also the Privy Council decision in *New Zealand Maori Council* v. *Attorney-General* [1994] 1 AC 466.

[57] For a summary, see OFTEL, *A Framework for Effective Competition* (London, 1994), 40. Unless otherwise specified, all papers cited in this book which were written by a regulator were published by the regulator him- or herself.

[58] Burns, P., Crawford, I., and Dilnot, A., 'Regulation and Redistribution in Public Utilities' (1995) 16 *Fiscal Studies* 1–22.

[59] Department of Trade and Industry, n. 40 above, conds. 1 and 17.

was tolerated; indeed, rather than seeing the prohibition as an attempt to outlaw social regulation, one commentator has seen it as a remnant of an older approach stressing equality of treatment rather than effective competition.[60] Moreover, the courts, in defining the concept of undue discrimination, though taking cost-reflectiveness as a starting point, adopted a highly flexible approach which is not incompatible with a degree of implementation of social policy even if undue discrimination provisions are viewed in isolation rather than as part of a constellation of duties, some with a social content.[61]

It would seem to make more sense to maintain that the two primary duties in the early legislation reflect two principles which are in tension; the financing of investment which would clearly make it unacceptable for a regulator to impose a set of social obligations which threatened the financial viability of the company or its ability to raise capital, and the concept of maximizing a universal right of access, including access where this might not be justified on straightforward commercial grounds. Indeed, the financing duty is expressed to be 'without prejudice to the generality of' the universal service duty.[62] Rather than mandating a single regulatory goal of efficiency maximization, the no undue discrimination provisions can rather be seen as early examples of regulation for competition by limiting the scope for unfair trading practices by the utilities where markets are potentially competitive; indeed, this is precisely what was envisaged in the Littlechild Report on British Telecom price control.[63] Later legislation has further emphasized

---

[60] Sharpe, T., 'Undue Price Discrimination and Undue Preference: A Legal Perspective' (1992) 2(1) *Consumer Policy Review* 33–5; see also Ogus, n. 18 above, 283–4.

[61] See, e.g., *Phipps* v. *London and North Western Railway* [1892] 2 QB 229; *Denaby Main Colliery Co.* v. *Manchester, Sheffield and Lincolnshire Railway* (1885) 11 App. Cas. 97; *A-G* v. *Long Eaton Urban Council* [1914] 2 Ch. 251; *A-G* v. *Wimbledon Corporation* [1940] 1 All ER 76; *South of Scotland Electricity Board* v. *British Oxygen Co.* [1956] 3 All ER 199 (HL); *London Electricity Board* v. *Springate* [1969] 1 SLR 539, and Sharpe, n. 60 above. For a recent OFGAS interpretation see OFGAS, *1997 Price Control Review Supply* (London, 1996), App. 4.

[62] Telecommunications Act 1984, s. 3(1)(b); a similar provision in the Gas Act 1986 was removed when the statutory duties were brought into line with those in electricity by the Gas Act 1995, though an equivalent survives in the Water Industry Act 1991, s. 2(2)(b).

[63] N. 11 above, para. 13.15.

the importance of regulating for competition by including this as a further regulatory goal.

The statutes will be analysed in detail in later chapters. The legal provisions quoted are ambiguous in important ways and open to various interpretations, but what emerges in general terms, however, is that regulatory goals are mixed and include irretrievably varied rationales, economic and social; for example, not only can universal service not be justified by efficiency maximization in every case, but neither can it be ignored by regulators, for it forms part of the constellation of duties to which they are subject. It surely makes much more sense to see this principle as expressing an egalitarian right of access to the basic means of communication or of fuel, a right of access to public services which prevails in certain circumstances over the maximization of efficiency. This legal principle gains greater force when one examines two other legal sources; the common law and the emerging law of the European Union.

Identifying Regulatory Rationales: The Common Law

It is interesting to discover that the legislative provisions concerning universal service closely reflect an older legal tradition in both English and Scots law which is concerned with access to monopoly services and in avoiding discrimination in the terms on which such access is provided, case law which has been the subject of renewed interest by commentators who have noted its relevance to the privatized utilities.[64] Probably the most important example was *Allnutt* v. *Inglis*,[65] in which it was held that a statutory dock monopoly was created for the benefit of the public as well as for the monopolist, and so the latter was not free to impose unreasonable charges which would prevent public access to his facilities: similar principles were applied to common callings such as carriers, innkeepers, and millers, and indeed to early public utilities.[66] As the works cited above document, these principles founded a developed body of constitutional law concerning regulation in the United States, but have been almost forgotten in England. In Scots law, a

[64] Craig, P., 'Constitutions, Property and Regulation' [1991] *Public Law* 538–54; Taggart, M., 'Public Utilities and Public Law' in Joseph, P. A. (ed.), *Essays on the Constitution* (Brooker's, Wellington, 1994), 214–64. These two articles deal with the cases with great sophistication and breadth, which permits me to include only a brief summary of the issues here.

[65] (1810) 12 East 527.   [66] See, e.g., *Harris* v. *Packwood* (1810) 3 Taunt. 263.

similar common law principle existed concerning the grant of monopoly rights for ports and for ferries as part of the *regalia minora*; for ports and harbours, in exchange for a monopoly right the proprietor was obliged to allow access by any member of the public prepared to pay charges, and these charges could not be set at a level which would prevent the public from having access.[67] Similar obligations applied in relation to the grant of ferry rights.

There are two ways of interpreting these cases. They can be seen either as an attempt to maximize efficiency through the imposition of rules limiting attempts by monopolies to restrict their output, or they could be seen as an expression of a socially-based right of public access to scarce resources. The phraseology of the decisions favours the latter interpretation.[68] Thus Lord Ellenborough CJ in *Allnutt* v. *Inglis* expressed the position as follows:

if, for a particular purpose, the public have a right to resort to his premises and make use of them, and he have a monopoly in them for that purpose, if he will take the benefit of that monopoly, he must as an equivalent perform the duty attached to it on reasonable terms.[69]

Similarly, Le Blanc J considered that 'where private property is affected with a public interest, it ceases to be juris privati only; and in cases of its dedication to such a purpose as this, the owners cannot take arbitrary and excessive dues, but the duties must be reasonable'.[70] The point also emerges strongly from one of the Scottish cases, in which Lord (Ordinary) Robertson decided that:

Rights of ferry are not only important to the party in whom they are vested, but are beneficial for the public interest. They impose on the parties possessing such rights a corresponding duty to accommodate the public, which private speculators, where their interests do not prompt them (as for example in plying the ferry in the winter season), are under no obligation to perform.[71]

What seems to be the basis of these cases is what Craig has termed some idea of public property rights which are triggered by the potential for restrictions on access to privately owned services

---

[67] See, e.g., *Aiton* v. *Stephen* (1876) 3 R (HL) 4, and Gordon, W., *Scottish Land Law* (W. Green & Son, Edinburgh, 1989), paras. 10–15 to 10–17.
[68] And see *Minister of Justice for the Dominion of Canada* v. *City of Levis* [1919] AC 505 (PC), discussed in Taggart, n. 64 above, 239–41.
[69] N. 65 above, 538.   [70] *Ibid.* at 542.
[71] *Magistrates of Kircaldy* v. *Greig* (1846) 8 D 1247 at 1248.

which are in some sense essential for users.[72] This is precisely what
the provisions in statutes and licences discussed above are attempting to achieve, and so there seems to be a degree of continuity from
the common law in the conception of regulation as involving a
number of goals, social as well as economic.

Identifying Regulatory Rationales: European Community Law

The third body of law to be examined is the still developing corpus
of European Community law. Here also it can be argued that the
regulatory principles are mixed; they include regulation for competition, especially in the liberalization of public utility services, but
also strong elements of social regulation through the acceptance of
an essential role for universal service.[73]

Of course, the body of Community competition law is extensive
and complex, and has been allied to policies of utility liberalization
in a number of areas.[74] Some of the resulting law resembles the
common law principles discussed above, for example the doctrine
of 'essential facilities' preventing the owners of such facilities from
denying access on reasonable terms to competitors. Thus in one
case the European Court of Justice decided that companies with
exclusive rights over port operations and the unloading of goods
would breach Article 86 of the European Community Treaty if they
engaged in overcharging, in failure to take up modern technology
or in undue discrimination. The Member State conferring the exclusive rights would also be in breach of Community law where the
conferral of such rights was liable to lead to such abuse.[75] This has
been developed in a number of Commission decisions concerning
the refusal of port owners to permit access by rival shipping lines

---

[72] Craig, n. 64 above, 54.

[73] For an excellent general survey of these issues see Scott, C., *Competition and
Coordination: Their Role in the Future of European Community Utilities Regulation*
(Centre for the Study of Regulated Industries, London, 1995); see also Scott, C.,
'Changing Patterns of European Community Utilities Law and Policy' in Shaw, J.,
and More, G., *New Legal Dynamics of European Union* (Clarendon Press, Oxford,
1995), 193–215. I shall merely outline the bare bones of this important subject here
postponing detailed discussion to later chs.

[74] See Whish, R., and Sufrin, B., *Competition Law* (3rd edn., Butterworths,
London, 1993), chs. 7–10 and Scott, *Competition and Coordination*, n. 73 above.

[75] Case 179/90, *Merci Convenzionali Porto di Genova SpA* v. *Siderurgica Gabrielli
SpA* [1994] 4 CMLR 422.

on reasonable terms,[76] and is of course closely linked to policies of Open Network Provision designed to provide standards and conditions for access to networks by competitors.

This is of course merely one small part of Community competition law designed to regulate for competition. However, more social objectives can also be detected. At the most general level, Article 90(2) of the EC Treaty provides a defence against proceedings for breach of the competition provisions where there is a conflict between the task assigned to the undertaking and the competition rules; this 'gives to courts the extremely difficult task of judging when performance of public obligations justifies breach of the competition rules, a task which might be thought more appropriate to a specialised regulatory agency'.[77] Of particular interest are the developments in the liberalization of telecommunications, posts, and energy markets within the Community. In many ways these reflect the model adopted in the United Kingdom in terms of opening up access to competing suppliers and separating regulation from the supply of services. However, in line with much continental jurisprudence, the concept of public or universal service and its variants is much more prominent in discussions of regulation than has been the case in the United Kingdom.[78]

The most advanced process of liberalization has occurred in the area of telecommunications. In this case the Commission identified the political goal of universal service as 'making available a defined minimum service of specified quality to all users at an affordable price', and as involving taking special account of 'the needs of more vulnerable or disadvantaged subscriber groups', and proposed a Council Resolution implementing these proposals.[79] Substantial developments since have culminated in a proposal for a directive on universal service for telecommunications in a competitive environment which will specify the types of service included and require

[76] See Hancher, L., 'Commission Decisions and "Essential Facilities"' (1994) 5 *Utilities Law Review* 62–4; Glasl, D., 'Essential Facilities in EC Antitrust Law: A Contribution to the Debate' (1994) 15 *European Competition Law Review* 306–14.

[77] Scott, *Competition and Coordination*, n. 73 above, 10.

[78] Again, only the barest outline will be given here, with details postponed to later chs. For the origins of the term 'universal service' see Mueller, M., 'Universal Service in Telephone History' (1993) 17 *Telecommunications Policy* 352–69.

[79] EC Commission, *Developing Universal Service for Telecommunications in a Competitive Environment*, COM(93)159 (final) (1993), 4, 6, 9.

steps to be taken to secure affordability.[80] The concept of universal service has become a cornerstone of Community telecommunications liberalization policy.

The proposals for postal services are much less well advanced, but the concept of universal service is if anything even more central to these. Thus in its initial Green Paper on this subject, the Commission stated:

> The cornerstone of the Community's policy for the postal sector should be the universal service. . . . The main concrete meaning of this universal service requirement is that there should continue to be a postal service available throughout the Community, both for national services within a Member State and for cross-border services linking two Member States. This universality implies certain more specific requirements: that the prices for the services should be affordable to all, that the service should be of good quality and it should be readily accessible to all.
>
> It is concluded that this universal service objective can justify the establishment of a set of reserved services . . . which would help to ensure the financial viability of the universal service network.[81]

As in the case of telecommunications, the universal service principle has been adopted by the Council, although more detailed proposals, including the adoption of minimum requirements for universal service, were not accepted after opposition from some Member States which considered the scope of universal service protection inadequate.[82] In this case the policy has also gained judicial support. In *Corbeau*[83] the European Court of Justice accepted that the normal principles of EC competition law could be limited to permit the conferral of exclusive rights to a state monopoly to the extent that this was necessary to preserve a universal service through cross-subsidy. As one commentator put it, 'the Court did

---

[80] EC Commission, *Proposal for a European Parliament and Council Directive on the Application of Open Network Provision to Voice Telephony and on Universal Service for Telecommunications in a Competitive Environment*, COM(96)419 (1996).

[81] EC Commission, *Green Paper on the Development of the Single Market for Postal Services*, COM(91)476 (final) (1992), 233.

[82] EC Commission, *Proposals for a European Parliament and Council Directive on Common Rules for the Development of Community Postal Services and the Improvement of Quality of Service*, COM(95)227 (final) (1995); see Estella, A., 'Commission Policy for the Postal Sector' (1996) 7 *Utilities Law Review* 64–6, 70; and *Community Postal Services*, Commission Press Release, 27 June 1996.

[83] Case C–320/91 [1993] ECR I–2533.

not forget to put the primary emphasis on the sustainability of universal service'.[84]

In the energy sector negotiations were hindered by fundamental disagreements between Member States, in part caused by the importance and difficulty of maintaining public-service obligations.[85] Thus the Council accepted proposals for draft directives on common rules for the internal markets in gas and electricity at the end of 1992. However, the Parliament proposed some 300 amendments, including the need for a clearer definition of public-service obligations. The Commission later introduced new proposals which include fuller reference to public-service obligations including the protection of small consumers; authorizations for new capacity and third-party access could be refused where they would prevent the performance of public-service obligations, and these obligations might also be reflected in tariff policy. The proposals would have permitted Member States to impose public-service obligations on undertakings operating in the gas and electricity sectors relating to the security, regularity, quality, and price of supplies.[86] Eventually, an agreement was reached by the Council in June 1996; this included acceptance that Member States may impose public-service obligations if they are clearly defined, transparent, and non-discriminatory.[87] Once more there is also some judicial support for this; in the *Almelo* decision the European Court of Justice specified that the normal competition rules could be modified if necessary in relation to energy-supply companies with public-service duties, in other words duties to ensure a continued supply of electricity, on demand, and to all types of consumers, on the basis of uniform tariffs and non-discriminatory conditions, throughout the area covered by their authorizations.[88]

It should finally be noted that, at the request of Jacques Delors, the former Commission President, the European Centre for

[84] Chung, C.-M., 'Recent Developments in EC Postal Liberalization' (1994) 4 *European Competition Law Review* 217–24 at 219.

[85] See Hancher, L., 'Towards a Unified European Electricity Market: The Commission's Latest Proposals' (1996) 7 *Utilities Law Review* 35–9.

[86] EC Commission, *Amended Proposals for a European Parliament and Council Directive Concerning Common Rules for the Internal Market in Electricity and Gas*, COM(93)643 (final) (1993).

[87] DG XVII, *Results of the Extraordinary Meeting of the Energy Council, Luxembourg 20 June 1996*, Press Release, 1996.

[88] Case C–393/92 [1994] ECR I–1477; see Hancher, L., 'Electricity and Competition' (1994) 5 *Utilities Law Review* 69–72.

Enterprises with Public Participation (CEEP) has been preparing a draft European Public Service Charter or European Charter of General Interest Services envisaged as striking a balance between principles of the market and of public service. While this could be dismissed as 'an interest group serving its members' interests in maintaining protected utilities monopolies', it has been welcomed by the outgoing Commission and the Parliament and has created much interest in Continental Europe.[89] In the context of the Intergovernmental Conference on reform of the European Treaties, CEEP has proposed that Article 90(2) of the Treaty be replaced by a new Article clarifying the objectives and obligations of services of general economic interest; more importantly, the Commission has itself proposed adding to the Treaty a new provision specifying 'a contribution to the promotion of services of general interest' as an activity of the Community.[90]

Conclusion

It should now be readily apparent that legal principles and provisions suggest that there is no single model or objective for utilities regulation. The regulation of monopoly is of course one central purpose for regulation; however, regulation for competition is also of considerable importance and, as has been less remarked, so is social regulation. In particular, concepts of universal service are of central importance to European Community policies on the liberalization of public utilities and their markets. When one adds to this the universal service provisions in domestic legislation and in the common law, it appears that a consistent legal principle exists enforcing access to these services. It therefore follows that the regulatory principles laid down for the regulators are not limited to those concerned with the maximization of economic efficiency (although these are of course important for regulating monopoly

[89] Scott, *Competition and Coordination*, n. 73 above, 12, 28; see also Egenhofer, C., 'Utilities Policy and the European Union—An Overview', in Centre for the Study of Regulated Industries, *Regulatory Review 1995* (Centre for the Study of Regulated Industries, London, 1995), 155–70; Hancher, L., 'Utilities Policy and the European Union', in Centre for the Study of Regulated Industries, *Regulatory Review 1996* (Centre for the Study of Regulated Industries, London, 1996), 119–42, 136–8.

[90] *CEEP Opinion on the Inter-Governmental Conference*, CEEP Press Release, 17 Apr. 1996; EC Commission, *Communication on Services of General Interest in Europe*, COM(96)443 (1996).

and regulating for competition), but include those based on more egalitarian or rights-based arguments; these are not simply imported through value judgements of particular regulators but have a sound foundation in legal principle.

The bulk of this book will be concerned to examine the decisions of different regulators in practice; I shall aim to identify the principles which they employ when faced with concrete problems, and any procedures which exist to render their decisions accountable. This is made all the more essential by the combination of the plurality of regulatory goals identified in this Chapter with the degree of personal discretion which has been entrusted to British regulators. Before this can be done, however, it will be necessary to describe the development of regulatory institutions in greater depth and detail.

2

The Development of British Regulatory Institutions

Introduction

Much of the recent writing on regulation has seemed to assume that it is a new phenomenon for the United Kingdom, one which has been a product of the privatization of public utilities since 1984. In fact, British regulation has a long history. The history is so long that it would be more accurate to see the period of nationalization of the major public utilities through use of the public corporation from the 1940s to the 1980s as the exception to longer periods of regulatory controls over private and partially public industries. In this Chapter, I shall provide a general survey of the institutions of regulation and will aim to illustrate this theme, whilst also showing how some of the problems of recent regulatory politics have much older roots. In particular, I shall attempt to demonstrate the essential pluralism of British regulation; a wide range of different institutional forms has been adopted with a variety of purposes and approaches, and no single rationale or type of institution has predominated. However, the creation of the utility regulators from 1984 involved a conscious rejection of earlier history and of overseas experience, making inevitable some of the problems which have arisen more recently. Moreover, the rejection of legalism in the creation of the new regulators rested on an assumption that legalism had been the chief reason for failures of earlier regulatory models, yet in fact there was a large number of different reasons for such failures, of which legalism was only one. Finally, this Chapter should act as a general introduction to the regulatory institutions to be analysed later.

Early Regulation

It has been well documented that much regulation has ancient roots; as Ogus has put it, '[t]he Tudor and Stuart periods gave rise to interventionist measures on an unprecedented scale. Under Tudor monarchs, about 300 statutes were passed to govern economic affairs and this figure does not include proclamations and other non-parliamentary instruments'.[1] Key areas of regulation were foreign trade, markets, prices, quality of products, employment and agriculture, and land use.[2] Moreover, self-regulation in something resembling its modern form also existed, notably through the guilds. Ogus concludes that '[a]t no time in English legal history has the law governing industry and commerce been so extensively and intensively penetrated by regulation as in the Tudor and Stuart periods'.[3] This is not however to suggest any great sophistication of institutional design during this period; as he also points out, the apparent extent of regulation was considerably weakened in practice by the lack of an adequate enforcement machinery.[4]

One view of history might see these controls as relics of an outdated mercantilism which were doomed to disappear with the growth of a more *laissez-faire* capitalism in later centuries, and it is true to say that these controls were not long-lived. However, as we saw briefly in Chapter 1, the common law itself developed principles which are directly analogous to some of the major (and controversial) principles of regulation today; by the early nineteenth century (though drawing on much older principles) the common law had regulated the use of monopoly power in such a way as to require it to be exercised for the benefit of the public and of other traders.[5] It has even been suggested that this amounted to the recognition of a form of public property right, which formed the basis for the much fuller development of such concepts by courts in the United States and indeed for much of the jurisprudence surrounding the panoply of US state and federal regulation.[6]

[1] Ogus, A., 'Regulatory Law: Some Lessons from the Past' (1992) 12 *Legal Studies* 1–19, 2.
[2] *Ibid.* 5–11.   [3] *Ibid.* 17.   [4] *Ibid.* 15–17.
[5] Craig, P., 'Constitutions, Property and Regulation' [1991] *Public Law* 538–54 at 539; the seminal case was *Allnutt* v. *Inglis* (1810) 12 East 527, further details of which are provided in Ch. 1 above.
[6] Craig, n. 5 above. For other discussion of common law as a source of regulatory principle see Taggart, M., 'Public Utilities and Public Law' in Joseph, P. A.

If the principles of the common law anticipated some of the key modern regulatory principles, institutional arrangements were of course very different, and appeared not to provide specialist means of enforcement. However, it is clear that the common law did not, even during the eighteenth and nineteenth centuries, preserve a monopoly of the regulation of economic affairs. As one of the leading legal historians of this period has argued at length:

making due allowance for a deficit of facts and for difficulties of interpretation, there are things we can say about law in the nineteenth century. It was complex, contradictory, and ephemeral—not simple, integrated and authoritatively established. Important decisions were made by people who were not judges, responding to rules not made by parliament, using structures and procedures not derived from or effectively subject to those of the formal legal system. People often ordered their affairs indifferent to and ignorant of that system, consciously or unconsciously responding to local custom, to business convention, to administrative expectations.[7]

Within this essentially pluralistic system he identifies institutions which are prototypes of modern independent regulatory commissions and also of self-regulation.[8] Examples of such bodies will be discussed more fully in a moment, but one theme about them is crucial to the argument in this book. This is that, to quote a contemporary issue of the *Law Magazine*, '[t]he duties attendant on these important enactments were so various and laborious, that it became necessary to form a kind of government in miniature . . . a commission'.[9] As this makes clear, the commissions were not simply established to implement a predetermined legislative mandate, but rather to engage in a range of different functions involving the interpretation of vague and often contradictory criteria and their own perception of the public interest. As we shall see again and again in this book, the lack of any clear structure for reconciling competing demands and providing authoritative guidance has continued to plague regulators to the present day; if they really are 'governments in miniature' how do they derive their legitimacy in

(ed.), *Essays on the Constitution* (Brooker's, Wellington, 1995); Daintith, T., 'Regulation by Contract: The New Prerogative' [1979] *Current Legal Problems* 41–64, esp. at 43, and his 'The Techniques of Government' in Jowell, J., and Oliver, J. (eds.), *The Changing Constitution* (3rd edn., Clarendon Press, London, 1994), 209–36.

[7] Arthurs, H., *'Without the Law': Administrative Justice and Legal Pluralism in Nineteenth-Century England* (University of Toronto Press, Toronto, 1985), 169.
[8] *Ibid.* esp. 115–29.   [9] Quoted in *ibid.* 117–18.

the absence of democratic credentials? Indeed, early in the nineteenth century this very problem was the cause of the demise of that
most notorious of the early commissions, the Poor Law
Commission of 1834.[10]

A second theme stressed in the historical study is also of considerable importance. This is the mutual hostility and incomprehen-
sion between the common law and other regulatory institutions.
Thus the same author documents attempts by the ordinary law to
take over other aspects of regulation at the expense of more pluralistic traditions; conversely, we see considerable hostility from
other jurisdictions towards the formality and 'legalism' of the common law. As we shall see below, these tensions have also continued
until the present day, and a mistrust of legalism has been a central
theme in the design of British regulatory institutions. However, we
should continue to bear in mind the basic theme in the historical
work, that of legal pluralism; just because regulation fell outside the
ordinary courts of common law did not mean that it did not have
a developed law through the activities of its own institutions.
Moreover, regulatory institutions did not fade away; 'the existence
of specialist bodies served to inject an almost unstoppable momen-
tum into the growth of regulatory law'.[11]

Regulatory Institutions in the Late Nineteenth and Early Twentieth Centuries

What were the institutions other than the courts and the common
law which administered regulation during this period? It should
perhaps first be noted that a point which has often been overlooked
is that important regulatory functions were undertaken directly by
government departments; examples included a range of functions in
relation to transport, public health, trade, and planning. Nor were
these simply matters of deciding high-level policy, for they often
included 'judicial' decisions, usually through determining appeals.[12]
Where specialist regulators were adopted, various solutions were
chosen in different areas of regulation. Perhaps the most celebrated

---

[10] See *ibid.* 118, 125–6, 134–5.
[11] Ogus, A., *Regulation: Legal Form and Economic Theory* (Clarendon Press, Oxford, 1994), 7.
[12] See Robson, W., *Justice and Administrative Law* (3rd edn., Stevens, London, 1951), 112–16, 150–3, 157–60, 164–85.

were those regulating the railways; these will be described in detail
in Chapter 7 below, but in brief the story was one of regulation by
Parliament, then by the courts of common law and finally by regulatory commissions, often involving proceedings with a high
degree of legal formality. None of these solutions was very satisfactory; the first stage, that of regulation through the granting of
an Act of Parliament which formed the equivalent of the contemporary licence, has been shown to have done nothing to promote
competition, not to have encouraged a reasonable rate of return on
capital in the long run, and to have lacked any effective enforcement mechanism.[13] The second stage of regulation through the
courts was, if anything, even less successful. The regulatory function 'was exiled, in 1854, into the wilderness of a reluctant and inept
Court of Common Pleas. There it languished for almost twenty
years, hostage to the notion that all adjudication is properly the
business of the courts, . . . the experiment of judicial involvement
proved a dismal failure'.[14] The successor Railway Commission 'was
dominated by the legal mind of its lawyer member and took a narrow view of its duty. The costs of litigation before it were almost
prohibitive' and the Railway and Canal Commission which in turn
followed as regulator 'is not a popular body. This is owing in part
to its complete aloofness and in part to the high degree of judicialization which results from the dominating influence of the High
Court judge who is its chairman'.[15] By contrast the Railway Rates
Tribunal, which took over price control from 1921 had a less formal procedure; in most cases lawyers did not participate, although
in important cases legalism remained a problem and its rules were
criticized as over legalistic.[16] Nevertheless, according to one commentator, the tribunal 'commands universal respect for impartiality and efficiency. It does admirably the job assigned to it'.[17]
However, as regards substantive regulatory principles, it was made
virtually powerless by a defective system of price control imposed
by statute which it had to administer.[18] As well as legalism of pro-

---

[13] Foster, C. D., *Privatization, Public Ownership and the Regulation of Natural
Monopoly* (Blackwell, Oxford, 1992), 35.
[14] Arthurs, n. 7 above, 126 (footnote omitted).
[15] Cushman, R., *The Independent Regulatory Commissions* (OUP, New York,
1941), 511–12, 516.
[16] Cf. *ibid.* 522; Robson, n. 12 above, 102–3; Foster, n. 123 above, 59–60.
[17] Cushman, n. 15 above, 523.   [18] *Ibid.* 517–24.

cedure, inadequate design of regulatory tools was thus a serious problem in railway regulation.

The well-known failures of railway regulation should not, however, blind us to the fact that there were different systems of regulation for other industries which may provide more useful lessons for the future. Thus in some areas quite sophisticated schemes for self-regulation were adopted; as an American writer put it:

British tradition and practice have long looked with favor upon giving important legal powers of self-regulation to organized groups. Self-regulation has always existed in the legal and medical professions, and has permeated many other fields in which regulation is thought necessary: it is somewhat reminiscent of the type of authority exercised for so long by the medieval guilds.[19]

A particularly important example of such self-regulation was that of the agricultural and other marketing boards, established in the 1930s under statutory powers, but which left the initiative for their establishment and their administration to producers themselves.[20]

Regulation of the public utilities took a variety of forms. One highly complex example is that of electricity generation and bulk distribution.[21] The Electric Lighting Act 1882 had instituted a licensing system by the Board of Trade for supply of electricity by local authorities or private companies; the licences were subject to numerous conditions. By the time of the First World War there were over 600 separate undertakings generating electricity, of a size far too small for efficient development of electric power. The Electricity Supply Act 1919 created the Electricity Commissioners to take over the licensing powers from the Board of Trade and also to serve as a national planning authority. In 1926 the Central Electricity Board was established as a national generating board, though distribution and sale were left in the hands of 635 different undertakers, municipal and private. The Board itself did not own or operate generating stations except in very exceptional cases but had absolute control over the decision-making of the stations remaining in private ownership; '[t]here is little left to the private ownership of the stations but the name, which remains as a

---

[19] *Ibid.* 550–1.   [20] For details see *ibid.* 550–73.
[21] A detailed history is Hannah, L., *Electricity Before Nationalisation* (Macmillan, London, 1979).

concession to certain trends of opinion'.[22] Initially the Commissioners had severe problems; their planning function was impossible due to lack of the power to compel amalgamations between the small companies and they had inadequate powers to control prices or service. After the 1926 legislation, however, their functioning seems to have been in marked contrast to the problems experienced in rail regulation; thus '[p]roblems of procedure before the Electricity Commissioners have never loomed very large'.[23] In law the Minister of Transport had wide powers of direction over matters of policy and also on specific minor matters, but in practice they enjoyed extensive independence on matters of day-to-day handling of cases; '[t]he success of the Electricity Commissioners within the scope of their present jurisdiction is admitted on all sides'.[24] Part of the reason for this is that they were businessmen and engineers rather than lawyers, and, though parties were sometimes represented by counsel at hearings before them, they avoided the excesses of legalism which had bedevilled railway regulation. Again, however, the Commissioners were let down by substantive regulatory problems; in the field of distribution and sale of electricity in 1934 over 600 companies still existed, of radically different sizes and with no uniformity in technical matters or in tariffs.

The lesson here seems to be that it is possible to have a form of regulatory commission which avoids undue legalism whilst maintaining a degree of independence from the sponsoring government department, although this does not mean that regulation will be successful if substantive questions of industry structure and of regulatory tools are not properly resolved. To consider the question of the type of regulatory tools which can be applied by agencies, the example of gas is of considerable interest. The industry was examined in detail in 1945 by a Committee of Inquiry which noted that the structure comprised no fewer than 1,047 undertakings, over a third of which were local-authority owned.[25] As with railways, early regulation took the form of private Acts of Parliament, and from 1840 the development of local monopoly caused these to include profit control limiting rates of dividend; this system was

---

[22] Cushman, n. 15 above, 577; for details of the arrangements see 529–41, 574–82.
[23] *Ibid.* 537.   [24] *Ibid.* 539.
[25] *The Gas Industry: Report of a Committee of Enquiry*, Cmd. 6699 (1945); for industry structure see paras. 57–80; for regulation see paras. 32–56.

standardized by the Gasworks Clauses Act 1847 to limit dividends to 10 per cent *per annum* and to permit consumers to petition Quarter Sessions to reduce prices if excess profits were made, though use of this latter provision was negligible. The maximum dividend was later reduced and maximum prices set; however these were of limited effect in a period of falling costs, and in 1875 a sliding scale system of control was introduced in an attempt to combine price control with incentives to efficiency improvements. In brief, this provided a standard dividend and a standard price; the dividend might be increased if the price fell below the standard price, but had to be decreased if the price rose above it; it was coupled with restrictions on the amount of capital issued and on the reserves which might be accumulated. This system of price and dividend control was supplemented by controls on quality, purity, and pressure standards backed up by machinery for testing and enforcement, and in 1871 the Gasworks Clauses Act introduced a form of universal service requirement by requiring supply to any consumer within twenty-five yards of a gas main subject to certain conditions.

Sliding-scale price control was initially regarded as highly successful;[26] however, in periods of falling costs such as the late nineteenth century it rewarded shareholders generously whilst penalizing them during inflationary periods such as the First World War, when in some cases it had to be suspended. Some companies secured from 1920 a new system of control known as 'the basic price system', which provided for a minimum dividend which could not be reduced due to price increases, plus a system of 'incentive payments' by which extra dividends could be paid in certain circumstances; interestingly, the system usually required that payments be made to employees through co-partnership schemes or bonuses equivalent to extra dividends paid. The new system served to encourage the supply of gas at a discount for industrial and other heating rather than the flat rate encouraged by the sliding scale control.[27]

The merits and demerits of sliding scale controls have again become a matter of considerable interest.[28] It should be noted now, however, that already in the nineteenth century attempts had been made to develop quite a sophisticated system of price control aimed

---

[26] *Ibid.* para. 44.　　　　　　　　　　　　　　[27] *Ibid.* paras. 45–6.
[28] Burns, P., Turvey, R., and Weyman-Jones, T., *Sliding Scale Regulation of Monopoly Enterprises* (Centre for the Study of Regulated Industries, London, 1995).

at combining consumer protection with the encouragement of efficiency improvement. Taken together with the institutional developments discussed earlier, this suggests that many of the themes of modern regulation had been anticipated in the nineteenth and early twentieth centuries, and that the solutions adopted had not been as universally unsatisfactory as the experience of the railways might suggest. The story was similar in the case of the other utilities; in the case of water and sewage there had been a combination of private and municipal ownership under private Acts, and a duty to supply had been imposed in 1847. Municipal provision rapidly became the dominant means of water supply and the sole means of sewerage disposal, though a number of private water companies survived municipalization and later nationalization, subject to statutory rate of return regulation. In the case of telecommunications, control took the form of licensing by the Postmaster-General under the Telegraph Acts of 1868–9, licences being granted to private companies and to the Post Office. The private companies merged in 1889 to form the National Telephone Company. The Post Office purchased the trunk lines by 1895 and agreed to purchase the whole system on the expiry of the Company's licence in 1911. Thus from the beginning of 1912 the system became publicly owned, with the exception of the Hull area which remained under municipal ownership. In the case of telecommunications, then, the period in private ownership was too short to enable any sophisticated regulatory arrangements to develop.

Regulation in the Period of Public Ownership

We now confront a paradox. It has been demonstrated that regulatory systems and controls of a considerable degree of sophistication had been developed before the 1940s, yet this has been neglected in later debate on this side of the Atlantic. However, the British experience was of great importance in shaping regulatory systems in the United States, especially in terms of the common law principles mentioned above which formed the basis for the development of US constitutional principles; as Craig has put it:

[a]ttempts at the regulation of private property in the United States were met by arguments that such regulation was unconstitutional. The battle over the constitutionality of the regulation was waged for more than 50 years, and the case law from the United Kingdom . . . was of seminal

importance in many of the cases decided by the American courts in those years.[29]

As he argues, in the United Kingdom these principles never acquired constitutional status, party of course due to different constitutional arrangements, but also because of the virtual disappearance of the principles themselves with the growth of public ownership. Similarly, in the regulatory bodies of the nineteenth and early twentieth centuries in Britain one finds the germs of the US regulatory commissions; yet on this side of the Atlantic they never achieved the degree of prominence of those in the New World. The reason for this is that the model of public ownership adopted in Britain left little room for discrete regulatory institutions or common law principles. Some of the early examples of municipal ownership mentioned above may have proved compatible with separate regulatory bodies, but this was not the case for the big nationalizations through the creation of public corporations from the 1940s.

It would of course be quite wrong to suggest that the public corporations established as a result of the nationalizations of the late 1940s and afterwards were unregulated by law; a number of important statutory and indeed common law principles were of importance to their operation.[30] Nevertheless, public ownership differed from previous forms of regulation in a number of important ways. First, it had only limited concern with institutional design; given that the public corporation or (in a very few cases) governmental acquisition of shares provided the basic structure for running the industry, why experiment with other institutional forms which could only complicate the task of government? Secondly and similarly, given that the relations between government and enterprises were largely determined by extra-legal factors giving government a considerable degree of flexibility on how it intervened, more specific regulatory tools were neglected; why bother with the complexities of price-control formulae when ministers could, and did, intervene directly?

The problems of accountability associated with public ownership on the UK model have been much discussed elsewhere and need

---

[29] N. 5 above, 538; see also 543–51.

[30] For details see Daintith, T., 'The United Kingdom' in Friedmann, W. (ed.), *Public and Private Enterprise in Mixed Economies* (Stevens, London, 1974), 195–287.

not be repeated here.[31] It should merely be stressed that one of the major problems was the lack of clarity of the respective roles of the industry boards, in formal terms granted a great deal of autonomy in management, and the pervasive influence of ministers who found it impossible to retain any degree of detachment or to develop a long-term policy framework for the industries. Nor did this confusion of responsibilities run only one way, for there is evidence that the industries were able to restrict effectively the abilities of ministers to impose unwelcome policies in certain areas;[32] indeed it can be suggested that on some crucial matters the industries were more autonomous under nationalization than under regulation after privatization. However, through blurring the distinction between regulation by ministers as an *external constraint* on enterprises, and the role of ministers as owners of the enterprises with resulting responsibilities for *internal control*, nationalization made it difficult to insist on information about plans and performance being made available outside the enterprise, or outside the closed circle of enterprise and ministers, who might both have a common interest in preserving such secrecy. One underlying problem also needs highlighting as it will reappear in our discussion of regulation later; this is that it was not possible to establish a single set of objectives for the industries. As Foster put it, the failures 'seem to have derived largely from the fact that not only was the influence of ministers not quite as it was . . . portrayed but also because the ministers, civil servants and public-sector managers had different primary or real objectives and none of these coincided with economic efficiency as seen by economists'.[33] The extent to which privatization has resolved the problem will be a central theme of this book.

The major institutional innovation in terms of regulatory controls with nationalization was probably the establishment of consumer councils for the major utilities; however these proved weak and ineffective, hampered by very limited powers to obtain information about the industries or to wield effective pressure towards them.[34] Nevertheless, elsewhere in the British economy there were some important new regulatory institutions created in the post-War

---

[31] See Prosser, T., *Nationalised Industries and Public Control* (Blackwell, Oxford, 1986); National Economic Development Office, *A Study of UK Nationalised Industries* (HMSO, London, 1976); Foster, n. 13 above, ch. 3.

[32] Foster, n. 13 above, 79–86.   [33] *Ibid.* 83.

[34] See Prosser, n. 31 above, chs. 8–9.

period. Both of the most important examples will be described in detail in later chapters, but their origins are worth a brief mention here as part of the pattern of regulatory development apart from direct public ownership.

The first example was that of the regulation of civil aviation; although public ownership was to play an important part in the operation of civil aviation, the international nature of the industry ensured that other forms of regulation were necessary.[35] This had initially taken the form of Departmental control, and indeed Government was to retain an important role through the negotiation of international agreements; however from 1938 an Air Transport Licensing Authority was set up, licensing services through formal hearings, no doubt influenced by the earlier examples of regulatory commissions discussed above. From 1947 an Air Transport Advisory Council was also established as an advisory and consumer representation body.[36] In 1960 the Licensing Authority became the Air Transport Licensing Board, which also retained some key elements of the earlier commissions; thus it was subject only to limited powers of direct governmental intervention and adopted a judicial approach, and according to Baldwin the two main features of its approach were the rejection of informal administrative guidance and the adoption of a court-like posture.[37] Indeed, to some degree the problems of the railway regulators were reenacted:

the ATLB experienced major difficulties in working alongside a central government department. In large part these problems stemmed from the way ATLB members saw the Board as a traditional tribunal. Because of such a conception, they saw no need to increase their secretariat and so their expertise (judges don't hear arguments, they don't research). They demanded independence of a formal kind from the Department but were in no position to sustain this.[38]

For want of a clearer structure of relations with government, the latter's policy was imposed *ad hoc* through allowing appeals from the Board and using other powers relating to traffic rights and international fares to negate its decisions. From 1972 the Board was replaced by the Civil Aviation Authority; its operation will be

[35] For an excellent account of the history of the regulation of civil aviation see Baldwin, R., *Regulating the Airlines: Administrative Justice and Agency Discretion* (Clarendon Press, Oxford, 1985).
[36] *Ibid.* 16–17, 20–1. [37] *Ibid.* 31, 32. [38] *Ibid.* 47–8.

discussed in detail in Chapter 8 below, but it should be mentioned here that it appeared to be a much more successful attempt to combine an open procedure using public hearings with a framework of governmental policy guidance, though the latter proved short lived. The model of a commission with a number of members responsible collectively for decision-making was retained, as was the system of licensing hearings.

Another important early example of a regulatory commission was the Independent Television Authority set up by the Television Act 1954.[39] Here the form of the commission was derived closely from the model of the public corporation used for public enterprises with a view to distancing the regulator from direct governmental intervention; the BBC Board of Governors was another important influence.[40] In this case a very extensive discretion was given to the Authority with limited guidance on how it should be exercised, and in marked contrast to the Civil Aviation Authority there was no provision for public hearings, and indeed any form of procedural fairness was noticeable by its absence.[41] The Authority became the Independent Broadcasting Authority and is now the Independent Television Commission; operation of the regulators will be discussed in more detail in Chapter 9 below.

A number of other bodies with regulatory functions were established during the late 1960s; examples listed by one commentator are the Highlands and Islands Development Board (1965); Race Relations Board (1965); Monopolies Commission (1965); National Board for Prices and Incomes (1966); Industrial Reorganisation Corporation (1966); Supplementary Benefits Commission (1966); Land Commission (1967); Gaming Board (1968); Community Relations Commission (1968); and the Post Office (1969).[42] It is striking that these were all examples of bodies set up by a Labour Government and might be seen as further growth of the interventionist state, especially in view of the large number of different subjects and types of activity covered. In fact, economic regulation was to flower further as a result of the privatization programme of the

---

[39] For the establishment of the Authority see Sendall, B., *Independent Television in Britain: Volume 1—Origin and Foundation, 1946–62* (Macmillan, London, 1982), 36–62.

[40] *Ibid.* 46.

[41] *Ibid.* 54–5, and see Lewis, N., 'IBA Programme Contract Awards' [1975] *Public Law* 317–40.

[42] Baldwin, n. 35 above, 12 (footnote omitted).

radical Conservative governments of the 1980s, and it is to these
that we shall now turn. To summarize the earlier discussion, previous examples of regulation in the United Kingdom had revealed a
number of serious problems, of which legalism in procedures was
merely one. Electricity and gas had suffered from difficulties of
industry structure and of substantive regulatory tools; civil aviation
from difficulties of relations with government and independent television from wide and non-transparent discretionary powers. All
these problems were to reappear with the post-privatization regulators; indeed, it could be suggested that the Government's concern
to avoid legalism in the procedures of the new regulators led to it
ignoring the likelihood of other familiar problems arising.

Regulation and Privatization

Improving regulatory systems was not of course a direct reason for
the development of a privatization programme by the Thatcher
governments; the programme started with the sale of council
houses, and then of enterprises operating in competitive markets
with no particular public-interest dimensions, so special regulatory
arrangements were not necessary. The need for bespoke regulation
arose with the sale of British Telecom in 1984 as the first of the public utilities to be disposed of. Nevertheless, improving the performance of public enterprise through new regulatory mechanisms was
used as one reason justifying the programme; as the Financial
Secretary to the Treasury put it, 'I firmly believe that where competition is impracticable, privatisation policies have now been
developed to such an extent that regulated private ownership of
natural monopolies is preferable to nationalisation'.[43] Perhaps
reflecting this relatively late development of improved regulation as
part of the rationale for privatization, the first characteristic of the
approach adopted was that regulatory institutions were improvised,
almost as afterthoughts to the main aim of successful privatization.
It is useful here to quote another commentator close to the political process of regulatory design:

the contrast with nationalization is instructive. The one [i.e. nationaliza-
tion], a long-standing commitment rubbed smooth to achieve consensus

---

[43] Moore, J., 'The Success of Privatisation' in Kay, J., Mayer, C., and Thompson,
D. (eds.), *Privatisation and Regulation: The UK Experience* (Clarendon Press,
Oxford, 1986), 95.

and mapped onto a [*sic*] already used civil service blueprint that reflected mainly administrative and some political considerations, quickly ran into difficulties and ended by pleasing no-one. The other, cobbled together in its formative stages mostly by hard-pressed civil servants under severe deadlines and at a time when they were most reviled by politicians who believed that among the other aspects of corporatism for which they were responsible was an over-regulated economy, was in the end more systematic and penetrating.[44]

Whether Foster's assessment of the success of regulation is accurate will be an important theme of this book. At this stage it is more important to note that the design of the institutions neglected the earlier history of regulatory commissions in the United Kingdom and, just as surprisingly, the experience of regulation elsewhere, notably in the United States. The model adopted was a more recent one, that of the Director General of Fair Trading. To quote Foster once more:

[i]t was a political decision that British Telecom should not be regulated by ministers. Instead, analogy suggested that the job should be done by the Director General of Fair Trading, who was in fact pressed to take it on. However, he decided that he had enough to do, so a specialist look-alike was invented, the Director General of Telecommunications.[45]

This model was adopted for later regulators, with the exception of airports regulation which passed to the Civil Aviation Authority. The key point to note is that it involved a rejection of the commission model, and legal powers were instead vested directly in a single, individual Director General. As we shall see, the resulting 'personalization' of regulation has been a heavily criticized feature of utility regulation in practice. When one examines the adoption of this model for the Director General of Fair Trading under the Fair Trading Act 1973 it is apparent that senior positions in his Office were to be filled by specialist outsiders from industry and consumer affairs and that the staff would represent the main constituencies affected by the activities of the Office. This did not occur in practice, but the appointment of outside experts has been one suggestion made for limiting the personalization of utility regulation.[46] The formal status of the regulators, as of the Director

---

[44] Foster, n. 13 above, 124.   [45] *Ibid.* 125.

[46] See Ramsay, I., 'The Office of Fair Trading: Policing the Consumer Marketplace' in Baldwin, R., and McCrudden, C. (eds.), *Regulation and Public Law* (Weidenfeld and Nicolson, London, 1987), 177-200 at 177–84; for comparison of

General of Fair Trading, was that of non-ministerial government department.

What were the tasks of the new regulators? The first point which should be made is that, although regulation was not to be carried out by ministers, the framework within which the regulators were to operate was very much a product of ministerial decisions. Thus the basic pattern adopted was that of licensing by the minister. Although licensing powers could be delegated to the regulator, the initial decisions on the amount of competition and industry structure were taken by ministers deciding how many licences should be issued. The most controversial examples were in the telecommunications and gas industries. In the former, the initial policy was to create a basic duopoly by restricting the provision of basic fixed services in the United Kingdom to British Telecom and Mercury. This was reviewed in a White Paper issued in 1991[47] which removed the duopoly through indicating the Government's willingness to consider other applications and its intention to issue a number of class licences, for example for private circuits; by 1996 there were more than 150 licensed public telecommunications operators. The advice of the regulator was central to the duopoly review, but the earlier decision to maintain the initial duopoly was very much a governmental one. In the case of gas, British Gas was privatized as a monopoly and regulatory activity since has been dominated by attempts to liberalize domestic markets. These came to fruition almost ten years after privatization through the passing of further legislation[48] creating the conditions for a liberalized domestic market. These examples show very clearly how decisions taken at the time of privatization determined the parameters within which regulators had to work.

This is also true as regards the chief regulatory controls on the privatized enterprises. The licences contained lengthy conditions determining the environment in which the enterprises were to operate. These conditions were not set by the regulator, but by the minister after private negotiations with the enterprise; for example, in

commissions and individual regulators see Breyer, S., and Stewart, R., *Administrative Law and Regulatory Policy* (3rd edn., Little, Brown & Co., Boston, Mass., 1992), 185–8.

[47] *Competition and Choice: Telecommunications Policy for the 1990s*, Cm 1461 (1991).

[48] The Gas Act 1995.

setting the licence conditions for British Telecom the Post Office Users' National Council, which had previously represented consumer interests, was not allowed to participate.[49] These conditions were of absolutely fundamental importance in determining the operation of the enterprises; in particular the conditions limiting price increases have proved the most controversial issue in the whole of utility privatization. As will be demonstrated in later chapters, there is ample evidence to suggest that the conditions were set too generously in an attempt to assist the privatization process, and much of the work of regulators has been to tighten the controls and avoid the prospect of unduly large profits being made by the companies.

If the government was the key actor in establishing the initial environment within which the regulators were to operate, what were the tasks of the regulators themselves? Three can be usefully identified here; enforcing licences, modifying licences, and protecting consumers. The enforcement of licences may involve the use of formal sanctions set out in the statute through the issuing of provisional and final orders creating rights to damages in private law.[50] However, the vast bulk of enforcement activity is informal; this has assumed a greater role with the development of liberalized markets, as much enforcement activity is concerned with policing competition, and, as we shall see in Chapter 3, in telecommunications where liberalization has been most effective new tools have been introduced for taking action against anti-competitive practices.

This may at first sight appear to create a clear division of functions between the minister who sets the rules and the regulator who enforces them. This is blurred, however, by the involvement of the regulator in licence modifications. These have been required very frequently and have often been highly controversial, for example in the case of modifications to price-control provisions. Two distinct procedures are made available. If the company holding the licence agrees to the modification, it can be made by the regulator subject only to limited requirements of notice and consideration of objections.[51] Modification without agreement cannot, however, be imposed unilaterally but requires a prior reference to the

[49] Post Office Users' National Council, *Annual Report 1983–4* (Post Office Users' National Council, London, 1984), para. 101.
[50] See, e.g., the Telecommunications Act 1984, ss. 17–18.
[51] e.g., the Telecommunications Act 1984, s. 12.

Monopolies and Mergers Commission (MMC); only after it has reported can the modification be made.[52] In the early years after privatization licence modifications were almost invariably made by agreement, if only to avoid the expenditure of company time involved in a reference to the MMC; however, latterly such references have become more frequent, as we shall see. The role of the MMC may be seen as some acceptance of the model of commission as regulator; however it is doubtful to what degree the MMC was expected at the outset to play a major role in the regulatory process. Rather, the procedure can be best seen as a form of appeal for the regulated company in relation to important regulatory decisions, and one which has the apparent advantage of being to a specialist body rather than to the courts. It was also influenced by the fact that the Director General of Fair Trading similarly refers monopoly and anti-competitive practice cases to the Commission, and so the institutional pattern for utility regulation reflected once more that of general competition law.

When it comes to consumer protection as a role for the regulators, greater uncertainty was apparent. Very different institutional arrangements were adopted for consumer representation for each utility; thus for telecommunications the regulator was advised by six Advisory Committees on Telecommunications and a network of some 160 local Telecommunications Advisory Committees. In the case of gas, a separate Gas Consumers' Council was established by statute, whilst for water the Director General established Customer Service Committees under statute, of which he appoints the members; an OFWAT National Consumer Council comprised of the Director and the Committee chairmen has also been created on a non-statutory basis. In electricity the arrangements were similar to those for water, with regional Electricity Consumers' Committees, though statute also required the appointment of a National Consumers' Consultative Committee composed of the chairs of the regional committees; this has been supplemented by a non-statutory Electricity Consumers' Committees Chairmen's Group. The difference in the arrangements sparked considerable debate about which is the most effective institutional means for consumer representation.[53]

[52] e.g., the Telecommunications Act 1984, ss. 15, 22, and 23.
[53] See Vass, P., 'Consumer Representation—Integration or Independence?' in Centre for the Study of Regulated Industries, *Regulatory Review 1995* (Centre for

Further problems in consumer protection were shown by the need as early as 1992 to pass new legislation in the form of the Competition and Service (Utilities) Act 1992 extending consumer-protection powers of regulators, especially in relation to the setting of standards of performance, the collection of information on performance, and the establishment of complaints procedures. Measures were also taken to improve the handling of individual disputes by the regulators, including the requirement that reasons be given.[54] In general, however, despite the stress on consumer protection as a key rationale for regulation, there seemed to be considerable uncertainty about how it should be implemented on the ground.

It is clear that the model of regulation adopted was deliberately distanced from experience elsewhere, especially from the regulatory institutions used in the United States. The lack of reliance on overseas models was no doubt in part due to lack of time, but also reflected a more general antipathy towards their regulatory style which was seen as over-legalistic.[55] The lack of study of such experience emerged clearly during the creation of the regulator for gas, when the Energy Select Committee of the House of Commons produced a pre-legislative report on the arrangements to be adopted for regulation. It received considerable evidence outlining advantages of the US system of regulation, and the Department claimed to have studied regulation in other countries in detail. The Committee recommended that an in-depth study of US experience should be carried out, and that information collected on foreign experience should be made publicly available. The Government replied that it had taken into account US practice but because of the diversity of sources in which it was contained the information could not be made available, and instead the Committee was referred to earlier evidence. This, however, deals with US experience in five brief paragraphs, only one of which refers to agency procedures, and that without any details.[56] Although it seems clear

the Study of Regulated Industries, London, 1995), 225–37; National Consumer Council, *Consumer Representation in the Public Utilities* (National Consumer Council, London, 1996).

[54] See the Competition and Service (Utilities Act) 1992, ss. 1, 5(1), 6(1), 7(1), 11, 16, 17, 23, 34, 36.

[55] See Foster, n. 13 above, 259–67.

[56] Energy Committee, *Regulation of the Gas Industry*, HC 15, 1985–6, para. 85 and *Minutes of Evidence*, 88–90; Department of Energy, *Regulation of Gas Industry*, Cmnd. 9759 (1986), para. 73.

that an apparent American culture of legalism was to be avoided, there were other reasons for attempting to avoid judicial involvement in the decisions of regulators:

[t]he decision to keep the courts out of the regulatory process was made not because of a wish to avoid the legalistic procedures of American legislation, though that was maintained later, but because at about the same time the Cabinet, considering changes to employment legislation, was persuaded of the harm past increases in the regulatory role of the courts had done to employer-employee relations.[57]

If there was little concern with learning from past or overseas principles in designing regulatory institutions, there seems similarly to have been little concern to specify purposes of regulation. As we have seen in the previous chapter, the nearest thing to a coherent vision was the first Littlechild Report presenting an economic rationale for regulation and suggesting that it would be a means of 'holding the fort' until competition arrived.[58] However, the range of statutory duties under which the regulators were to work was far too varied to correspond to such a vision.[59] Nor did the essentially stopgap role of the regulator sufficiently recognize the complexity of the regulatory task. In later chapters we shall see that, in particular, insufficient thought was given to securing the availability of information to the regulators, not so much in terms of their formal powers to demand information, but in ensuring that the information was recorded in ways which would facilitate the regulatory task. Nor was much thought given to the role of the regulator in policing competitive or partly-competitive markets as the extent of monopoly was reduced (regulation of competition rather than as a surrogate for competition); this is particularly surprising when the model adopted for the institutional arrangements was the Director General of Fair Trading and when regulation was initially seen as a stopgap before the introduction of competition. This issue has become of especially great importance with the full opening of gas and electricity markets to competition; as we shall see in Chapters 4 and 6, this involves a radical change of role for their regulators.

---

[57] Foster, n. 13 above, 125.
[58] Littlechild, S., *Regulation of British Telecommunications Profitability* (Department of Trade and Industry, London, 1983).
[59] Cf. Foster, n. 13 above, ch. 9, esp. 315, and Ch. 1 above.

Problems of Regulatory Legitimacy

In view of the lack of thought given to matters of institutional design or regulatory rationale it is not surprising that the first ten years of the regulatory institutions have been characterized by serious questions about their legitimacy.[60] Some of these have concerned substantive issues; for example the effects of decisions about the electricity market on the coal industry which raised questions of both the powers and the competence of the electricity regulator,[61] criticisms about the inability of the regulators to influence decisions on directors' pay, and questions of price rebalancing with regressive distributional consequences. Some of these criticisms were unfair, as they related to matters clearly outside the jurisdiction of the regulators such as directors' pay; however, underlying concerns reflected uncertainty about the relationship between regulators and government in determining industrial policy. This raises the question whether provision should be made for the issuing of a general framework of policy guidance for the regulators by government, a question which will be considered in Chapter 10 below. Other criticisms concerned the substantive regulatory tools available to the regulators, such as the efficacy of the RPI–X formula and their access to information; yet others concerned the question whether the industry-specific model of regulator was appropriate or whether they should be merged into sectoral agencies covering, for example, energy and communications.

Many of the criticisms however concerned regulatory accountability. The new legislation in 1992 did not stem the criticism which has embraced a large number of themes. These include the above-mentioned personalization of regulation, the extent of the discretion vested in the regulators, lack of transparency in the form of open hearings or of reasons for decisions, and the division of responsibilities among the regulators themselves. It is striking that these proposals have come from both the liberal right and from the

---

[60] From an extensive literature cataloguing criticisms of the regulators, good accounts of some of the overall themes are to be found in Helm, D., 'British Utility Regulation: Theory, Practice and Reform' (1994) 10 *Oxford Review of Economic Policy* 17–39 and Graham, C., *Is There a Crisis in Regulatory Accountability?* (Centre for the Study of Regulated Industries, London, 1995).

[61] See the Report of the Trade and Industry Select Committee, *Energy Policy and the Market for Coal*, HC 237, 1992–3.

left, suggesting that criticism does not only reflect directly substantive political agendas.[62] Moreover, criticism of existing institutional arrangements has come from some of the regulators themselves.[63] Further discussion of reform proposals will be postponed to Chapter 10 below; it is enough at this stage to note the fact that the arrangements adopted after privatization have now faced extensive criticism from a range of sources and cover a large number of different issues. This book is not alone in addressing these questions; the National Audit Office and Public Accounts Committee are undertaking a study of regulation of the utilities,[64] and the European Policy Forum and the Hansard Society have set up a Commission on the Regulation of the Utilities.

One further point needs to be made. It was briefly noted above that one of the most important aims of regulatory design at the time of privatization was to avoid involvement by the courts in the decisions of regulatory bodies, both because of antipathy towards the US model of regulation and because of other reasons for finding judicial involvement unhelpful. For some time this was largely successful; although there were a few judicial review cases brought, they did not have any great effect beyond establishing some procedural requirements to be followed in determining individual disputes.[65] Moreover, a decision of the House of Lords concerning an attempt to challenge the award of a broadcasting licence also suggested that the courts would be most reluctant to second-guess regulatory bodies on substantive issues.[66]

There is some evidence however that this may be changing. A more recent decision of the House of Lords has shown a more interventionist approach to substantive review, and moreover

[62] e.g., Veljanovski, C., *The Future of Industry Regulation in the UK* (European Policy Forum, London, 1993); Hain, P., *Regulating for the Common Good* (GMB, London, 1994); Corry, D., Souter, D., and Waterson, M., *Regulating Our Utilities* (Institute for Public Policy Research, London, 1994).

[63] See, e.g., the views of the Director General of Gas Supply: 'Watchdog Stirs Up a Row Over Reform of Regulation' and 'Gas Regulator Turns Up Heat on Rules Debate', *Financial Times*, 18 Apr. 1995.

[64] National Audit Office, *The Work of the Directors General of Telecommunications, Gas Supply, Water Services and Electricity Supply*, HC 645, 1995–6.

[65] See *R. v. Director-General of Gas Supply, ex parte Smith*, CRO/1398/88, QBD, 31 July 1989; *R. v. Director-General of Telecommunications, ex parte Let's Talk (UK) Ltd.*, CO/77/92, QBD, 6 Apr. 1992.

[66] *R. v. Independent Television Commission, ex parte TSW Broadcasting Ltd.*, [1996] EMLR 291.

approved the use of the ordinary procedure by originating sum-
mons to challenge a determination of the Director General of
Telecommunications relating to the terms of a contract, even
though this involved interpreting the licence granted under statute.
The effect of this procedure may be in some circumstances to avoid
the protections to public bodies afforded by the judicial review procedure, and this is likely to make challenge easier and more common.[67] More importantly, the decision also indicated a greater
willingness to overturn substantive decisions; in the words of Lord
Slynn, with whom the rest of their Lordships agreed, '[i]f the
Director misinterprets [conditions in a licence] and makes a determination on the basis of an incorrect interpretation, he does not do
what he was asked to do'.[68] Thus it seems that interpretation of
licences is to be treated as a question defining the jurisdiction of the
regulator, and not as something in relation to which he has discretion, and so subject to a lower standard of review. The decision
apparently had the effect that the Telecommunications Regulator
doubled his legal staff, though it has not yet been the case that there
has been an outburst of challenges following it.[69] In view of the
continuing criticisms of the operation of the regulators and the possibility of greater legal challenge, the time seems particularly ripe
for the sort of examination carried out in this book.

Regulation and the European Community

So far discussion has concerned developments in the United
Kingdom with some brief reference to US experience. However, it
is important to stress that regulatory developments in the European
Union are also becoming extremely important, although their
effects are sometimes uncertain due to the disparities in progress
amongst different Member States.[70] Perhaps the most striking
developments have been in environmental matters; these are largely
outside the scope of this book, but, as Chapter 6 will show, in the
case of water and sewerage disposal European quality standards

---

[67] *Mercury Communications Ltd.* v. *Director General of Telecommunications* [1996]
1 All ER 575 (HL); for a forceful criticism of the decision see McHarg, A.,
'Regulation as a Private Law Function' [1995] *Public Law* 539–50.
[68] N. 67 above, at 582.   [69] McHarg, n. 67 above, 550.
[70] For an excellent brief account of this subject see Scott, C., *Competition and
Coordination: Their Role in the Future of European Community Utilities Regulation*
(Centre for the Study of Regulated Industries, London, 1995).

have been the driving force behind much regulatory development, including the degree of new investment needed, and so pricing for consumers.

More directly relevant are the processes of liberalization of telecommunications, energy, and posts spearheaded by the European Commission. This is at its most developed by far in the case of telecommunications, and as a result some important regulatory requirements have already been imposed on national authorities. Thus, for example, the basic Commission Directive on Competition in the Markets for Telecommunications Services requires Member States to 'ensure that the conditions for the grant of licences are objective, non-discriminatory and transparent, that reasons are given for any refusal, and that there is a procedure for appealing against any such refusal'.[71] Similarly, it also requires that the grant of operating licences is carried out by a body independent of the telecommunications organizations which provide telecommunications services.[72] These requirements have not been met in all Member States; indeed, it was found in 1995 that the separation between regulators and operators was not sufficiently clear in at least five Member States, and at the end of that year the Commission proposed a new directive requiring Member States to establish national regulatory authorities legally distinct from and functionally independent of telecommunications organizations; where Member States retain ownership or a significant degree of control of telecommunications organizations effective structural separation must be ensured between the regulatory function and activities associated with ownership or control. Finally, a right of appeal must be provided to an independent body.[73]

This does not of course require the adoption of a regulatory commission on the UK model, and the European Court of Justice has confirmed that, on existing law, control by a ministry is acceptable, especially where the operator is controlled by private shareholders. If the ministry has a controlling interest in the operator regulatory powers must be granted to an independent body, although an administrative separation between the two functions within the

---

[71] Commission Dir. 90/388/EEC [1990] OJ L192/10, art. 2.

[72] *Ibid.* art. 7.

[73] EC Commission, *Proposal for a European Parliament and Council Directive for the Purpose of Adaptation to a Competitive Environment in Telecommunications*, COM(95)543 (final).

ministry will be acceptable where there is real separation, financial independence, and when movement of personnel is subject to special scrutiny.[74] This is the model adopted in France through the use of a directorate within the Ministry of Telecommunications.[75] Nevertheless, the effect of the developing law of utility liberalization in the EU is to bring regulatory matters into the open much more clearly, and the stress on the requirements of independence in regulation are, in the long term, likely to result in further use of the independent commission model, whether as a bespoke regulator for a particular area or as a more general competition authority. For example, Italy has passed the enabling legislation for the establishment of independent regulatory authorities for energy and telecommunications influenced considerably by the UK model, and legislation will establish a similar model in Ireland on privatization of the telecommunications utility.[76]

An allied point is however worth making here; the process of European liberalization is likely to increase the importance of law in relation to regulatory authorities in two ways. The first is simply that litigation on the basis of Community law is a well-recognized technique for both affected companies and different Member States, and the nature of the law lends itself to development through litigation much more than has the highly discretionary domestic regulatory law. This reinforces the suggestion made above that regulation is likely to become more litigious, with a greater role for the courts. Secondly, the principles of Community administrative and competition law are considerably more sophisticated and more far reaching in their implications than are those of domestic administrative law.[77] The result may be somewhat paradoxical; although European law requires the development of new regulatory

---

[74] Case C–69/91 *Decoster* v. *Commission* [1993] ECR I–5335; Case C–92/91 *Taillandier* v. *Commission* [1993] ECR I–5383; and see Sauter, W., 'The Status and Implementation of Services Directive 90/388' (1995) 6 *Utilities Law Review* 81–2.

[75] See Maisl, H., 'La régulation des télécommunications, changements et perspectives', *RFD adm.* 11 (3), mai–juin 1995, 449–61.

[76] For the Italian model see *Legge 14 novembre 1995, n. 481; Norme per la concorrenza e la regolazione dei servizi di pubblica utilità. Instituzione della Autorità di regolazione dei servizi di pubblica utilità Gazzetta Ufficiale n.* 270, 18. 11.1995; for the Irish plans see Hackett, F., 'The Changing Face of Telecommunications in Ireland' (1996) 7 *Utilities Law Review* 230–3.

[77] For discussion of these principles see Schwartz, J., *European Administrative Law* (Sweet & Maxwell, London, 1992) and his 'Developing Principles of European Administrative Law' [1993] *Public Law*, 229–39.

institutions, there is not yet much sophistication in what is actually required by way of institutional design. However, the legal principles which will apply to, and be applied by, these institutions are sophisticated and potentially demanding.

Conclusion

This brief summary of the development of regulatory institutions in the United Kingdom has revealed a number of themes which will be important to this work as a whole. First, Britain has a rich heritage of regulatory institutions showing a considerable degree of pluralism in their design; although later attention has been concentrated on the common law and the more legalistic of the regulatory bodies, there were others. In fact, legalism was only one of many problems encountered in earlier regulatory experience; others included inappropriate regulatory tools and industry structure, unpredictable government intervention, and lack of transparency in regulatory procedures. One of the effects of nationalization was to conceal the importance of other types of regulatory technique. When the regulators of the privatized utilities came to be established, the process was conducted in considerable haste and was characterized by a neglect both of previous history and of overseas models; instead the competition authorities provided an institutional model. An important reason for not adopting older or US models was a desire to avoid judicialization of regulatory procedures and to prevent the courts from having a major role as a means of challenge of regulatory decisions. There are signs however that, after initial success, this is beginning to change, both because of the greater willingness of domestic courts to permit challenge and because of the potential use of a range of administrative-law principles opened up by European Community law. It is also reinforced by a growing crisis in regulatory legitimacy. It seems likely that future regulation of the utilities in the United Kingdom will be very different from that experienced in the years since 1984. I shall now proceed to examine the practice of regulation in each sector.

3

Telecommunications: Managing Competition and Universal Service

Introduction

With the privatization of British Telecom in 1984, the Government faced a new challenge; how to devise regulatory arrangements for what was widely regarded as a public utility with inevitable elements of natural monopoly remaining for the foreseeable future. Although the provision of telecommunication services is not commonly bracketed with water and fuel as part of the essentials of life, the ubiquity of the telephone and its role in access to emergency services and as a lifeline for the isolated meant that this privatization was very different from those which had preceded it, not only in scale but in testing the ability of the Government's programme to secure continued provision of a public service. Yet at the same time this service was one where technological change was providing a rapidly shifting environment, and one in which competitive service provision was far more of a possibility than in other cases which would follow. Indeed, the actual growth of competition has been very considerable; thus by 1994–5 British Telecom's market share had fallen to 70 per cent in the case of outgoing international calls and was continuing to fall in almost all areas. Nevertheless, it retained 94 per cent of residential exchange lines, and the result was that regulation has, in telecommunications more than any other sector, necessarily concerned both the control of monopoly and regulating for competition.

The basic structure of the institutional response to this challenge has been described in the previous chapter, but at this point it is necessary to describe some of the peculiarities of telecommunications which were of importance in shaping this particular regulatory regime. The first point to note is that the history of telecommunications services had been different from that of other nationalized industries in the United Kingdom. Provision of these services had commenced privately, with early Post Office involvement and a regime of licensing by a minister. However, with the exception of the provision of services in the Hull area, nationalization had replaced this from 1911 and done so in a peculiar institutional form; that of a government department with responsibility for both posts and telecommunications headed by a responsible minister, the Postmaster-General. Conversion to the usual public corporation form had occurred as late as 1969, and separation from the Post Office into a separate telecommunications business only took place under the British Telecommunications Act 1981. Thus in one sense telecommunications could be seen as particularly closely linked to public-service ideals through an earlier identification with the state and with the symbolism of the Royal Mail services to which it had for so long been bedfellow.

On the other hand, the pace of technological change was particular rapid in relation to telecommunications. This had two particularly important consequences. The first was that behind the move to privatization lay a need for massive capital investment to replace outdated equipment.[1] Attempts had been made to provide for mixed public/private financing though the proposed 'Buzby bonds', but these had fallen foul of the Treasury and full privatization was seen as the best means to provide access to capital. Ensuring a rate of return which would permit access to massive amounts of such capital inevitably provided one of the parameters of future regulatory policy.

Secondly, technological development meant that opportunities for early competition were far greater than was to be the case for other privatized utilities. This is not to say that the recent revolution in information technology could be foreseen in 1984, nor that the related blurring of the boundaries between telecommunications, broadcasting, and information technology was apparent at privatization. Nevertheless, it was already clear that a competitive environment of some kind was just around the corner, and that any regulator would have to be concerned not simply with public-interest goals but with the development of competition. Thus already in 1981 an official report had urged unrestricted resale of voice telephony,[2] and in

---

[1] See Foster, C. D., *Privatization, Public Ownership and the Regulation of Natural Monopoly* (Blackwell, Oxford, 1992), 114–16.
[2] Beesley, M., *Liberalisation of the Use of British Telecommunications' Network* (HMSO, London, 1981).

that year the British Telecommunications Act had made provision for
the Secretary of State to license competing telecommunications systems and to develop standards for the approval of privately supplied
apparatus to be connected to the system. The 1984 Telecommunications Act not only provided for the privatization of British
Telecom but removed its monopoly of supply for the first telephone,
enabled a general licence to be issued for value-added services, and
most importantly permitted the licensing of a major competitor in the
form of Mercury. This duopoly was to last only until 1991, when the
growth of technology meant that a relatively stable duopoly would be
untenable, and it was replaced with a policy of full liberalization.[3]

Regulatory Institutions

As we saw in previous chapters, a further important element in the
process of designing the regulatory structures was the Littlechild
Report of 1983 which established key regulatory values which were
to influence all regulatory systems adopted after privatization.[4] It
will be recalled that this proposed a local tariff reduction scheme
which became the celebrated RPI–X model of price control, aiming
at limited regulatory discretion and at enabling sharing of efficiency
gains. The institutional model adopted for the regulator, as we also
saw in the preceding chapter, was that of a single Director General
modelled on the Director General of Fair Trading, supported by the
Office of Telecommunications (OFTEL), a non-ministerial government department. Both the operation of the price control and the
working of the regulatory institution will be described in detail
below; however a preliminary point must be made here. The Director
General is only one actor amongst many in a complex regulatory
process. Government has had a key role in determining the amount
of competition (the 1991 duopoly review was a governmental
decision taken on the advice of the Director General) and in determining the initial operating environment of the privatized enterprise
through setting licence conditions, notably the initial value of the
efficiency improvement X figure in the price formula. Indeed, the
Secretary of State still retains the licensing powers, and has not del-

---

[3] *Competition and Choice: Telecommunications Policy for the 1990s*, Cm 1461
(1991).
[4] Littlechild, S., *Regulation of British Telecommunications' Profitability*
(Department of Trade and Industry, London, 1983).

egated them to the Director General. Other regulatory bodies have also become closely related to telecommunications regulation with the convergence of media technology, notably those regulating broadcasting, especially the Independent Television Commission; this has given rise to boundary disputes. The Director General has also been assisted by a number of advisory committees; for example, consumer representation has partly operated through advisory committees for England, Scotland, Wales, and Northern Ireland, as well as specialist committees for small businesses and the elderly and disabled. One hundred and sixty four local Telecommunications Advisory Committees were also recognized to represent the interests of consumers, although this system is under review with the aim of making it more focused and effective.[5] Other aspects of regulation have passed to non-statutory committees; for example, most regulation of premium-rate services is carried out by the industry's own self-regulatory body, the Independent Committee for the Supervision of Standards of Telephone Information Services (ICSTIS); further use of committees of this kind is likely in developing areas to be described below such as universal service. When one remembers from the previous chapters that regulation at a European Union level has also become very important, the reality is that of a considerable degree of regulatory complexity rather than the concentration of monolithic powers in the Director General and OFTEL.

A constellation of elements thus shaped the regulatory system for telecommunications. On the one hand, the adoption of certain public-service goals was inevitable, given the history of the provision of telecommunications services in the United Kingdom; yet opportunities for both the encouragement of private capital and the growth of new competition were particularly strong. As we shall see, the encouragement of competition rapidly became the major concern of the regulator. First, however, it is necessary to assess how the constellation of tasks lying behind the regulation of telecommunications under these conditions became translated into legal duties for the regulator.

The Legislation

The previous chapters have described how the model of regulatory institution adopted in telecommunications provided a blueprint for

---

[5] Telecommunications Act 1984, ss. 27, 54.

the other regulators of privatized utilities. To a large extent this is also true of the regulatory duties contained in the Telecommunications Act 1984 and the licence granted to British Telecom under it.[6] In this section I shall outline the relevant duties before examining in more detail the ways in which they have been worked out in practice by the regulator, building on the discussion of statutory duties in general contained in Chapter 1.

The legislation imposes two primary duties on the Director General of Telecommunications (they also apply to the minister). The first is:

(a) to secure that there are provided throughout the United Kingdom, save in so far as the provision thereof is impracticable or not reasonably practicable, such telecommunications services as satisfy all reasonable demands for them including, in particular, emergency services, public call box services, directory information services, maritime services and services in rural areas.[7]

The second primary duty is:

(b) without prejudice to the generality of paragraph (a) above, to secure that any person by whom any such services fall to be provided is able to finance the provision of those services.[8]

The two primary duties are supplemented by a series of secondary duties; these include 'to promote the interests of consumers, purchasers and other users in the United Kingdom (including, in particular, those who are disabled or of pensionable age) in respect of the prices charged for, and the quality and variety of, telecommunications services provided'[9] and 'to maintain and promote effective competition between persons engaged in commercial activities connected with telecommunications in the United Kingdom.'[10] These are explicitly made subject to the two primary duties of universal service and of ensuring that service providers are adequately financed.[11]

It was argued at some length in Chapter 1 above that the statutory duties do not provide the basis for an unambiguous programme

    [6] Department of Trade and Industry, *Licence granted by the Secretary of State for Trade and Industry to British Telecom under Section 7 of the Telecommunications Act 1984* (HMSO, London, 1984).
    [7] Telecommunications Act 1984, s. 3(1)(a).
    [8] Telecommunications Act 1984, s. 3(1)(b).   [9] S. 3(2)(a).
    [10] S. 3(2)(b).   [11] S. 3(2).

of efficiency maximization by the regulator; whilst it is an exaggeration to claim that '[t]he Telecommunications Act imposes on the regulator a set of objectives reminiscent of 70s industrial policy',[12] it does seem to include a number of different regulatory rationales with potentially contradictory policy implications. This is reinforced by provisions in the British Telecom licence; these include those relating to regulation of monopoly through price control, those concerned with regulation for competition through prohibiting undue preference and setting the terms for interconnection, and those with more social goals such as requiring the provision of emergency services, services in rural areas, and public call box services.[13]

As we saw in Chapter 1, historical developments in the common law and modern developments in European Community law would seem to reinforce this presence of economic and social goals in the provision of public services; indeed, European Community law is now of the first importance in telecommunications regulation and, as we shall see below, this also contains both economic and social goals. It now remains to examine the way in which the regulators have interpreted their various duties in practice.

The Regulators

One of the main themes in the literature of British utility regulation is that a great deal of personal discretion is conferred on each Director General. It is thus important to say a little about the background and views of each. Telecommunications regulation is of particular interest in an examination of the approaches of the utility regulators, not merely because it was the first regulatory regime to be established after privatization, but because of the especial importance of Sir Bryan Carsberg influencing regulators who came after him; in the words of his acting successor, '[d]uring the eight years he ran OFTEL, Sir Bryan was the embodiment of the regulatory regime, and he created a model for others to follow in the UK and internationally.'[14] From the outset he emphasized his

[12] Veljanovski, C., *The Future of Industry Regulation in the UK* (European Policy Forum, London, 1993), 14.
[13] N. 6 above, conds. 2, 6, 11, 14, 17, 24; several of these conditions have been substantially amended since the original version of the licence was issued.
[14] OFTEL, *Annual Report 1993*, HC 298, 1993–4, 1.

pro-competition approach; 'I believe that the regulator should endeavour to press competition to its economic limits'.[15] It was this strong competition orientation which made his contribution highly distinctive. However, from the beginning, it was clear that this did not prevent the making of difficult and complex regulatory decisions; as Sir Bryan put it in his first Annual Report:

although I believe that a presumption exists in favour of competition, and careful consideration must be given to the justification for any inhibitions of competition, nevertheless some planning of the path to competition and some limitation of the ultimate scope of competition is likely to be in the public interest.[16]

This also influenced his perception of the relationship between economic and social goals; as he put it:

I do not think it would be appropriate for me to seek to impose a balance of prices in a way that is motivated primarily by a desire to achieve some particular redistribution of income . . . nor do I think my powers would permit me to do this. I must limit my studies to economic factors and to such matters as the adequate provision of adequate services in rural areas and for elderly and disabled people—matters explicitly referred to in my duties under the 1984 Act. I do not believe . . . that I could properly put forward a proposal for a rule that all people on low incomes should be given telephones free of rental: such a proposal would involve arbitrary judgements about matters of income redistribution and my making it would involve the usurping of the proper role of government.[17]

As we shall see in considering pricing policy and social obligations, this apparent stress on the economic rationale for regulation was not as simple as it might seem. The key point however is that the early statements from Sir Bryan emphasized strongly his role as an economic regulator with competition as the first choice for maximizing consumer welfare, though in practice this did not enable the regulator to stand back and let competition come naturally into play; it involved active policy-making to achieve the conditions in which competition could grow.

After an interregnum under Sir Bryan's deputy as acting Director General, he was succeeded by Don Cruikshank, who had previously been managing director of the Virgin Group and of Times

[15] OFTEL, *Annual Report 1985*, HC 461, 1985–6, para. 1. 21.
[16] OFTEL, *Annual Report 1984*, HC 457, 1984–5, paras. 1.4–1.5.
[17] *Ibid.* 10–11.

Newspapers, and most recently Chief Executive of the National Health Service in Scotland. The emphasis under his leadership remained similar; he also had a strong commitment to competition as the best means of consumer satisfaction. To choose one statement of this from many, 'we have seen no reason to alter our overall goal. OFTEL's role will principally be to extend customer choice so that value for money and quality decisions are increasingly made by customers from a choice of providers promoted, and if necessary policed, by OFTEL'.[18] As we shall see in detail later, he also undertook a number of procedural reforms which, apart from their inherent importance, made public his key objectives and those of OFTEL. Thus from 1995 a detailed OFTEL management plan was published, setting out goals and objectives; these are backed up by accounts of progress and current projects.[19] One effect of this greater clarity in the setting of objectives is that the relationship between economic regulation, competition, and social obligations has had to be identified much more clearly. As the Director General put it in his Annual Report for 1993:

[s]ocial provision in the UK is an area where the nature of OFTEL's role is less clear. We will begin a review in 1994 of the fundamental questions raised by this issue before we come to a view on what should be done. We will consider the extent to which OFTEL should actively promote social objectives and what level of social provision is desirable. One central question is how social provision, if it is desirable, should be funded. . . . Another point to consider is whether other bodies more directly involved with groups affected, such as elderly and disabled people and those who have difficulty affording a telephone, are better placed to view telephony as a right or at least a basic necessity.[20]

As we shall see, this resulted in an extended consultation on universal service. Similarly, greater clarity in the role of the regulator in policing competition led to proposals and a further consultation exercise on making OFTEL into a specialist competition authority through a new condition in the licences of dominant operators, in effect incorporating European Community competition law to be directly implemented by the regulator.

---

[18] OFTEL, *Annual Report 1994*, HC 340, 1994–5, para. 1.2.
[19] OFTEL, *OFTEL Management Plan* (London, 1985 and updated. It is also available over the World Wide Web).
[20] OFTEL, n. 14 above, 10.

What we see in this case is, then, a growing acceptance that regulation has a variety of goals, both economic and social. This means that it is important to retain regulatory discretion; as Don Cruikshank put it, '[t]he UK framework raises arguments over the discretion of the regulator. I have found it very important for discretionary powers to be both flexible and widely drawn. The only alternative to this is, in effect, to leave this discretion in the hands of the regulated company.'[21] Yet the exercise of the discretion is being structured and made more predictable through analysis of different regulatory rationales and purposes, and through the adoption of open procedures. How successive Directors General have exercised their discretion in practice will be the theme of the rest of this Chapter.

Regulating Monopoly: Price Control

It was of course apparent from the outset that, given the initial monopoly elements in British Telecom's business, price regulation would be a central concern of the Director General. It is worth reminding ourselves at this point of how the model of price regulation was originally designed to work according to the Littlechild Report. It was to provide a stable environment for the enterprise subject to review only every five years, probably through automatic reference to the MMC. This would reduce the discretionary role of the regulator; '[t]he DGT does not have to make any judgements or calculations with respect to capital, allocation of costs, rates of return, future movements of costs and demand, desirable performance, etc.'.[22] The reality has been very different.

The original price control imposed on BT on privatization in 1984 limited the weighted average price increases for a basket of services to RPI–3. The prices included in the basket were local exchange line rental, and tariffs for directly dialled local calls and national calls, except those from public call boxes; an additional voluntary constraint limited exchange line rental increase for residential customers to not more than RPI+2. By 1996 the basic value of RPI–X had been changed three times, culminating from 1993 in a value of RPI–7.5. The basket of services had widened to include

[21] OFTEL Press Release 46/95, *Don Cruikshank Speaks Out on Telecoms Regulation.*
[22] Littlechild, n. 4 above, para. 13.20.

operator-assisted calls, private circuits, international direct dialled calls, connection charges, and some special services; additional constraints had been introduced for individual prices in the basket, low users, and individual private circuits. The effect was that the amount of BT turnover covered by price control had increased from 48 to 53 per cent in 1984 to 64 to 67 per cent. A further revision of the price formula will come into effect in 1997.[23] For this OFTEL's final proposals (accepted by BT) are for radical change adopting a cap of 4.5 per cent (equivalent to 7 to 8.5 per cent on the previous basis) but applying only to residential and small business users, so reducing coverage to 26 per cent of BT's turnover. It is thus clear that price control is anything but an automatic process subject to occasional review, and involves an extensive degree of discretionary judgement by the regulator; none of the changes had involved a reference to the MMC.

What approaches have underlain the price reviews? Here it is of course impossible to point to a single basis for the decisions, but what has been consistently noted by commentators is that the process of determining price controls has come increasingly to resemble US-style rate of return regulation:

[t]he key components are: the operating expenditure . . . ; the capital expenditure . . . ; the asset valuation; and the cost of capital. In *all* regulatory systems, the adjudicators are required to adjudicate—implicitly or explicitly—on *all* of these items. The difference between the British price cap and the US rate of return regulation is not one of kind, but of degree.[24]

The situation was complicated by the political context of criticisms of the size of BT profits and the effects of rebalancing of tariffs between small, mainly domestic, and large, mainly business, users. Thus as early as December 1985 the Director General issued a statement on the BT price increases in the previous month. Whilst declining to amend the price-control rule he undertook to keep the situation under review and to consider the need to propose a licence amendment if BT's rate of return were to show a further significant increase or if rebalancing were to be carried out beyond the point justified on economic grounds.[25] In the case of the next round of

[23] For details of the complex changes see OFTEL, *Pricing of Telecommunications Services from 1997* (London, 1995), Annex B, Table 1.

[24] Helm, D., 'British Utility Regulation: Theory, Practice, and Reform' (1994) 10 *Oxford Review of Economic Policy* 17–39, 21: emphasis retained.

[25] OFTEL, *British Telecom's Price Changes*, 1985.

increases in November 1986 the Director General examined the rate of return on capital of BT and determined that, as it was acceptable, there was no case for changing the price-control formula. The changes had involved a very substantial rebalancing; the Director General considered that as the rates of return on local and long-distance calls were close to equal no amendment to the formula was justified, though further substantial increases in local call charges should not be needed; further investigation would be needed into the question whether action should be taken on the balance of prices between exchange line rentals and call charges.[26]

The first revision of the price-control formula took effect from the end of July 1989. In setting this the Director General once more took into account a reasonable rate of return for the period to be covered; as he put it, 'I do not believe that the rate of return is the only criterion that should be taken into account in chosing [sic] the price-cap, although I think it is the most important'.[27] On the basis of the analysis carried out the most appropriate price cap appeared to be one of RPI–4.5 per cent to apply for four years with some extended coverage. An individual price cap was applied to exchange line rentals to aid the transition to rebalanced tariffs reflecting costs. However, one significant new element appears in the process. As the Director General stated:

I have been discussing with BT the introduction of a special new tariff for low users. BT has been working on proposals for such a tariff but has not yet finalised them. However, it has agreed that it will introduce such a tariff as part of the agreement on new price controls. The special tariff will involve a reduced exchange line rental of not more than 60% of normal residential exchange line rentals. This new low user scheme would take the place of the existing low user rebate but would be better targetted and would enable people with low incomes to avoid the difficulties associated with high exchange line rentals.[28]

This was justified mainly on the basis of maximizing the value of the telephone network as a national resource through encouraging as many people as possible to be connected to it by a reduced line rental for those most vulnerable to increases. However, given the background of political and distributive concerns about BT profits, it can also be seen as a more socially-directed response. I shall

[26] OFTEL, *Review of British Telecom's Tariff Charges*, 1986.
[27] OFTEL, *The Control of British Telecom's Prices*, 1988.   [28] *Ibid.*

return later to this special tariff and its implications; the point for now is that the process of price control was far more complex than had ever been envisaged when the system of regulation had been established, and involved detailed investigation of rate-of-return considerations and operated in a political context of the high profitability of BT and the effects of rebalancing.

The second price review was implemented in 1991 as part of the duopoly review, and followed the announcement in 1990 by the Director General that international charges needed to be brought within the price-control formula; despite competition from Mercury, BT had made excess profits on such calls and this had meant that the overall rate of return on capital during 1991 was higher than the estimate made at the time of the previous setting of the price formula of BT's cost of capital. Thus a transitional control was put in place including international calls within the basket and tightening the overall control to RPI–4.5 per cent. On rebalancing, the Director General stated: '[a]t present, local prices are uneconomically low and long distance prices are too high. Altering the balance of these prices would increase the encouragement given to competition at local level. However, such a change would also affect residential customers detrimentally, and vociferous objections would be likely to ensue.'[29] Further developments also took place in relation to the low user scheme, and these will be dealt with below.

A further revision took effect in 1993. In his consultative document on the review, the Director General once more stressed rate of return factors, and noted the similarity between price-control and rate-of-return regulation, stating that the essential distinction lay in the time period over which the controls operate, price control delaying the need to consider rate-of-return considerations to the time of the periodic reviews and giving the firm an incentive to cut costs between reviews. Nevertheless, it was accepted that even in the United Kingdom difficult assessments had to made at the time of the review about the admissibility of items of investment and cost; not only was determination of the appropriate rate of return necessary, but also determination of the asset base to which it would apply.[30] RPI–X, then, was no longer being justified as a

---

[29] Quoted in Burns, P., Crawford, I., and Dilnot, A., 'Regulation and Redistribution in Utilities' (1995) 16 *Fiscal Studies* 1–22, 6.
[30] OFTEL, *The Regulation of BT's Prices*, 1992.

simple or near-automatic regulatory tool, but for different reasons; it provides a structure for taking the difficult discretionary decisions involved in price regulation periodically, and enables efficiency savings to be shared between the enterprise and consumers. The actual price formula set involved an overall price cap of RPI–7.5 per cent with a number of sub-price caps, including RPI+2 per cent on exchange line rentals to protect residential customers from steep rises in rentals.

Finally, a further general review of BT prices took place during 1995–6 to become operative in 1997. It was undertaken using the sophisticated consultative procedures introduced by Don Cruikshank, and these will be discussed below. As a result of a separate review of competition issues, the RPI–2 constraint on line rentals had already been lifted in 1996. In brief, the first consultative document proposed that the pricecap form of regulation be retained, but stressed that; '[t]he distinction between rate of return regulation and price cap regulation should not, however, be taken too far. In setting the price cap an assessment of the firm's expected efficiency gains has to be taken together with assessments of its investment needs and its likely profitability.'[31] This included a survey of the comparative efficiency of other operators and of British Telecom's historical performance, as well as complex financial modelling to determine the appropriate costs of capital. It also involved some attention to distributional issues:

> OFTEL wants to ensure that better quality of service, choice and value for money are available to *all* groups of customers. OFTEL is concerned, for example, that residential customers should secure a reasonable share of the benefits of competition compared with business customers; and that customers living remote in rural areas, the elderly, people with disabilities and people on limited incomes also get a fair deal.[32]

Similar points were made in the second consultative document, proposing a broad basket of charges subject to a four-year pricecap with X set at 5 to 9 per cent.[33] The final proposals were radically different from this, however.[34] At first sight they appeared deregulatory, in that the new price cap would apply only to residential and

---

[31] OFTEL, n. 23 above.   [32] *Ibid.* para 2.26 (emphasis retained).

[33] OFTEL, *Pricing of Telecommunications Services from 1997, Second Consultative Document*, 1996.

[34] OFTEL, *Pricing of Telecommunications Services from 1997, OFTEL's Proposals for Price Control and Fair Trading*, 1996.

small business customers, thus covering only 26 per cent of BT revenues as opposed to 64 per cent earlier.[35] However, the controls came as a package with a new condition prohibiting anti-competitive behaviour which will be considered below. The rate of X was to be 4.5 per cent, although this represented an equivalent of 7 to 8.5 per cent to earlier controls, and was proposed on the basis of comparative examination of possible efficiency improvements, financial modelling of the future cost of capital and asset valuation to establish an asset base, all elements which the Littlechild Report had claimed would be unnecessary. The regulator also expected to receive an undertaking from BT that each residential customer would not experience a real increase in bills, the aim being to ensure that the abolition of sub-caps contained in the new proposals would not disadvantage low-spending customers. Perhaps the most interesting aspect of the proposals was the radical change made to them during the consultation process; it really did seem that this process mattered in shaping the complex price-review decisions.

It should already be clear from this discussion that the role of the Director General in price review has not been one of making periodic reassessments of the price formula in a technical way; it has involved a number of different considerations centred around the inevitably highly complex, and to some degree subjective, matter of determining an acceptable rate of return for the business, an asset base, and possible efficiency savings. There has also been some concern with distributive considerations; although the Director General initially explicitly stated that such concerns were outside his terms of reference, the issue of rebalancing of charges has invitably brought such considerations into play, something which will be confirmed in the discussion of low-user tariffs below. Indeed, this accurately reflects the constellation of statutory duties applying to the Director General which, as we have seen, do not limit themselves to requiring efficiency considerations alone to be taken into account. Most recently, the regulator has emphasized that he must have substantial discretion, but has sought to increase the transparency of its exercise through open procedures; we shall look at the procedures in more detail towards the end of this Chapter.

---

[35] *Ibid.* para. 2.13.

Regulating Monopoly: Quality of Service

Pricing policies are not the only important concern of a regulator which may have an impact on consumers. In one sense quality of service is intimately tied up with price control for, as the Director General noted early on, a decline in service standards may in effect be a disguised price increase; this means that quality of service is best treated as regulation of monopoly alongside price control.

The issue of quality of service emerged very early as a result of the 1987 'quality crisis'.[36] A strike early in that year had caused a backlog in maintenance and in the connection of new customers, a problem exacerbated by the introduction of new exchanges. This coincided with difficulties for the regulator in obtaining adequate information. On privatization BT had ceased to publish performance indicators relating to quality of service. The Director General responded by organizing a quality-of-service survey using volunteers from local advisory committees and some of BT's own statistics; 'after bringing considerable pressure to bear'[37] he then obtained the Company's agreement to republication of quality-of-service information. He made quality of service a priority issue in 1987, and obtained much improved information from BT. As Foster has noted, the essential problem was the absence of proper requirements in the licence for quality of service to be treated as an integral part of price control.[38]

Since the events of 1987, Directors General have issued annual reports on quality of service by BT. One striking element in this has been the breadth of matters which the Directors General have been prepared to consider as raising questions of quality; for example, from the 1989 report Sir Bryan Carsberg noted that 'telephone selling is extremely unpopular with telephone customers on the whole and that it may be regarded as diminishing the quality of service a customer receives from the telephone';[39] telephone selling and nuisance calls have remained a major concern. Another expression of a broad concept of quality in a different context concerned premium-rate 'Chatline' services; the Director General expressed himself concerned that they decreased quality of service and concerned

[36] See Foster, n. 1 above, 214–15.
[37] OFTEL, *Annual Report 1987*, HC 432 1987–8, para. 1.3.
[38] N. 1 above; 214–5, 305.   [39] OFTEL, *Telephone Service in 1989* (1990).

'about the danger that these services can diminish the quality of telephone service by subjecting vulnerable people to—or encouraging them to participate in—obscenity, pornography and other hazards'.[40] This was the reason for a reference to the MMC in 1988; the latter rejected the Director General's recommendation that such services be available only through 'contracting in' and with itemized billing, and instead recommended regulation through a code of practice and a compensation fund, this regulation to be monitored by the Director General. There have been a number of later developments relating to such services, but their importance here is to show the breadth of the concept of quality of service.

The quality-of-service problem has in many respects been resolved by more recent legislative changes to bring the powers of the Director General of Telecommunications up to the level of those of later regulators. These were implemented through the Competition and Service (Utilities) Act 1992. The Act empowered the Director General to make regulations prescribing standards of performance in individual cases and to determine disputes about service problems and compensation, a power to determine and enforce standards of overall performance, to collect information on performance and to compel its publication, and to oblige operators to establish effective complaints-handling procedures. In fact, both individual and general standards had been agreed voluntarily, but nevertheless the power to do so was a potentially important additional weapon for the Director General; as he put it in his 1991 Annual Report:

[w]e have made excellent progress on quality of service in telecommunications, including the introduction of BT's plan for compensating customers for certain kinds of poor service, without formal regulatory powers. However, I welcome the provision of powers because the need for further action may arise in the future and the existence of formal powers is likely to make it possible to secure further improvements and resolve future problems with a minimum of difficulty and delay.[41]

By 1996, it had proved possible to publish comparable performance indicators from different telecommunications operators; they covered measures of service provision, customer-reported faults, fault repair, complaint handling, and bill accuracy. In

[40] OFTEL, *Annual Report 1989*, HC 491, 1989–90, 12.
[41] OFTEL, *Annual Report 1991*, HC 42, 1992–3, 7.

addition, BT quality-of-service indicators covered network reliability, performance in fault repair, speed of response of operator services and directory inquiries, and availability of itemized billing.[42] BT and other operators also offered Customer Service Guarentee Schemes, providing, for example, that unrepaired faults would attract compensation of £5 per day or, in some circumstances, of actual financial loss. Quality of services is thus a matter in relation to which the regulator has achieved considerable success, and there is no doubt that the quality of service has improved greatly since privatization. Moves are also developing at European Community level to require the drawing up and monitoring of service standards; the Voice Telephony Directive requires Member States to set a number of indicators, and improved monitoring arrangements are now proposed.[43]

Regulation for Competition: Interconnection

Despite the lack of a primary duty to promote competition in the Telecommunications Act, we have seen that the promotion of competition has loomed large in the objectives of the Directors General, and that a substantial body of their work has concerned creating and policing competitive opportunities, indeed so much that a substantial section of the 1995 OFTEL *Annual Report* is entitled 'OFTEL as a Competition Authority'. To a considerable degree the competitive framework is influenced by government, especially in this case through the duopoly review. The area of greatest importance in competition promotion by the regulators themselves has been that of interconnection; as one commentator has put it, '[a]ll roads in telecommunications regulation seem now to lead to interconnection, which has become the central issue in regulating for the development of a competitive market in telecommunications'; this applies also to work by the European Commission.[44] Far from

[42] For details see OFTEL, *Annual Report 1995*, HC 295, 1995–6, App. 2.

[43] Dir. 95/62/EC [1995] OJ L32116; for future plans see *Communication from the Commission of the European Communities on Universal Service for Telecommunications*, COM(96)73 final (1996), and *Proposal for a European Parliament and Council Directive on the Application of Open Network Provision to Voice Telephony and on Universal Service for Telecommunications in a Competitive Environment*, COM(96)419 (1996).

[44] Scott, C., 'Blizzard from OFTEL Addresses Interconnection and Deregulation Process' (1996) 7 *Utilities Law Review* 47–8.

minimizing the role of the regulator, interconnection has posed important new problems.

Apart from issues of avoiding undue discrimination between different operators, the particular problem raised initially was that of the access deficit contribution. Rebalancing of BT prices to bring them into line with costs was not completely achieved, and as a result BT incurred a shortfall between its revenues and access costs. This was funded from profits. However, where its system was used by other operators they were expected to contribute to these costs in the form of access deficit contributions which thus formed, in effect, contributions to the costs which BT incurred in meeting its social obligations and were a central element in calculating costs of interconnection for new operators. Inevitably, such contributions could act as a deterrent to operators otherwise able to enter the market, and in 1991 the Director General decided to waive them for firms with a small market share. As a result, only Mercury paid the contributions for the time being, and this only for its international traffic.

As competition and its potential have developed further, the issue has become crucial and controversial in determining the future competitive structure of the telecommunications industry. One illustration of this is the litigation brought by Mercury concerning the extent of the Director General's powers to set interconnection terms.[45] The Director General and OFTEL have also undertaken much work on their own behalf on the problems, and an important fruit of their work was a statement from the Director General issued in March 1994. It set out new interconnection principles requiring accounting separation between network, access, and retail BT businesses and new rules to avoid undue discrimination, far greater transparency in the calculation of interconnection charges, and new methodology in calculating them.[46] Many respondents in the consultation process urged that the future of access deficit contributions be reviewed as soon as possible, and two further consultative documents were issued.[47] Key proposals included a general

---

[45] *Mercury Communications Ltd* v. *Director General of Telecommunications* [1996] 1 All ER 575 (HL); cf. *Telecom Corporation of New Zealand* v. *Clear Communications Ltd*, 19 Oct. 1994 (LEXIS) (PC).

[46] OFTEL, *Interconnection and Accounting Separation: The Next Steps* (1994).

[47] OFTEL, *A Framework for Effective Competition* (1994); *Effective Competition: Framework for Action* (1995).

prohibition on anti-competitive behaviour and further clarification of universal service; these will be analysed in the following sections. On interconnection, the 1995 document proposed limiting the Director General's direct regulatory role through his withdrawal from setting interconnection charges in most cases; future controls would be considered as part of the price review, with the introduction of a charge cap formula for them similar to those used to control retail prices. Access deficit contributions would be abolished and replaced by a universal service fund supported by operators.[48] At first sight this might seem to represent straightforward deregulation, with the regulator withdrawing from the setting of detailed controls. However, it is better seen as a change of regulatory form away from direct regulation of monopoly to policing competition and protecting social interests through the universal service obligations, an important part of the proposals. One advantage of the consultation process carried out is that it has enabled the issues to emerge with a clarity which has permitted the different types of regulation involved to become evident. Action has also been taken at a European level with interconnection a key element of open network provision to complete the liberalization of telecommunications markets.[49] Work was also carried out on the application of the competition rules of the EC Treaty to interconnection agreements. It is thus necessary for me to proceed to discuss issues of more general competition regulation and of universal service, as interconnection cannot now be considered in isolation.

Regulation for Competition: Anti-competitive Behaviour

From the outset, the telecommunications operator had responsibility for dealing with anti-competitive behaviour in the telecommunications market, particularly through the enforcement of licence conditions. In 1995, 103 complaints on competition issues were dealt with, most of them alleging undue preference or discrimination, cross-subsidies or predatory behaviour, and for the first time provisional and final enforcement orders were issued against BT. However, responses to the 1994 consultation had shown widespread dissatisfaction with the effectiveness of the regime in dealing with anti-competitive behaviour, and it was announced in 1995

[48] OFTEL, *Effective Competition: Framework for Action*, n. 47 above.
[49] See the references in n. 43 above.

that a new approach would be adopted through fuller publication of information about the enforcement process and other internal reforms; most importantly, however, the Director General proposed a new licence condition on anti-competitive behaviour. The proposed condition was modelled on Articles 85 and 86 of the EC Treaty and would prohibit any abuse of a dominant position by a telecommunications operator and any anti-competitive agreement between undertakings materially affecting competition in the UK telecommunications market. It would be accompanied by published guidelines (and copies of these were made available in draft with the proposed condition) and a greater involvement of experts in an advisory commitee. Breach of the condition would enable enforcement action to be taken under the 1984 Act, and so would avoid the complexity caused by the difficulties of prohibiting particular types of anti-competitive conduct by specific licence conditions in a rapidly changing environment. The condition was to apply to all operators including BT, Mercury, Kingston Communications, and the mobile operators.[50] It was the subject of OFTEL's first public hearing, but was opposed by BT because it considered that the discretion conferred on the Director General was excessive and that there was no adequate appeals mechanism; it became closely linked also to the pricing formula as the Director General made it clear that he could not agree to a less interventionist form of price control without acceptance of the new condition; '[i]f OFTEL does not have the powers necessary to deal quickly with anti-competitive behaviour then it would bring forward very different price control proposals.'[51] The condition was finally accepted by the company along with the new pricing formula; no formal appeal right could be established without a change in the statute, but arrangements were to be made for reference of cases to the advisory committee either by the Director General or by the company, and clearly its views would have considerable weight.

What is important here is the acceptance that the role of the regulator is changing from that of a regulator of monopoly to that of a specialized competition authority, and that this requires new regulatory techniques and rules, though it is doubtful whether the

[50] For details of the proposed condition see OFTEL, *Effective Competition: Framework for Action*, n. 47 above, sect. II and Annex C.

[51] OFTEL, n. 34 above (1996), para. 2.23; ch. 3 of this document discusses the proposed conditions in detail.

Telecommunications Act provides an adequate enforcement base for a full competition authority.[52] The change of regulatory style is also apparent in the seemingly very different, but in practice closely linked, matter of social regulation and universal service, and it is to this that I shall now turn.

Social Regulation and Universal Service

A number of different matters are linked together under this head; what they have in common is that they are all concerned with access to the telecommunications system, especially by the economically underprivileged; the Director General has characterized it as 'securing a fair distribution of benefits to customers' through universal service.[53] The first example is that of disconnection, which has been far more controversial in the energy and water utilities, as we shall see below. Nevertheless, the licence conditions of both BT and Mercury require the publication of Codes of Practice on consumer affairs, including guidance on the handling of disputes and complaints. That for BT is included in all telephone directories, and includes a section on difficulties in paying a bill, making provision for the giving of advice so as to avoid disconnection. In 1992 the Director General agreed new procedures under the 1992 Act to avoid disconnection during a dispute.[54] By 1995 he had secured the publication of disconnection statistics (they showed 60–70,000 domestic customer disconnections by BT each month) and proposed that by the end of 1997 the barring of outgoing calls should be required rather than disconnection.[55] A related problem has been the requiring of deposits before telephone services will be provided. This was also the subject of concerns by the Director General, and as a result deposit-taking was significantly reduced; it has now been replaced by a new system of call levels which have largely removed the need for deposits for residential customers.

One particular area of concern relating to access is that of the provision of public call boxes. At the time of privatization strong fears were expressed that it would lead to a loss of call boxes, especially in

[52] See Scott, C., 'Deregulation of BT's Pricing and the New Fair Trading Requirements' (1996) 7 *Utilities Law Review* 176–7.
[53] OFTEL, n. 42 above, para. 1.65.
[54] OFTEL, *Annual Report 1992*, HC 718, 1992–3, 69.
[55] OFTEL, *Universal Telecommunications Services*, 1995, paras. 5.4–5.5.

rural and low-income areas. To avoid this, complex provisions were
included in the BT licence somewhat analagous to those applying to
the closure of uneconomic railway lines.[56] At the time of the 1987
'quality crisis' a report from the Director General noted that urgent
action was needed from BT to improve the quality of these services,
hardly surprisingly as surveys had shown that almost 50 per cent of
regular call-box users had had difficulty in finding a working box the
last time they had tried.[57] In October 1987 BT set itself the target of
having 90 per cent of boxes working by the end of March 1988; this
was achieved, and reliability figures have remained high, with figures
of over 90 per cent reliability in most periods afterwards.[58] The number of call boxes has also grown considerably, from under 80,000 in
1987 to almost 124,000 in 1994. BT retained a market dominance of
98 per cent. In the revised definition of universal service which will be
discussed below, OFTEL proposes to include 'reasonable access to
public call boxes' in licence conditions for BT and Kingston
Communications, and provision of public pay-phones is included in
the European Community definition of universal service.[59]

Moving for the moment away from physical access to affordability, a number of developments also occurred in relation to the
low-user rebate scheme. The first Director General had stressed
that his approach to rebalancing was essentially economic rather
than social; as he put it at the time of the 1986 price review, 'I do
not think it would be proper for me to attempt to redistribute
wealth by my policy on telephone pricing.' However, some restraint
on increases in line rentals could be justified by the argument that
the more customers who join the telephone network the more valuable it is for all customers.[60] As mentioned above, a low-user tariff
emerged from discussions leading to the 1989 review of the price
formula, and involved a reduced line rental of not more than 60 per
cent of the normal rate. During the next price review in 1991, the
Director General noted that:

[a]lthough the typical residential customer is experiencing a lower level of
increase in telephone prices than the general level of inflation, OFTEL is
aware that the higher than average increase in exchange line rentals affects

---

[56] Department of Trade and Industry, n. 6. above, cond. 12.
[57] OFTEL, *Quality of Telecommunications Services* (1986), para. 23.
[58] OFTEL, *Telephone Service in 1993* (1993), table 7.
[59] See the references in n. 43 above.
[60] OFTEL, *Review of British Telecom's Tariff Changes* (1986).

low users of the telephone service particularly harshly and that low users
are often elderly people and others with low incomes. In order to help such
people, the Director General discussed with BT its plans to replace its Low
User Rental Rebate Scheme with a better focused scheme for low users
which would avoid giving benefits to customers whose low usage arises
because the line concerned is a second line.[61]

Thus the scheme was being phased out in favour of a new scheme
called Supportline which was considerably more generous;
'Supportline will make an important contribution to ensuring that
the rebalancing of prices does not alter the burden of costs in such
a way that the telephone service can no longer be afforded by the
poorest members of the community'.[62] The change in emphasis is
striking; it suggests a move towards a special tariff system targeted
to meet the demands of social policy rather than simply reflecting
the economics of maximizing the value of the system.

By 1993 it was estimated that no fewer than 1.5 to 2 million customers were benefiting from low-user schemes; thus the low-user
schemes were hardly marginal adjustments to the general tariff policy but applied to a substantial group of domestic consumers.
Further changes were made at the beginning of 1994 with the introduction of a Light User Scheme designed to extend coverage further; however, there continued to be strong criticism of their
effectiveness on both economic and social grounds.[63] The future of
the schemes become part of a much more general and extended project of OFTEL on the future of universal service, and it is in this
context that it must now be examined. The European Commission
had already been undertaking work on the concept of universal service as part of its preparations for telecommunications liberalization. For example, it had produced a definition of universal service
in 1993 defining the political goal of universal service as 'making
affordable a defined minimum service of specified quality to all
users at an affordable price', thereby combining both physical
access and affordability; the definition was accepted in a Council
resolution in 1994 adding that it should be based on the principles
of universality, equality, and continuity.[64] Considerable work has

---

[61] OFTEL, n. 41 above, 22.   [62] *Ibid.*
[63] Fitch, M., 'BT's Light User Scheme' (1994) 5 *Utilities Law Review* 162–4.
[64] *Developing Universal Service for Telecommunications in a Competitive Environment*, COM(93)159 final (1993); *Council resolution of 7 February 1994 on universal service principles in the telecommunications sector* [1994] OJ C48/1; for the background to these principles see Ch. 10 below.

been carried out since to develop this definition and to determine its applicability to new services.[65]

OFTEL included questions on the definition and funding of universal service in its 1994 consultation paper on interconnection.[66] Universal service was defined in terms reminiscent of the work by the European Commission referred to earlier as:

the requirement to provide consumers with direct access to a switched telephone network, and the ability to make and receive voice calls, at a reasonable price. The obligation to provide reasonable access implies some intervention to ensure that telephone service is available for high cost customers (for example, those living in remote rural areas, or those with special needs), and also for customers for whom price might otherwise be a barrier

and the basic principles were distilled into three; geographic accessibility, that access should be affordable, and that access should be equitable for those with special needs.[67] The priority was to be the separate identification, costing, and funding of universal service.

A further document incorporated a study of the costs of universal service which suggested that they were much smaller than expected; with net costs possibly as low as zero and certainly no higher than £22 million. Consultation had shown strong support for the proposition that the costs should be funded by the industry as a whole; further consultation then took place on these findings.[68] The final document in the series was concerned wholly with universal service.[69] It noted the close connection between the European developments and the OFTEL proposals, and that they would produce similar outcomes. The policy objectives were to be geographical accessibility, affordability, and equal opportunities for customers with special needs, and the definition of universal service was to be 'affordable access to basic telecommunication services for all those reasonably requiring it regardless of where they live'.[70] This was the basis for proposals for a universal safety net including free itemized billing and selective call-barring; disconnection was to be replaced

---

[65] See for an overview Sauter, W., 'The Evolution of Universal Service Obligations in the Liberalisation of the European Telecommunications Sector' (1996) 7 *Utilities Law Review* 104–10, and the references in n. 43 above.
[66] OFTEL, *A Framework for Effective Competition*, n. 47 above, para. 12.1.
[67] *Ibid.* paras. 12.3, 12.10.
[68] OFTEL, *Effective Competition: Framework for Action*, n. 47 above, ch. 4.
[69] OFTEL, n. 55 above. [70] *Ibid.* para. 4.3.

by the barring of outgoing calls and reasonable access to public call-box services was to be assured. Affordability meant that a more effective alternative to the existing Light User Scheme be developed; a number of alternatives for this were put forward, such as a fixed-sum package for a basic service; further consultation was to take place on the options. A special definition of universal service was to apply to those with severe hearing loss or speech impediment requiring availability of a text relay service. A Universal Service Fund was to be established into which all operators would pay contributions in proportion to basic network service revenues; the fund would compensate operators incurring a net loss through delivering universal service to customers. Thus, on the principle of 'pay or play', any operator could participate in universal service delivery. All these proposals were consistent with similar proposals in the European Community.[71]

Most innovatively of all, special levels of universal service were to be set for educational institutions giving affordable access to a wideband or broadband network, reasonable network access and usage charges, and dedicated external high speed network links. In the case of persons with special needs and of education superhighway services, then, universal service went well beyond provision of basic telecommunications services alone. However, it was later decided that enhanced access for educational establishments and public libraries should be pursued separately from the work on universal service; reasons for this included the fact that the special needs of such institutions could not be limited to the narrow range of services under the Telecommunications Act and that the proposed European directive on open network provision would restrict the possibility of formally defining a higher level of universal service for selected classes of customer. Instead, the Director General chaired a task force including industry and consumer members to assess the needs of educational institutions and libraries and to consider a voluntary scheme based on similar principles to the universal service fund.[72]

It is very evident that universal service issues have moved on in a way which is radically different from the concerns in early regulation, partly influenced by developments in the European

[71] See n. 64 above.
[72] OFTEL, *Improving Access to the Information Society for Education and Public Access Points* (1996).

Community approach. At first, the issue was of relatively limited attempts to lower the charges for access to the telecommunications system for the economic reason of enhancing the value of the whole network. Now the concern is much more clearly social; the first consultation paper commenced discussion of universal service by acknowledging that 'OFTEL has a responsibility to promote the interests of all consumers, including people with a disability or of pensionable age, and a general duty to regulate in the public interest. A fair and equitable balance needs to be struck between the interests of different groups'.[73] This does not exclude an economic justification for universal service, and indeed the case for this has been set out in the consultation documents, but suggests that regulatory purposes are not solely economic. If it is correct to suggest that there is a plurality of regulatory purposes, it becomes essential to examine the procedures used for regulatory decisions; this will be my final concern in this Chapter.

Regulatory Procedures

One of the early criticisms made of the regulators was that they operated in a way which was secretive and unaccountable. This was partly unfair; much more information was available and much more consultation undertaken than in the days of public ownership when disputes on, for example, tariffs were settled in secret between minister and board.[74] Indeed, the First Director General of Telecommunications had promised openness in his first *Annual Report*:

I have made a commitment, in public statements, to be as open as possible in the discussion of issues arising out of my functions and duties. I intend to make public statements about issues under review and to invite representations from interested parties; I intend to establish contact with individuals, companies and representative bodies with interests in telecommunications so that I may become fully aware of their views on important issues; and I intend to give the fullest possible explanation of the basis for my conclusions, subject only to the need to respect commercial confidentiality.[75]

---

[73] OFTEL, *A Framework for Effective Competition*, n. 47 above, para. 12.1.
[74] For examples see Prosser, T., *Nationalised Industries and Public Control* (Blackwell, Oxford, 1986), 63–74.
[75] OFTEL, n. 16 above, para. 1.27.

Steps taken to implement this undertaking included the issue of consultation documents on which representations were invited and the calling of meetings of representives of the industry and other groups. Representations made during consultation were made public except where the Director General was requested not to do so, and he published his advice to the Secretary of State except where commercial confidentiality was involved. However, the giving of reasons was not always as consistent as might have been assumed from the statement; thus on making the crucial first interconnection determination the Director General did not give reasons after legal advice and for fear that a legal challenge would delay the introduction of competition to BT; this fuelled much of the criticism of allegedly unaccountable regulators.[76]

The most important procedural developments have occurred, however, under the Directorship of Don Cruikshank; the openness of decision-making has been nothing less than revolutionary for British public administration. One aspect of this has been straightforward provision of information; OFTEL has established an excellent site on the World Wide Web containing consultative documents, responses to them, and other information. Since 1995 an annual operating plan has been published setting out objectives, priorities, and a work programme; in many respects this is similar to the annual regulatory plan to be submitted by the US agencies as part of the Clinton Administration's regulatory reform to be discussed in Chapter 10.

The most important innovations concerned consultation procedures. It has already been noted that frequent consultation documents had been published and representations invited and published. In March 1995 the result of a review of the consultation process was announced, applying both to statutory consultation and informal consultation. All responses to consultations were to be made public unless clearly marked confidential; respondents were asked to avoid such markings and warned that confidential representations from an operator might in some circumstances nevertheless be published by using the regulator's statutory powers. Further, 'responses (or parts of responses) which are not put into the public domain and are therefore untested by other participants in the industry, may in particular cases be considered by the

---

[76] Veljanovski, n. 12 above, 63.

Director General to have less probative value, and accordingly to carry less weight'.[77]

Secondly, future consultations would incorporate a second consultation stage; after representations had been received, the Director General would be prepared to receive further comments on them within fourteen days; this would provide an opportunity for review of comments made in order to assist analysis of the formal submissions. Finally, the regulator committed himself to providing full explanations for decisions; these would include references to the arguments of parties consulted and a summary of views submitted. In practice a further innovation was introduced; public hearings to consider issues on which consultation was taking place, the first concerning the proposed condition on anti-competitive practice; others related to the proposed price control provision. Once more these reforms are reminiscent of the rule-making procedures of the US agencies to be considered more fully in Chapter 10 below.

A little needs to be said about how these procedures have worked in practice. The most important example is probably that relating to the price controls and the related fair trading condition. An initial consultation document of sixty-eight closely-printed pages was issued in December 1995. The initial consultation period ran to 2 February 1996, with fourteen days for further comments on the submissions, which were published. A second document of ninety-five pages was published in March 1996 setting out further proposals, including indicative values for X in the price formula and responding to comments received in the first consultation. A further consultation period ran until 26 April 1996, followed by the customary two weeks for comments on the submissions made. Five open hearings were heard in April and early May in London, Glasgow, Cardiff, Belfast, and Birmingham. They commenced with statements from OFTEL, British Telecom, other operators, and consumer organizations and then took views from the floor; a summary record of the hearings was published as an annex to the next consultative document. More detailed proposals were included in a two-volume document issued in June 1996; comments were invited by 1 July, with a period up to 15 July for further submissions on them. Final proposal were put to BT by the end of July.[78]

[77] OFTEL, *Consultation Procedures and Transparency*, 1995.
[78] OFTEL, n. 34 above.

Two things are particularly striking about this procedure, apart from the simple mass of information made public. The first is the opportunity provided for exchange of views by participants through the double consultation procedure and the public hearings; consultation moved from a passive receipt of information by the regulator to his encouraging an active debate amongst those interested and responding to them in successive papers. As described in the discussion of pricing proposals above, the plans did change radically during the consultation process, and this must be a tribute to its effectiveness. Secondly, a strict timetable was adhered to successfully; the process took less than eight months, and the most serious possible delay would not have been because of consultation but would have occurred if BT had chosen to require an MMC reference. It should also be mentioned that this is only one example of a number of exercises in extended consultation; for example, universal service proposals had first been the subject of consultation in December 1994 with further consultative documents in July 1995 and December 1995; firm proposals were to follow in late 1996 with implementation for 1997. At each stage a similar consultative process to that for the price controls had taken place; this included a workshop in which a range of interested groups was represented. A further consultative technique is the creation of working groups of industry and consumer members; apart from that on access to services by educational institutions and libraries mentioned above, others considered disconnection and services for the disabled. As also mentioned, a panel of expert advisers will have a particularly central role in the implementation of the new fair trading condition.

Conclusions

It has been possible in this Chapter to cover only some aspects of the work of the Director General of Telecommunications; important areas have been omitted, including, for example, number portability, the issue on which the first important reference in telecommunications to the MMC had been made. Nevertheless, the most important theme to emerge is the complexity and diversity of his task. Regulation of monopoly is only one part of it, and indeed a part declining in importance with the growth of competition; the Director General considers that the 1997 retail price control will be the last. On the other hand, the policing of competition has grown dramatically as a regulatory task and OFTEL is rapidly coming close to being a specialist competition authority, a process only underlined by the proposals for the adoption of a general prohibition of anti-competitive behaviour adopted from the law of the European Community. Whether there is a case for such a specialist competition authority rather than leaving policing to the general competition authorities in London and Brussels will be discussed in Chapter 10; for the moment it should be said that the case for specialism is convincing. Finally, social regulation has achieved a much greater importance than some writers had expected; the concept of universal service will continue to be important in the future as new types of telecommunications and other services develop, and future regulation will be closely linked to actions taken by the European Community.

What is very evident is that regulation is not withering away. It may be changing its form with the growth of competition and of new types of service, and this raises interesting questions about the best type of institution to carry out regulation. Nevertheless, regulation appears to be a permanent phenomenon. Moreover, the issues raised are not susceptible to technical solutions; whilst economic analysis is obviously crucial in, for example, determining the cost of capital in price control, social and distributional considerations have also played a part in the Director General's work. Just as the constellation of duties applying to the regulator reflect a number of different purposes, so does the practice of regulation. Given this necessity to consider a range of apparently incommensurable considerations, the regulator has opted for a procedural solution through extended and sophisticated consultation procedures. These appear to be highly successful. It is perhaps ironic, given the Government's determination to avoid US models at all costs in establishing the regulatory framework that the best contributions of US-style rule-making seem to be finding their way into telecommunications regulation through the voluntary establishment of procedures by the Director General of Telecommunications.

4

Gas: Regulating Monopoly and Managing Liberalization

Introduction

The gas industry after privatization is in many respects in marked contrast to the telecommunications industry discussed in the previous chapter. Some common origins exist in early local-authority ownership and participation; even in the nineteenth century the regulation of gas companies also posed some interesting regulatory problems.[1] At the time of nationalization by the Gas Act 1948, ownership remained extremely fragmented; thus there were 269 municipal operations, five joint boards, 264 private companies under the control of eleven holding companies, and 509 independent private companies; these last supplied 52 per cent of all gas.[2] As a result of this pattern, gas was not so closely associated with public-service ideals as was telecommunications whilst the latter formed part of the Post Office, and universal service could not be so fully applied given the difficulties and expense of supplying isolated rural areas with gas. Nevertheless, gas came to be seen as one of the more successful nationalized industries, especially given the successful implementation of the nationwide conversion from town to natural gas. This is not to say that the characteristic problems of the public enterprises did not apply here; for example, controversy existed over the setting of price levels reflecting negative external financing limits in the mid-1980s.[3] Competition with other gas suppliers before privatization was extremely limited, although of course gas did compete with alternative fuels, especially electricity and oil, and

---

1 See Ch. 2 above and Foster, C. D., *Privatization, Public Ownership and the Regulation of Natural Monopoly* (Blackwell, Oxford, 1992), 61–2.

[2] *The Gas Industry: Report of the Committee of Inquiry*, Cmnd 6699 (1945), para. 57.

[3] Prosser, T., *Nationalized Industries and Public Control* (Blackwell, Oxford, 1986), 63–4.

some restrictions were loosened by the Oil and Gas (Enterprise) Act 1982. This in theory permitted producers to negotiate direct sales of gas to larger consumers, but had minimal practical effects in liberalizing gas supply. The highly monopolistic character of the industry was changed to only a limited degree at privatization. The enterprise was not split up, but privatized as a single unit, a decision much criticized from the outset; as early commentators put it, 'British Gas offers all the disadvantages of the nationalised structure combined with much weaker controls . . . it is difficult to see why, by any measure of efficiency, allocative or managerial, it is likely to become more efficient'.[4] The regulatory story after privatization has largely been one of attempts to correct the difficulties this posed; in a stronger sense than in the case of the other utilities, the form of privatization determined the regulatory task.[5] As we shall see, this initially took the form of a confrontational regulatory attempting to act as a surrogate for the competition which had not been created at the time of the sale of the company, together with determined attempts to enforce fair-competition requirements in the liberalized industrial market, and latterly has included ambitious steps to liberalize the domestic, or tariff, market also. Regulation for competition has necessarily been slower to develop than in telecommunications, but has rapidly taken off with the liberalization of the domestic market.

The lack of a strong perception of a public-service tradition in the sense of that associated with the Post Office, for example, does not mean that social considerations have not loomed large in relation to regulatory concerns. Much more than in the case of telecommunications, the availability of fuel is seen as an essential of life, and so access and disconnection issues have had a much higher profile, as has the possible ending of cross-subsidy to poorer consumers due to the liberalization of the domestic market. The availability of fuel to poorer consumers also has a strong political resonance, as evidenced by the Government's being forced to

---

[4] Price, C., and Gibson, M., 'Privatisation and Liberalisation 2: British Gas' in Whitehead, C. (ed.), *Reshaping The Nationalised Industries* (Transaction, Oxford, 1988), 158–9 at 178; see also Vickers, J., and Yarrow, G., *Privatization: An Economic Analysis* (MIT Press, Boston, Mass., 1988), 268–71.

[5] For a concise account of the privatization process see Ernst, J., *Whose Utility? The Social Impact of Public Utility Privatization and Regulation in Britain* (Open University Press, Buckingham, 1994), 8–14.

abandon the second stage of the imposition of VAT on fuel in 1994. Both these influences have meant that social issues have had a high salience after privatization. Moreover, in the case of telecommunications universal service and a low standing charge could be justified by the economic argument that the more people connected to the system the greater its value for other users, an argument inapplicable to gas and which has required direct distributive justifications for these policies. Social regulation has emerged as a particularly strong concern in designing the arrangements for liberalization of the domestic market in order to prevent cream skimming and lack of service to the least profitable consumers. Finally, energy efficiency has occupied a particularly controversial role in gas regulation, raising directly the authority of the regulator to act for other than economic goals.

Regulatory Institutions

The institutional structure adopted for the gas industry broadly followed that for telecommunications discussed in the previous chapter; perhaps the most interesting point was that the incremental structure of privatization resulted in an industry-specific regulator rather than one across the energy sector. There were however certain important differences which should be signposted from the outset. A separate Gas Consumers Council was established with the duties of investigating complaints apart from those relating to the enforcement of authorizations, of advising the regulator, and of generally representing consumer interests.[6] The Council has been able to achieve a high profile in this activity; its future was for a while uncertain and under review by government, but it campaigned for its own continued future partly by contrasting its performance with the relatively weak one of the less independent Electricity Consumers' Committees. The Government accepted that it should continue in its present form.[7] Secondly, the Monopolies and Mergers Commission was much more actively involved in the regulatory practice than was the case with the other regulatory regimes. Thus soon after privatization vociferous complaints were received from industrial users about British Gas's pricing policy,

---

[6] Gas Act 1986, ss. 2, 32, 40, Sched. 2.

[7] *Government Observations on the First Report of the Trade and Industry Committee*, HC 291, 1994–5, para. 10.

and this resulted in a reference from the OFT to the MMC which made a number of important recommendations, including gas pricing according to a published schedule to avoid discrimination.[8] Responsibility for implementation of the recommendations was given to the DGFT and the Gas Regulator; they did not prove easy to implement. Even more importantly, a series of references to the Monopolies and Mergers Commission was made in 1992 by the Regulator relating to the possible separation of transport from other aspects of the British Gas business, and by the President of the Board of Trade at the request of British Gas itself after it had not felt able to accept the reviewed pricing policy. This enabled the Commission to undertake comprehensive review of the industry, and its Reports[9] formed the basis for far-reaching Government proposals for the opening up to competition of the domestic market, a subject which will be examined in more detail below. It is evident from this that the Government has also been an important regulatory actor, and its proposals differed in very important respects from those of the MMC. Notably, it decided on a faster timetable for domestic liberalization, and this may have contributed to British Gas's serious financial problems caused by entering into long-term contracts with gas producers on the assumption that it would retain its monopoly position.[10] Institutional complexity has thus been particularly marked as a potential source of difficulties in the regulation of the gas industry; as the Gas Consumers Council put it, '[f]rom the consumer viewpoint it is important that regulation should henceforth be a matter for the Regulator. Separate but uncoordinated interventions, by OFT, DTI and OFGAS, have produced market distortions.'[11] However, governmental powers have actually been increased in one respect by the 1995 Gas Act which gives the Secretary of State power to veto licence modification references to the MMC.[12] It should finally be added that, although the European Community has succeeded in agreeing a directive to improve the transparency of industrial pricing,[13] liberalization in the Union has so far been much less marked

---

[8] *Gas*, Cm 500, 1988.   [9] *Gas*, CM 2314–7, 1993.
 [10] See Fitzpatrick, J., and Dow, S., 'The UK Gas Contract Dilemma: Who Dares Wins?' (1996) 7 *Utilities Law Review* 82–7.
 [11] Trade and Industry Committee, *The Work of OFGAS*, HC 185, 1993–4, *Minutes of Evidence*, 20.
 [12] Sched. 3, para. 21, inserting a new s. 24 into the 1986 Act.
 [13] Council Dir. 90/377/EEC [1990] OJ L185/16.

due to difficulties in negotiating linked plans for electricity with
other Member States. Liberalization may proceed more quickly
with agreement having been reached in mid-1996 on liberalization
plans in the Council, but substantial problems still remain.

The Legislation

In gas, we have a unique opportunity to compare two pieces of
legislation nine years apart. The Gas Act 1986 was to a considerable degree modelled on the telecommunications legislation, but, as
with the institutional arrangements, there were some important differences. Thus the general duties of the Director and the Secretary
of State were expressed to be 'to secure that persons authorised by
or under this Part to supply gas through pipes satisfy, so far as it
is economical to do so, all reasonable demands for gas in Great
Britain'[14] and 'without prejudice to the generality of paragraph (*a*)
above, to secure that such persons are able to finance the provision
of gas supply services'.[15] The same general principles applied as in
telecommunications, although the first duty was qualified in such a
way as to reflect the added expense of adopting universal service in
the gas infrastructure. The secondary duty was 'to protect the interests of consumers of gas supplied through pipes in respect of the
prices charged and the other terms of supply, the continuity of supply and the quality of the gas supply services provided',[16] to promote efficiency and economy on the part of gas suppliers, to protect
the public from dangers arising from gas transmission, distribution,
or use, and, in the industrial market (that for customers using more
than, at first, 25,000 therms per year, then 2,500), to enable suppliers to compete effectively.[17] The protection of consumers was also
expressed to require the regulator and Secretary of State to 'take
into account, in particular, the interests of those who are disabled
or of pensionable age'.[18]

A further provision in the Act required a public gas supplier (in
effect, British Gas), to supply premises within twenty-five yards of
a gas main, again reflecting the limits imposed by the technology of
gas supply on universal service.[19] The Competition and Service
(Utilities) Act 1992 conferred on the Gas Regulator additional
powers in relation to service standards and disputes in terms sim-

[14] S. 4(1)(a).   [15] S. 4(1)(b).   [16] S. 4(2)(a).   [17] S. 4(2)(b)–(d).
[18] S. 4(3).   [19] S. 10.

ilar to those for telecommunications, whilst also giving the Secretary of State power to reduce the 25,000 therm threshold for tariff customers and imposing a new primary duty on the regulator and Secretary of State to exercise their functions in the manner best calculated to ensure effective competition between gas suppliers.[20] Further provisions were of course contained in British Gas's authorization, as the licence was termed in this case.[21]

Important changes were made to the statutory duties by the Gas Act 1995 in preparation for domestic liberalization. The first primary duty is changed to require that the Minister and regulator 'secure that . . . all reasonable demands for gas conveyed through pipes are met'; the financing duty is unchanged, but a third primary duty is added; this is 'to secure effective competition in the carrying out of activities' which are to be licensed under the Act.[22] Changes have also been made to the secondary duties; most strikingly, a duty to secure effective competition in the conveyance of gas to pipe-systems and to areas where it has not previously been conveyed is added, as is the duty to take into account the interests of the chronically sick.[23] Very importantly, the duty to supply referred to above is replaced by a duty on the part of a public gas transporter merely to connect premises.[24] At first sight this appears a revolutionary change, ending universal service as a statutory requirement.[25] However, universal service is maintained by other means designed to prevent 'cream-skimming' of profitable consumers at the expense of those less profitable to supply. Thus a licensing system is set up for gas suppliers, and the issue of licences and their conditions are extensively regulated by statute and standard conditions issued by the minister. Thus no licence may be granted if, in the opinion of the regulator, it is framed artificially to exclude premises likely to be owned or occupied by persons who are chronically sick, disabled, or of pensionable age, or who are

---

[20] Ss. 11–19, 37–8.
[21] Department of Energy, *Authorisation Granted by the Secretary of State for Energy to the British Gas Corporation Under the Gas Act 1986* (HMSO, London, 1986) as amended.
[22] S. 1, inserting a new s. 4(1) into the 1986 Act.
[23] S. 1, inserting a new s. 4(2) and 4(3) into the 1986 Act.
[24] Sched. 3, para. 4.
[25] Spring, P., 'The Restructured Gas Industry 1994–5' in Centre for the Study of Regulated Industries, *Regulatory Review 1995* (Centre for the Study of Regulated Industries, London, 1996), 33–57, 44.

likely to default in the payment of charges.[26] Standard conditions
to be included in all supply licences also require the supply of gas
to all domestic customers connected to the network without undue
preference or undue discrimination in the processing of applications; they also empower the regulator to direct a supplier to supply domestic customers in the case of another supplier's default,
thus maintaining security of supply.[27] These provisions and other
social goals will be discussed further when universal service is examined in more detail below.

What we see here, then, is initially a similar mix of duties to those
in the case of telecommunications, with some downplaying of the
elements of universal service; as befits an enterprise privatized in the
form of an almost unbroken monopoly, regulating monopoly was
the main legislative rationale. Nine years later, regulation for competition has emerged and the statutory duties have been changed to
reflect this; new forms of protection have been provided to make
universal service compatible with a competitive market. We thus
once more have a mixture of monopoly, competition, and social
obligations applying to the gas regulator, and the rest of this
Chapter will examine the way they have been worked out in practice.

Before doing so, however, I should make one particular point
about the legal role of the Gas Regulator. This is that the possibility of judicial review seems to have loomed particularly large in
regulatory perceptions. As the first regulator put it, 'OFGAS is
driven by statute . . . our measuring point should be the stage at
which we would become vulnerable to judicial review, . . . OFGAS
has been brought under this particular spotlight on two occasions
and it is far from being a pleasant experience. . . . The cost to us in
time and money was much greater than the outlays involved in a
Monopolies and Mergers Commission case'.[28] In the first case[29]
judicial review was sought of a refusal by the regulator to order
reconnection of supply to the applicant's home after allegations of

[26] S. 6(1), inserting a new s. 7A(8) into the 1986 Act.

[27] Department of Trade and Industry, *Gas Act 1995. Determination of the
Standard Conditions of Public Gas Suppliers' Licences* (HMSO, London, 1996),
conds. 2 and 5.

[28] McKinnon, J., 'Conference on Regulatory Reform' (1993) 4 *Utilities Law
Review* 119–22 at 119–20.

[29] *R.* v. *Director-General of Gas Supply ex parte Smith*, CRO/1398/88, QBD, 31
July 1989.

meter tampering. The application was successful, although all grounds alleging substantive illegality were rejected, the court stressing the broad discretion conferred on the regulator and his autonomy as regards questions of fact. The successful ground was that of procedural impropriety because the applicants had been given no opportunity to comment on evidence obtained by the regulator from a meter reader. If the outcome suggests that the fears of the regulator were somewhat exaggerated, it makes it clear that he was very conscious of the legal duties confining his powers; as we shall see, this has also re-emerged in the context of energy efficiency in relation to his successor.

The Regulators

I mentioned above that the privatization of British Gas as a single unified company set the style for regulation. It is clear that the first regulator was very conscious of this; as he put it, '[t]he privatisation of the British Gas Corporation in 1986 as a single entity conferred PLC status on the enterprise and set the stage for the type of interaction between the newly created Office of Gas Supply . . . and the 100 per cent monopolist.'[30] Added spice was given to this style by the fact that, unlike the other first wave of regulators, Sir James McKinnon came from a background in private business. The result was that under his regime a far more adversarial relationship existed between regulator and regulated company than in other cases. This was largely due to the perception of the regulator that his role was to act as surrogate competition for British Gas; in other words, the competition not created by restructuring would be supplied by regulatory pressure; '[t]here is no real likelihood of an alternative public gas supplier challenging British Gas in gas to gas competition. . . . The next best thing is to simulate competition and that is the task that confronts OFGAS.'[31] Relations further deteriorated with initial difficulties for the regulator in obtaining information from British Gas.[32] As a result of these problems it is

[30] McKinnon, J., 'Office of Gas Supply: Regulation of the Gas Sector' in Veljanovski, C., *Regulators and the Market* (Institute of Economic Affairs, London, 1991), 94–8, 94.

[31] OFGAS, *Annual Report 1988*, HC 197, 1988–9, 9.

[32] For a summary of the deterioration in the relationship see McKinnon, n. 28 above, (1993).

unsurprising that the references to the Monopolies and Mergers Commission proved necessary, and that relations were more confrontational here than elsewhere; nowhere else has a regulator criticized the regulatory industry, for example, for its 'intransigence . . . and its continued desire to retain protection of its profits rather than to have to compete for them as the rest of British industry has to do'.[33] A similarly forceful approach was taken by the regulator in relation to the industrial, or contract, market, where provisional and final enforcement orders were issued against British Gas after complaints of discrimination in contracting and pricing.[34]

The dominance of surrogate competition does not however imply that the regulator ignored more social considerations. For example, he stated that:

[w]hile British Gas should not have to subsidise its consumers, it could be expected to make it easier for them to remain customers. For instance, it might offer a package under which it provided a minimum level of heating, along with both advice and installation of optimal energy efficiency measures, so that the minimum level of heating was provided at the lowest effective cost.[35]

Sir James McKinnon was followed as regulator on 1 November 1993 by Clare Spottiswoode. She had previously worked in both the private and the public sectors; rather surprisingly, she obtained the job after having contacted headhunters; 'I rang them up on one Friday evening, they sounded extremely enthusiastic about my background and said they had the ideal job for me, which was actually this one.'[36] We do not have the benefit of a published management plan as we do in telecommunications; nevertheless, evidence to Committees makes very clear her commitment to competition; '[t]he key thing is to get the structure of the industry right and introduce competition in a way which will really work';[37] '[w]e believe all gas consumers should be able to enjoy the benefits of competition at the earliest possible opportunity'.[38] Initially she appeared to adopt a more conciliatory attitude; no doubt this was

[33] OFGAS, *Annual Report 1991*, HC 193, 1991–2, 25.　　　[34] *Ibid.* 30–2.

[35] OFGAS, *Annual Report 1989*, HC 142, 1989–90, 8–9.

[36] Environment Committee, *Energy Efficiency: The Role of OFGAS*, HC 328, 1993–4, *Minutes of Evidence*, 66.

[37] Trade and Industry Committee, n. 11 above, 5.

[38] Trade and Industry Committee, *The Domestic Gas Market*, HC 681-ii, 1993–4, 84.

facilitated by the fact that the MMC recommendations provided a clearer basis for liberalization than had been available to her predecessor, and anyway relations with British Gas had improved with greater willingness to supply information even before this. However, two areas of great controversy emerged. The first was that of energy efficiency, which she considered a matter for the market or for fresh legislation rather than for regulatory intervention; we shall examine this in detail later. Secondly, she strongly supported domestic liberalization, and, contrary to the views of the Gas Consumers Council, believed it would not result in large price increases to small consumers. Her support for a rapid timetable for such liberalization,

led some industry executives and observers to criticise Ms Spottiswoode for having allegedly fallen under the spell of one particular 'Austrian' school of economic theory. This say her critics, extols the virtues of competition at any price. The result, they say, is that OFGAS views the world through academic eyes, and fails to understand the commercial realities and compromises which characterise competitive markets.[39]

Once again, I shall examine this process in detail later.

Regulating Monopoly: Price Control

As in the case of telecommunications, the first tariff formula was set not by the regulator but by the Secretary of State. It is worth reporting the views of the first regulator on this:

The opening price control formula was prepared in advance of the formation of OFGAS. When, in 1986, I asked if I could have a set of working papers on the construction of the formula I was told that certain forecasts had been made by industry experts and it had been, in the final analysis, a judgement call. In the circumstances, I accepted this, but when I pursued the issue to try to understand the general thrust of the judgement I was slightly disturbed to hear the value of 'X' had been set, 'To get the company off to a good start'.[40]

The initial formula was (for tariff customers, i.e. those consuming fewer than 25,000 therms per year) RPI–2, but with provision for the passing through to consumers of any increases or decreases

---

[39] Corzine, R., 'Lion-tamer Holds the Ring', *Financial Times*, 29 Apr. 1996 (supplement).

[40] McKinnon, n. 28 above, 120.

in the purchase price of gas from off-shore suppliers. This did indeed get the company off to a good start, especially given a fall in world oil prices and gas purchase costs, though domestic gas prices also fell by 10 per cent in real terms from 1986 to 1989.[41]

The formula was to last to April 1992, and in 1990–1 the regulator undertook detailed analysis of British Gas's finances as a basis for its replacement. It was made clear that the decision would be largely based on rate of return considerations:

[a]s part of its review, OFGAS looked specifically at the rate of return which British Gas ought to be able to earn on its tariff business, to ensure that the level of prices set by the formula is enough to give a fair rate of return for British Gas and its shareholders and no more. . . . In particular, it looked at the rates of return employed by comparable businesses in the United Kingdom and overseas, in terms of accounting rates of return and of market rates of return. Taking account of all these factors, OFGAS reached the conclusion that a rate of return of around 5% to 7% in current cost accounting terms would be appropriate for the tariff business.[42]

The Director General proposed a new formula based around RPI–5 with the ability to pass through increases in gas costs limited by a price cap and with provision for recovery of costs associated with energy efficiency measures approved by the regulator. This formula was greeted as far more demanding than its predecessor; the measures 'constitute in aggregate a far superior settlement for the domestic consumer than that achieved at privatisation'.[43] Nevertheless, there were difficulties in implementation, and enforcement action had to be threatened by the Regulator; the company requested a reference to the MMC in June 1992, much to the annoyance of the Director General.[44]

This put many issues into the melting pot, and the Commission recommended divestment of British Gas's trading business by March 1997 and then gradual liberalization of the domestic market. To take account of the first stage of liberalization the tariff formula was to be adjusted from RPI–5 to RPI–4, and a new control based on rate of return was to be set for transportation charges. The Government did not require divestment, but merely internal separation of the businesses, but decided that the monopoly would end in 1996 with full competition phased in over two years from

[41] See Ernst, n. 5 above, 108–10.   [42] OFTEL, n. 33 above, 12.
[43] Ernst, n. 5 above, 113–14.   [44] McKinnon, n. 28 above, 121–2.

that date. The tariff formula was revised to RPI–4 until April 1997 (the coverage of the tariff customer monopoly had been reduced in August 1992 to those customers using 2,500 therms per year or less) and a separate transport price control formula was set at RPI–5 per cent for the period from October 1994 to the same date. In addition to these controls, since privatization standing charges had been subject to a supplementary price cap equivalent to the RPI. In fact, standing charges had been increased by a lower figure. In 1994 the regulator had to determine the transportation part of the standing charge and set it at £15 with a volume charge of 4.19 pence per therm. This was substantially lower than the figure proposed by British Gas and even by independent producers, and has been criticized as perpetuating a large subsidy to domestic users for social reasons, though OFGAS maintained that it was set at this level to enhance prospects for competition.[45]

New, separate, formulae had to be set for transport and supply to take effect from April 1997; going further than the internal separation required by the Government after the MMC report, in February 1996 British Gas announced that it would demerge into two separate companies, TransCo International for transport and production, and British Gas Energy for supply, retail, and service. The new price formulae were, as proposed by the regulator, the most demanding and controversial of all. For transportation, the way was paved by the issue of a consultation paper in June 1995 on the issues to be addressed, followed by two progress reports with detailed initial proposals published in May 1996; final proposals followed in August and were rejected by the company, a reference to the MMC being made in October.[46] The control was to last for five years to March 2002. The most important element in the process was the commissioning of Coopers and Lybrand to carry out an efficiency study of TransCo's forecast operating expenditure; this considered that efficiency improvements of 4 per cent per year could be achieved. A separate study was carried out by consultants of the efficiency of forecast capital expenditure; as a result,

[45] Burns, P., Crawford, I., and Dilnot, A., 'Regulation and Redistribution in Utilities' (1995) 16(4) *Fiscal Studies* 1–22 at 4–8; see also Trade and Industry Committee, *The Domestic Gas Market*, HC 23, 1994–5, paras. 22–7.

[46] OFGAS, *1997 Price Control Review British Gas Transportation and Storage: The Director General's Initial Proposals*; and *The Director General's Final Proposals* (London, 1986).

TransCo's forecasts were reduced by 30 per cent on the basis of previous overestimates. A cost of capital of 6.5–7 per cent was considered appropriate (using as a precedent the MMC report on Scottish Hydro-Electric). Most controversially of all, an opening regulatory value (asset base) of £9–11 bn was proposed for the company based on market value in 1991 and deducting full current cost depreciation to the period up to 1997; the value was set so as to correct the effect of the discount to shareholders on privatization. TransCo suggested a figure of £14.2 bn. The result would be a fall in average prices to TransCo's customers of 20–28 per cent in 1997–8 with an annual price cap of RPI–5 thereafter. Unsurprisingly, TransCo reacted violently to the proposals, claiming that they represented 'one of the biggest smash and grab raids ever' and that they would result in the loss of half TransCo's workforce, a claim disputed by the unions.[47] The final proposals adopted a figure of 7 per cent for cost of capital and the asset base was raised to £11.7 bn, as well as including a number of detailed changes, such as risk-sharing arrangements where costs were particularly uncertain, and permitting TransCo to choose to have the formula reviewed after three or four years. Nevertheless, British Gas did not accept the final proposals, and a reference to the MMC was made; the Director General made it clear that she would argue for the original, stricter proposals before the Commission. Initial-supply price proposals were published in June 1996, after a consultation paper in November 1995 and a progress report and summary of responses.[48] The price cap was to be set for three years in this case to allow subsequent price control to reflect the experience of domestic competition. The 1997 controls would take the form of caps on the four tariffs presently offered, with freedom to rebalance within them and to offer alternative tariffs; they would allow pass-through of TransCo charges and of gas-purchase costs subject to an economic purchasing requirement. Once more, consultants (in this case Arthur Andersen) were used to review forecast supply costs, and British Gas's estimates were revised downwards. The proposals were accepted by British Gas after some revisions in the

---

[47] 'TransCo Prepares to Fight Smash and Grab Raid', *Financial Times*, 14 May 1996.

[48] OFGAS, *1997 Price Control Review Supply at or below 2,500 Therms a Year— British Gas Trading: The Director General's Initial Proposals* (London, 1996).

efficiency targets and acceptance of greater freedom to set additional tariffs.[49]

Initially, there were a number of similarities between price control in gas and that in telecommunications. Thus the initial formula was extremely generous, and much of the effort of the Director General has been spent in trying (with particular difficulty in the case of gas) to correct this. Tariff regulation has proved to be anything but a mechanistic process, and the determination of an appropriate rate of return and especially the asset base has been central to the process. There have been a number of distinguishing features, however. Initially, there was a particularly adversarial relationship between regulator and dominant company (itself largely due to the way in which British Gas had been privatized); there was also institutional complexity with the involvement of the OFT, the MMC, and the Secretary of State, again largely a result of the adversarial relations with the regulator. The simple message of early price control was that the form in which the enterprise was privatized was the key element in determining the regulatory task. In the most recent round of proposals, the asset-base controversy was also largely determined by decisions taken as part of the privatization process; another striking characteristic was the use of outside consultants to examine efficiency in detail and to propose efficiency savings. These have produced proposals of unprecedented severity for the regulated company. This re-emphasizes the message from my examination of telecommunications; the use of the RPI–X formula does not remove the need for detailed regulatory examination of possible efficiency savings, and this involves a considerable effort in analysing the company; it is certainly in no sense a mechanistic process.

Regulating Monopoly: Quality of Service

Just as was the case in telecommunications, a major concern of the Regulator has been quality of service. Two particular aspects of this are of particular interest; the building in of service standards during price review, and the continuation of service standards into the competitive market. During the price-review process in 1991 British Gas agreed to implement a package of proposals on supply service

[49] OFGAS, *1997 Price Control Review Supply: The Director General's Final Proposals* (London, 1996).

standards; this contained ten key standards identified by OFGAS as the principal points of interaction with customers. It was made clear that if standards were not achieved this would constitute grounds for reconsideration of the price formula and possible reference to the MMC, and a compensation scheme was introduced similar to that already existing in the water and electricity industries. A package containing further standards was implemented from April 1992, and in the following year British Gas agreed to introduce a set of standards for transportation and storage. Further supply standards were also introduced at the end of that year, bringing the total number of service standards to thirty-nine.

Performance fell short of the levels expected in 1994 and 1995 in two key areas, and British Gas voluntarily relinquished its Charter Mark for delivery of high standards of public service at the end of the period. With the separation of supply and transportation, the standards of service were reallocated between the two new enterprises, and transport standards were reviewed after poor performance in relation to suppliers was identified; transportation standards were incorporated into the Network Code which came into effect in March 1996 (see below) and are likely to continue indefinitely. TransCo now had two sets of service standards, one for public service and one for performance to other companies using its network. In the supply review, in addition to the service standards which will apply to all domestic gas suppliers, additional standards for British Gas were to continue, and provision was to be made for tightening the operation of the price formula if service standards were not met.[50] Thus in both transportation and supply, some standards reflect the dominant position of British Gas, whereas in supply other standards will be part of the conditions applying to all competing suppliers. This brings us to the role of the regulator in facilitating and policing competitive markets.

Regulation for Competition: The Industrial Market

This can be covered briefly as, despite considerable activity by OFGAS here, most of the controversy has concerned the domestic market. From privatization, the industrial market of consumers who used more than 25,000 therms per year was liberalized,

---

[50] For details of all the standards, see *1997 Price Control Review Supply—Initial Proposals*, n. 46 above, ch. 3 and App. 2.

although earlier attempts to encourage competition had had minimal success; the floor was reduced to 2,500 therms in 1992. This did not prevent the emergence of a large number of regulatory problems, including the first reference of British Gas by the Office of Fair Trading to the MMC which concerned discriminatory pricing, lack of transparency, the conditions under which interruptible gas was supplied, and the pricing policy for power schemes. The Commission's recommendations included that gas should be priced according to a published price schedule with an obligation not to discriminate between customers, that more information should be published by British Gas, and that the company should be required initially not to contract for more than 90 per cent of deliveries from the UK continental shelf. As mentioned above, this then encountered serious difficulties of implementation.[51] The lesson is that even where liberalization has taken place important regulatory policing duties will remain. Even in 1992 the regulator found cause to complain that '[a]ccess by competitors to parts of the market is . . . still denied as a result of the anticompetitive behaviour of British Gas'.[52] However, by mid-1994 45 per cent or more of the industrial market was served by British Gas's competitors; in October of that year the requirement of published schedules was suspended for customers on firm contracts, and for all customers in June 1995 subject to undertakings by British Gas, whose market share had dropped to a mere 35 per cent.[53] OFGAS also established a new system for dealing with complaints arising from the industrial and commercial market; in 1995 it dealt with 2,975 inquiries and complaints. Steps were taken to ensure the effective separation of TransCo from the British Gas trading business; these included an amendment to the authorization to include a non-discrimination provision and the erection of 'Chinese walls' to prevent the flow of inappropriate information between the businesses.

With the separation out of the transportation and storage business, it was also necessary to establish open and non-discriminatory access to it. This took the form of agreeing the Network Code. The Code was treated as primarily a matter for commercial negotiation between TransCo and gas shippers, though OFGAS set an overall

[51] See Graham, C., and Prosser, T., *Privatizing Public Enterprises* (Clarendon Press, Oxford, 1991), 205–6.
[52] OFGAS, *Annual Report 1992*, HC 385, 1992–3, 12–13.
[53] OFGAS, *Annual Report 1995*, HC 128, 1995–6, 12–13.

framework and gave direction to the project, resolved disputes referred to it, and chaired the steering group and panel responsible for drawing up the Code. It was also given the statutory power to determine the terms of transportation in the event of an appeal to the regulator.[54] Thus, even in the industrial market, it is clear that the achievement of effective competition has been dependent on important initiatives by the regulator who will have a clear continuing role in policing competition.

Regulation for Competition: The Domestic Market

With the second set of MMC Reports, controversy passed to the question of the liberalization of supplies to tariff customers.[55] Though they did not find the domestic monopoly as such to be against the public interest, the 1994 reports proposed the divestment by British Gas of its trading business by 1997, followed by a phased opening up of the domestic market over the following three to five years; 'no decision should be taken as to the timing of the complete removal of the tariff monopoly except after a most careful assessment of the consequences'.[56] In December 1993 the Government announced that, while British Gas would be required to separate its transportation and trading businesses rather than to divest the latter, competition in the domestic market would be introduced much more quickly with the market opened up progressively from April 1996 and fully from April 1998. The implications of the proposals were examined in detail by the Trade and Industry Select Committee. It quickly became clear that the major concern was that of avoiding cream-skimming of the most profitable customers at the expense of the less well-off, raising the question of social obligations which will be discussed in detail in the following section.[57] The Gas Act 1995 was passed to pave the way for the changes, and trial areas were established from 1996 in the south west, being extended to cover two million customers in the

[54] Gas Act 1986 s. 19, as inserted by the Gas Act 1995, Sched. 3, para. 16. For a summary of issues arising in relation to the Network Code see OFGAS, *Annual Report 1995*, HC 128, 1995–6, 27–31.

[55] For a comprehensive analysis of the liberalization of domestic energy markets see Corry, D., Hewett, C., and Tindale, S. (eds.), *Energy '98: Competing for Power* (Institute for Public Policy Research, London, 1996).

[56] MMC, *Gas*, Cm 2314, (1993), i, para. 1.9.

[57] Trade and Industry Committee, n. 45 above.

south west and parts of the south east in 1997, with full liberalization in 1998. The choice of trial areas was influenced by their distance from the sites at which gas is landed, so that they incur the
greatest transport costs for their gas.

The 1995 Act amends that of 1986 to create a complex system
of licensing. Three new classes of licence are created, for public
gas transporters, gas shippers, and for gas suppliers, and it is the
latter which are of the greatest interest here. No holder of such a
licence will be able to hold a transportation licence, so there will
be clear separation between the two types of business. Licences are
issued by the regulator; however, the Secretary of State has issued
detailed standard conditions to be included in all licences, which
will be considered in detail in the following section as they have
been used to impose uniform social obligations.[58] The regulator
may however modify the standard conditions to meet the circumstances of the particular case, and may impose additional conditions.[59]

Before considering the conditions in detail it is worth reiterating
an important point. The first Director General of Gas Supply concluded a survey of his role as follows:

As the level of competitive activity in the industrial sector grows so will
customer choice become wider. This process will bring advantages in terms
of price and quality of service to the customers and additional efficiency to
the operations of suppliers. As if this were not enough, there will be the
added bonus of the disappearance of the regulator.[60]

This now seems a wildly over-optimistic (or simplistic) view. In the
industrial market continued policing of anti-competitive behaviour
has proved necessary, and this has involved the regulator rather
than the ordinary competition authorities. Even after the separation of the transport and trading businesses, the former will remain
a monopoly and will require continued regulation, in particular,
price control and control of anti-competitive practices. As regards
the domestic market, the introduction of competition gives major
new licensing and licence-modification powers to the regulator, as
well as the responsibility of policing licensing obligations; as one

[58] Gas Act 1995, s. 8, inserting a new s. 8 into the Gas Act 1986; for the standard conditions, see n. 27 above.
[59] Gas Act 1995, ss. 7(4), 8(3), inserting new s. 7B into the 1986 Act.
[60] McKinnon, n. 30 above, 97.

commentator has put it in relation to the 1995 Act, '[t]he Director's power to modify conditions is but one example of the wide discretion granted to the Director under the new regime. . . . The personality of the Director becomes an increasingly important element in the regulatory regime'.[61] The licence conditions for domestic liberalization are of particular interest in enforcing social obligations, and it is to these that I shall now turn.

Social Regulation and Universal Service

In the discussion of the legislation above, it was noted that a number of social obligations exist in relation to gas, although they are modified by the technological nature of the product and its supply. A further contrast with telecommunications is the absence of an economic argument to justify a low-user tariff on the grounds of easier access to the network, increasing its value to users as a whole; nor does such a tariff exist, although, as mentioned above, it has been suggested that the low site charge set for TransCo in 1994 may have been an attempt to keep low the bills of low users on distributional or political grounds.[62] Nevertheless, a number of social concerns have arisen similar to those in telecommunications, and the issues of access and universal service have arisen in different forms for this industry as well as for telecommunications. Universal service was implemented during the domestic monopoly by requiring British Gas to provide quotations in response to any request for a new gas supply; this was supervised and complaints resolved by OFGAS, which could independently determine the connection charge. Substantial success had been achieved in extending coverage; by 1994 gas was supplied to 91 per cent of households.[63] Even before domestic liberalization, however, the issue of disconnection was controversial.[64]

After privatization, gas disconnections rose, increasing from 35,626 in 1985 to 60,778 in 1987.[65] In April 1989 the Director

[61] Dow, S., 'Licensing of the Gas Supply Industry Under the Gas Act 1995' (1996) 7 *Utilities Law Review*, 31-4 at 34.

[62] Burns *et al.*, n. 45 above, 4–8.

[63] Trade and Industry Committee, n. 11 above, 1.

[64] For a detailed account of disconnection policy and its background, see Rowlingson, K., and Kempson, E., *Gas Debt and Disconnection* (Policy Studies Institute, London, 1993).

[65] Ernst, n. 5 above, 139.

General announced a modification of British Gas's authorization
introducing new procedures aimed at limiting disconnections. This
new Condition 12A effectively prevented disconnection unless the
customer had first been offered a pre-payment meter as an alternative. Payment thus changed from being by credit to in advance with
the meter set to recover past debt.[66] Despite some implementation
problems, the effect was radically to reduce disconnections, with
the numbers dropping from 61,796 in the year ending 31 March
1988 to 19,266 in the year ending 31 March 1990.[67] Later years
have seen further reductions, with 14,511 disconnections in 1995,
the lowest number since privatization; 566,092 prepayment meters
were in use.[68] This has not solved all the problems, of course, for
difficulties have remained both in cases where it proved impossible
to contact defaulting customers, so making disconnection
inevitable, and in cases of self-disconnection, in other words inability to pay with a prepayment meter.[69] Nevertheless, OFGAS considered that the effect of the changes had been to produce
considerable improvement in procedures:

OFGAS believes that a combination of the legal requirement now contained in the Authorization, backed by a considerable training effort and
changed attitudes from within British Gas has been responsible for ensuring greater consistency in the operation of debt collection policies.
Customers are no longer wholly dependent on British Gas's interpretation
of a voluntary Code of Practice and have a right to expect sympathetic
treatment at all times.[70]

As we shall see in a moment, the existing protections are being
extended to new suppliers in the newly competitive domestic market.

Other types of social obligation supplemented the rules on disconnection. One innovation after privatization was the introduction of a Gas Care Register to ensure that the elderly and disabled
enjoy special consideration through, for example, free safety checks
and free adaptations to appliances; over 900,000 elderly and disabled people were on the register by 1993, and once more existing
obligations are extended to new suppliers in the competitive domestic market.

---

[66] *Ibid.* 141.   [67] *Ibid.*   [68] OFGAS, n. 53 above, 23.
[69] See Ernst, n. 5 above, 142 and Rowlingson and Kempson, n. 64 above.
[70] OFGAS, *Annual Report 1990*, HC 158, 1990–1, 33.

It will already be apparent that issues of universal service and other social obligations were a dominant theme in the debates around in the proposals for liberalization of the domestic market. In particular, there was a fear that in a competitive market new suppliers could 'cherry-pick' the most profitable customers. Not only would this mean that the opportunities offered by competition were only available to the most prosperous, it could, in a manner familiar from telecommunications, prevent the continuance of existing cross-subsidies and require price increases to the less well-off. Before liberalization, cross-subsidies existed between different parts of the country, from large customers to small ones, between those with even load requirements and those whose demand varies seasonally, and between good payers and bad payers.[71] While not all of these are defensible (for example the subsidy to bad payers), others clearly raise distributive issues. The Select Committee recommended that such cherry-picking be prevented by prohibiting licensees from discriminating unfairly between customers using fewer than 1,500 therms per year on the basis of the customer's level of consumption, and that OFGAS should examine any discount system to ensure that it was fair to those with prepayment meters.[72] A second aspect of the same problem concerns customers with special needs. The danger here once more was that customers such as the elderly, the disabled, and those on low incomes would be avoided by new suppliers. The solution chosen by the Government was to continue a form of universal service obligation, but one applying to all suppliers; as the Select Committee put it:

suppliers will be obliged to publish their tariffs and to supply any customer within their licence area who requests a supply, though not necessarily on credit. . . . Also the DTI states that 'geographical licences will cover areas with a reasonable cross-section of types of customer'. Standardised debt and disconnection procedures will also be important. *We regard the principle of equal obligations on all suppliers as an essential feature of the new competitive market.*[73]

These principles have been implemented in a number of ways. First, and as mentioned early in this Chapter, the 1995 Act forbids the regulator from framing a licence in such a way as artificially to exclude premises likely to be occupied by persons who are chroni-

---

[71] Trade and Industry Committee, n. 45 above, para. 20.
[72] *Ibid.* paras. 27, 29.   [73] *Ibid.*, para. 40, footnotes omitted, emphasis retained.

cally sick, disabled, or of pensionable age, or who are likely to default in the payment of charges; this will thus prevent a new supplier artificially excluding the inner city from his area, for example.[74] Secondly, the standard conditions to be included in all licences require that all domestic customers in the licence area must be supplied with gas without undue preference or undue discrimination in the processing of applications; a dominant supplier is also prohibited from undue preference or undue discrimination in charges.[75] This will mean that the dominant supplier at least must retain cost-reflective tariffs and so cannot impose highly onerous pricing conditions to deter customers of a particular type.[76] In a manner reminiscent of telecommunications, the Government also accepted that a levy on gas suppliers might prove necessary if British Gas or any other supplier were to bear an unfair share of the burden of less economic customers. The standard conditions provide for suppliers to make claims for 'special customer payment claims' which must be approved by the Director General and the Secretary of State, though it seems unlikely that this power will be used.[77] The standard licence conditions also require all suppliers to comply with other social obligations, including services for pensioners and the disabled and disconnection procedures. Finally, it should be noted that the individual price caps agreed for supply from 1997 to 2000 include a specific cap on the prepayment tariff, thereby providing protection to prepayment meter customers.

The conclusion to this section is somewhat ironic in that it reverses some of the original assumptions about utility regulation, in particular, that regulation withers away with the growth of competition, and that it is concerned with economic rather than social obligations. We will of course see some withering; thus price control of supply will not ultimately be required in a competitive supply market, although TransCo will need to be subjected to price control indefinitely. Supervision of contractual arrangements between the different operators within the competitive gas industry will also be required to ensure fair competition, for example by settling disputes arising from the Network Code. But, crucially, the regulation of suppliers to enforce licence requirements concerning

---

[74] S. 6(1), inserting a new s. 7A(8) into the Gas Act 1986.
[75] Department of Trade and Industry, n. 27 above, conds. 2, 13.
[76] See Corry, Hewett and Tindale, n. 55 above, 74–5.
[77] Department of Trade and Industry, n. 27 above, cond. 6.

social obligations is likely to become more, not less, important. Where a monopoly has existed it has been possible to maintain protections serving social functions through cross-subsidy and through the remnants of commitments dating back to nationalization. Competition will require deliberate action by the public authorities in the form of licence conditions and regulatory supervision to protect the vulnerable and maintain universal service. It has yet to be seen how effective the provisions designed to implement such protections will be, particularly if a levy is not implemented.[78] Nevertheless, not only are we unlikely to see an end to regulation, but that which remains will become increasingly concerned with two themes: policing competition and enforcing social obligations.

Energy Efficiency

Gas regulation has offered us an opportunity to observe the relationship between economic and social or political goals in a dispute concerning the powers of the regulator to promote energy efficiency. This is not to say that such promotion is not in itself an economic goal; clearly energy efficiency can of course be seen as an economic goal designed to promote the optimum distribution of resources and to ensure that pricing reflects the real value of a limited resource. Nevertheless, there is also a social element involved, through, for example, aiding low-income consumers to make their homes energy efficient. Moreover, differences between the regulators are of interest in showing their personal conceptions of their roles in a particularly clear way.[79]

The Gas Regulator is under a statutory duty to promote 'the efficient use of gas conveyed through pipes'.[80] The issue of energy efficiency arose in 1989 when it became apparent that a number of customers were wasting gas in order to move from the tariff to the contract market through increased consumption, so as to benefit from lower prices. In 1990 proposals were put forward by the regulator to prevent the wasteful flaring of gas by customers seeking to enter the contract market, and they were adopted in a mod-

---

[78] See Corry, Hewett and Tindale, n. 55 above, 74–6, 84, 136.

[79] For a very clear analysis of this dispute see Tierney, S., 'OFGAS and the Energy Efficiency Debate' (1996) 7 *Utilities Law Review* 15–21.

[80] Gas Act 1986, s. 4(2)(b), as amended by the Gas Act 1995, s. 1; previously the same duty applied but referred to gas 'supplied' through pipes.

ified form in 1991. A Code of Practice on energy efficiency was also agreed in 1990, with British Gas agreeing to provide information to customers, to provide staff training, and to provide packages including easy payment methods designed to be particularly attractive to low-income consumers.[81] In 1991 a new statement of intent was agreed between the regulator and the company enabling the Director General to determine standards of performance in connection with the promotion of the efficient use of gas;[82] statutory powers to determine and monitor such standards were added by the 1992 Act.[83]

Thus from early on in the regulatory regime there were modest but useful attempts to promote energy efficiency by the regulator. Much more controversial was the use of the price formula to fund energy efficiency schemes. The new price formula agreed in 1992 included provision for the pass-through of energy efficiency costs (the E-factor). This was intended to enable expenditure on energy-efficiency measures to be commercially appealing in the same way as new gas purchases, through permitting the regulator to permit pass-through of such expenditure. British Gas did introduce two schemes promoting the use of condensing boilers and residential combined heat and power, however the major controversy arose in relation to the Energy Saving Trust with the appointment of Clare Spottiswoode as Gas Regulator. The Trust was established by the Government and the energy utilities with the aim of increasing financial resources available for promoting energy efficiency, and, in particular, implementing the Government's strategy for the reduction of carbon dioxide emissions agreed at the World Summit in Rio in 1992. The E-factor and its equivalent in the electricity industry were seen by the Trust as key means of doing so.

The new Director General had doubts whether her powers permitted her to approve this. As she put it in evidence to the Trade and Industry Select Committee:

My main concern about the E factor is that it has become a political means of funding the Energy Savings Trust and dealing with the CO2 limits, which are Government policy, and there appears to have been an assumption that the regulator would just take on Government policy and fund it. I have two problems about that. Firstly, it actually requires raising taxes

[81] OFGAS, n. 70 above, 12–13.   [82] OFGAS, n. 33 above, 36–7.
[83] Competition and Service (Utilities) Act 1992, s. 15.

on gas consumers generally and . . . [s]econdly, raising taxes is actually a Parliamentary decision, not a regulatory decision.[84]

She was then called to give evidence before the Environment Select Committee, which was astonished to hear evidence from her to the effect that her predecessor had acted outside his powers in his application of the E-factor to support expenditure by the Trust.[85] Unsurprisingly, this provoked an explosive response from Sir James McKinnon.[86] Ms Spottiswoode then withdrew her allegation after receipt of Counsel's opinion to the effect that the principle of law preventing the levying of taxation without Parliamentary authorization would not be breached by the use of the E-factor to fund Trust schemes, and that the matter was for the discretion of the regulator. According to the opinion, rather than imposing a public-law obligation on British Gas to support the Trust and so amounting to unlawful taxation, the E-factor merely involved lifting the ceiling on a regulated price which the company might or might not choose to pass on to customers. Nor did the scheme involve disregard of any of the regulator's statutory objectives.[87]

In evidence to the later Select Committee inquiry on the domestic gas market, the Trust described the arrangements as unsatisfactory for all parties, and it recommended the amendment of the statute to permit the support of such schemes by the Secretary of State; the Committee recommended that the Government take such a power to impose an energy efficiency levy on gas.[88] However, no steps were taken to do so in the 1995 Act. In 1994 British Gas had proposed five energy-efficiency schemes for funding from the E-factor as part of a strategic plan prepared by the Energy Saving Trust; after some delay the Director General rejected funding for almost all of them.[89] Her obvious reluctance to approve such measures, even once it was clear she had the legal power to do so, appears clearly from her evidence to the various Select Committees, for example:

I, first of all, have to ask why is the scheme not being done commercially, if it is truly to the benefit of all consumers; if it requires a subsidy then I

[84] Trade and Industry Committee, n. 11 above, *Minutes of Evidence*, Q. 92.
[85] Environment Committee, n. 36 above, *Minutes of Evidence*, Q. 88.
[86] *Ibid. Minutes of Evidence*, 43–5.
[87] *Ibid.* 50–7. Cf. Corry, Hewett and Tindale, n. 55 above, 108.
[88] Trade and Industry Committee, n. 45 above, paras. 44-5.
[89] OFGAS, n. 53 above, 19–20.

have to justify that subsidy and say that there are externalities involved in this decision, over and above the normal financial costs and benefits to consumers, and, therefore, I am taking policy decisions on either environmental concerns or on industry concerns, but I am actually taking policy decisions that are normally the prerogative of Parliament.[90]

No equivalent for the E-factor is proposed for the set of price controls commencing in 1997.

This dispute raises a number of issues concerning the role of the regulator within the regulatory framework. It has underlined the personalized nature of regulation; what is quite clear is that, as one commentator has put it, 'the discretionary freedom permitted by existing legislation has allowed considerable scope for the political values of the regulators to influence the decision-making process, even to the extent of undermining existing Government policy'.[91] This is particularly striking when it is noted that the Electricity Regulator had not found any difficulty in accepting that legitimacy of support for Energy Saving Trust schemes from the electricity equivalent of the E-factor. One point which is also underlined, however, is that the legislative framework does not simply require efficiency-maximizing solutions; the advice received by the Gas Regulator made it quite clear that a broad discretion was conferred on the Director General, and this need not be influenced solely by economic considerations; in balancing improved energy efficiency and the interests of consumers in relation to gas prices, the Director General has a 'wide discretion'.[92]

Regulatory Procedures

As with the other utility regulators, both of the Directors General of Gas Supply have made public commitments to be as open as possible in their decision-making. For example, soon after her appointment, a member of the Trade and Industry Committee suggested to Ms Spottiswoode that there should be consultation procedures and reasons given in relation to all decisions; she agreed strongly.[93] Compared to OFTEL, less ambitious steps have been taken to implement this openness through formal consultation

---

[90] Environment Committee, n. 36 above, *Minutes of Evidence*, Q. 448.
[91] Tierney, n. 79 above, 20.
[92] Environment Committee, n. 36 above, *Minutes of Evidence*, 57.
[93] Trade and Industry Committee, n. 11 above, *Minutes of Evidence*, Q. 35.

procedures. OFGAS has not published a management plan, nor does it have a home page on the World Wide Web; moreover, its annual reports are noticeably briefer than those from the other utility regulators (in 1995, forty pages compared to eighty-three for OFWAT, 144 for OFTEL, and 151 for OFFER). Nevertheless, it should be underlined that far more information has been made available than before privatization, when pricing decisions, in particular, were shrouded in secrecy.[94] The first review of the price formula was criticized because the regulator took the issue out to consultation only after reaching agreement with British Gas. However, as was shown earlier in this Chapter, more recent price-control decisions have involved the issue of several consultation documents, progress reports, and proposals setting out a number of options. Responses have also been made publicly available unless otherwise requested, and the views of British Gas and of participants in consultative procedures have been summarized in final OFGAS proposals. What does not yet exist is a procedure for debating different inputs into the consultative process, either in the form of hearings (which OFGAS has no plans to use) or in the form of a second round of notice and comment during each stage of consultation, as implemented by OFTEL. This could assume particular importance given the heavy reliance on outside consultants in recent price reviews. Such use of consultants is extremely valuable in providing an independent viewpoint in the process and as reducing the regulator's reliance on information from the regulated company. However, given the strong weight given to consultants' views, some opportunity to debate them is essential, and this will require full access to consultants' reports by other participants in the consultative process, except where strong reasons of commercial confidentiality suggest otherwise. One of British Gas's complaints in the price review was that it was not afforded such access to key consultants' reports relating to capital and operating expenditure for TransCo; it noted that in the Electricity Regulator's review of the transmission price control such access was provided.[95] Summaries were however published as part of the consultation process, with some figures removed at TransCo's request for reasons of commercial confidentiality, so it is not just OFGAS

---

[94] For examples see Prosser, n. 3 above, 63–6.

[95] British Gas, *Response to OFGAS's Initial Proposals for the Control of British Gas TransCo's Prices* (London, 1996), para. 1.25 and ch. 4.

which could be accused of lacking a full commitment to transparency.

Extensive consultation has also taken place in relation to other regulatory developments. Thus, in the case of liberalization of the domestic market, a detailed joint consultation document was issued by the Department of Trade and Industry in May 1994.[96] In 1994, OFGAS published fourteen consultation documents and discussion papers relating to the changes to be made by the 1995 legislation, and 165 formal responses were received to the consultation. Seven conferences were also held as part of the consultation exercise. Consultation documents were also issued on a range of other subjects; for example, in 1996 three were issued on competition in parts of TransCo's work.[97]

Conclusions

Three themes have emerged clearly from this Chapter. The first is that OFGAS will have a continuing role in price control, for some years at least in gas supply, and indefinitely in transportation. It has adopted an ambitious approach to this work, using consultants extensively as a means of obtaining views from a source other than the regulated company, and making detailed analyses of the economic issues involved. It is clear from this that price control cannot be in any sense a mechanistic or simple process, even under the RPI–X formula; the attraction of this formula lies rather in postponing regulatory decisions to periodic intervals, and in permitting the sharing of efficiency gains.

Secondly, as with OFTEL, the regulator in gas is assuming an important role as a competition authority, in relation to both the industrial and the domestic markets. This will also continue well into the future. Thirdly, and interestingly, the opening up of a competitive domestic market has not resulted in the end of social obligations. Rather they have become implemented in new ways; through licence conditions drawn up by government with the regulator's advice and incorporated in all licences. This is particularly true in the case of universal service, where the effectiveness of the

---

[96] DTI/OFGAS, *Competition and Choice in the Gas Market* (DTI/OFGAS, London, 1994).
[97] OFGAS, *British Gas TransCo Metering; Storage; Connection and System Extensions: Regulating for Competition* (London, 1996).

conditions has yet to be tested. Again, the regulator will retain an important role in the enforcement of these conditions, and in policing other service standards.

One difference from telecommunications is that, given the absence of competing transportation systems, regulation of monopoly will continue indefinitely. However, regulation for competition has become increasingly important, and it is probable that in the future social regulation in the competitive market will also have a higher profile. Regulation is certainly not withering away, but changing its form. This makes a concern with regulatory procedures all the more important, and the record is mixed. A strikingly large amount of information is now made available in price reviews, though devices such as hearings to test opposing views have not been used and there has been criticism of lack of access to all-important consultants' reports.

5

Water: Regulating Without Competition

Introduction

There is once more a striking contrast in the nature of the regulated industry; water is very different from the other privatized utilities for a number of reasons, notably the much stronger natural monopoly characteristics present and the pervasive interaction of economic and environmental regulation. It should be mentioned that, whilst the word 'water' is used as shorthand to describe the industry, the most important enterprises are both water and sewerage companies, and regulation covers both aspects of their business.

As with other enterprises described, there was a history of local-authority ownership.[1] Water supply had been undertaken by private companies and municipal corporations under local Acts in the early nineteenth century, and a statutory duty to supply on request was imposed in 1847. By 1913 local authorities were providing 80 per cent of supply, though twenty-nine private companies survived under strict regulation until after the privatization of the rest of the industry. After the Second World War the number of suppliers was rationalized, falling from over 1,000 to 150 in thirty years. Sewerage disposal had been exclusively the preserve of local government and was undertaken in a highly fragmented way; by 1974 there were still no fewer than 1,393 sewerage authorities in England and Wales.[2]

The system was entirely transformed by the Water Act 1973, which established ten Regional Water Authorities which assumed the responsibilities previously undertaken by all the bodies mentioned except the private water companies. The Authorities also had regulatory responsibilities for river management and land drainage; the radical reform in the Act was intended to introduce the principle of 'integrated river-basin management' with a single

---

[1] For a historical summary see Saunders, P., and Harris, C., *Privatization and Popular Capitalism* (Open University Press, Buckingham, 1994), 34–8.
[2] *Ibid.* 36.

body responsible for the entire water cycle in each river-basin region. Initially local authorities retained some agency responsibilities for sewerage and had a majority of seats on the new Authorities; however in 1983 both of these were ended, and the Authorities came closer to the standard model of nationalized industry. Inevitably, given the need for large-scale capital investment to renew ageing infrastructure and improve environmental quality, problems in raising investment funds from public finance became serious, and privatization emerged out of these difficulties.[3] A discussion paper was issued by the Department of the Environment in April 1985, and a White Paper in February 1996, both proposing privatization of the Authorities in their existing form, retaining both operational and regulatory responsibilities. This combination of gamekeeper and potential poacher in the same organization was strongly opposed by affected interests, including business, farmers, and landowners, and was potentially in conflict with European Community obligations; the situation was complicated by the granting of leave for a judicial review action by the trade unions relating to the *vires* of preparations for privatization. The Government changed its plans in July 1986, and announced in its 1987 election manifesto that the Authorities would be privatized stripped of their regulatory powers, which would be passed to the new National Rivers Authority. Despite strong initial opposition from the Authorities, this went ahead; the new system was established by the Water Act 1989 (now consolidated into the Water Industry Act 1991 and the Water Resources Act 1991), and all the shares in the new water and sewerage companies were successfully floated in December 1989. Finally, under the Environment Act 1995 the National Rivers Authority was subsumed into the new Environment Agency designed to offer a 'one-stop-shop' for environmental, though not economic, regulation.

The peculiar elements of the water industry derive to a large degree from this history. First, public-service perceptions remain strong, reflecting both a history of local-authority management until fairly recent times, a type of management which survived until 1996 in Scotland, and perceptions of water as essential for any acceptable standard of living and for preventing ill health, not only for individual consumers but for others through infection and epidemics. This is reflected in the virtual achievement of universal

[3] *Ibid.* 38–9, 40-4.

service; before privatization, 99 per cent of households in England and Wales had been connected to the water system, and 96 per cent to that for sewerage.[4] Despite the large number of organizations involved in water and sewerage, this had not led to the establishment of any real degree of competition; indeed the post-1973 structure emphasized economies of scale and integrated management in a way which was strongly antipathetic to competition. As a result, natural monopoly was far stronger in the case of the water industry than in any other to be examined in this book. As the regulator put it:

[c]onsumer sovereignty is a far cry from the water industry. The provision of water and sewerage services is a statutory, and water distribution is a natural, monopoly. . . . Unlike telecoms, gas and electricity, there is no national network to act as a common carrier for competing suppliers. It may be possible to develop such competition, but, in the absence of structural change, only in the longer term.[5]

Such competitive developments as have proved possible have been at the margin or have involved the technique of 'yardstick' or 'comparative' competition rather than creating directly competitive conditions, as we shall see. This has been exacerbated by a charging system for domestic consumers which has traditionally been based not on usage but on rateable values, thus making it difficult directly to respond to consumer demand; as we shall see also, the quest for an alternative charging method has been one of the most controversial regulatory activities.

Regulatory Institutions

A further, very important, effect of the structure and history of the water industry has been to require a highly complex regulatory structure with responsibilities divided several ways. In brief, regulation of drinking-water quality is carried out by the Drinking Water Inspectorate (and this has not been transferred to the new Environment Agency). Water-pollution control, abstraction licensing, and other resource management and drainage and flood protection were the responsibility of the National Rivers Authority,

---

[4] *Ibid.* 35.
[5] Byatt, I., 'OFWAT: Regulation of Water and Sewerage' in Veljanovski, C., *Regulators and the Market* (Institute of Economic Affairs, London, 1991), 119–31, 121.

and, since 1 April 1996, of the Environment Agency. Quality-standard setting is carried out by the Secretary of State for the Environment, and underlying much of this is the implementation of targets and standards set by the European Community. It should be obvious that this complex division of functions cannot be free from conflicts. The Director General of Water Services is responsible for economic regulation, but even this is not solely a matter for him. The Monopolies and Mergers Commission plays its usual role in licence modification; however, the key factors in price control are treated not as simple licence amendments but as determinations under the licence which can be made by the MMC on reference by the regulator at the request of the company. In this case the Director General must implement the MMC decision.[6] The Commission has a special role for water, in that mergers between large water companies are automatically referred to it to establish whether the merger will make yardstick competition more difficult.[7] Yet another different model has been adopted for consumer representation. The regulator is obliged to establish customer service committees, of which he appoints the members; the Committees are responsible for reviewing matters affecting the interests of consumers and investigating complaints.[8] Ten such committees have been established.[9] An OFWAT National Consumer Council has also been established on a non-statutory basis as a means for the Chairmen of the Committees to speak nationally, and the Director General has expressed strong support for this model as enabling a more direct input for the consumer voice in monitoring company performance; as we shall see, the Committees played a particularly important role in the price control process.

Already this regulatory complexity has caused problems. The most celebrated has been that involving the European Community. Community law has a very different role from that discussed earlier in the context of telecommunications, for economic regulation

---

[6] See Water Industry Act 1991, s. 12.

[7] See Water Industry Act 1991, ss. 32–5.

[8] Water Industry Act 1991, ss. 29–30; for a detailed account of consumer representation in the water industry, see Ogden, S., and Anderson, F., 'Representing Customers' Interests: The Case of the Privatized Water Industry in England and Wales' (1995) 73 *Public Administration* 535–59.

[9] For information on composition see Ernst, J., *Whose Utility? The Social Impact of Public Utility Privatization and Regulation in Britain* (Open University Press, Buckingham, 1994), 171–2.

at the level of the Community is very limited due to the lack of interstate trade in water. Instead, environmental regulation has been of the utmost importance. This is not the place to outline the general problems of compliance with Community law as regards water quality and sewerage treatment,[10] but it is worth noting that the regulator has gone so far as to criticize European Commission standards in public. In a document leading up to the periodic review of prices he stated:

[c]lear signals are emerging from the market research which companies have carried out about the limited extent to which customers are willing to pay for improvement. Without some moderation in respect of timing or implementation of new obligations bills could rise at the same rate as in the first five years of regulation or even faster. . . . I believe that the Secretaries of State should consider going as far as renegotiation of European standards, where obligations, and particularly the speed of their implementation, place an unmanageable burden on customers.[11]

In response, the Secretaries of State accepted the principles argued for by the regulator and issued a document setting out the quality requirements.[12] Similar concerns about the cost of quality standards also led to conflicts with the National Rivers Authority,[13] though the problem may now be partially alleviated through the imposition on the Environment Agency of a duty to take into account the likely costs and benefits of the exercise of its powers; previously, the environmental duties had not been so constrained.[14] The different but related matter of paying for water, and in particular the question of compulsory metering (which will be discussed below) also led to some tension early on with some Customer Service Committees, and in one case the Chair of such a Committee did not have her contract renewed after controversial opposition to such metering, though according to the regulator this was not the cause of the failure to renew; relations with the Committees are now good.[15] In public provision as controversial as water, it is

---

[10] For a general account see Kramer, L., *EC Treaty and Environmental Law* (2nd edn., Sweet & Maxwell, London, 1995).

[11] OFWAT, *Paying for Quality—The Political Perspective* (1993), 13.

[12] Secretary of State for the Environment and Secretary of State for Wales, *Water Charges: The Quality Framework* (Department of the Environment, London, 1993).

[13] See, e.g., Environment Committee, *The Work of OFWAT, Minutes of Evidence*, HC 346(I), 1993–4, 5, 13–14.

[14] Environment Act 1995, s. 39.

[15] Environment Committee, n. 13 above, 2–3.

hardly surprising that conflict between different regulatory bodies will frequently emerge, especially given the varied objectives of each of them. Given the general theme of this book, I will concentrate on the role of the economic regulator and omit any detailed account of the environmental regulators or the environmental role of the Secretaries of State except where they impinge on the work of the former.

The Legislation

The legislative structure is more complicated than in the case of the other utilities already discussed because of the complexity of different regulators and the importance of environmental as well as economic considerations. The different types of duties have been highlighted, with the separation in 1991 of the legislation into two consolidation Acts, the Water Industry Act and the Water Resources Act, whereas previously both types of duty had been contained in the Water Act 1989, together with a large number of other pieces of legislation; further complexity has been added by the amended duties contained in the Environment Act 1995. Thus the Environment Act imposes a number of general environmental and recreational duties on the Environment Agency, for example its primary duty is to discharge its functions so as to protect and enhance the environment and contribute towards the achievement of sustainable development, and further environmental duties apply specifically in relation to water; as we saw above, there is now also a general duty to weigh costs and benefits in the exercise of its powers.[16] Both the Environment Agency and the ministers are required to have particular regard to duties imposed by the Water Industry Act on the water and sewerage undertakers.[17] However, this applies to duties directly imposed on the undertakers in Parts I to IV of the Act, including those included in licences and the general duty to maintain a water-supply system, and excludes the general duties applying to the Director General by virtue of Part I of that Act. The environmental regulators are thus obliged to take into account the regulatory framework, but the two schemes are essentially subject to separate legislative provisions.

When it comes to the duties imposed on the economic regulator

---

[16] Ss. 4(1), 6, 39.   [17] Water Resources Act, s. 15.

by the Water Industry Act, to some degree a common pattern is taken from the other duties applying to utility regulators described in the previous two chapters; there are however some striking differences. Thus the Secretary of State and the Director General of Water Services are obliged to exercise their powers in the manner they consider best calculated 'to secure that the functions of a water undertaker and of a sewerage undertaker are properly carried out as respects every area of England and Wales'.[18] This is somewhat different from the universal service provisions encountered previously which referred to the meeting of reasonable demands. The financing duty is similar; 'without prejudice to the generality of paragraph (a) above, to secure that companies . . . are able (in particular, by securing reasonable returns on their capital) to finance the proper carrying out of the functions of such undertakers',[19] though here once more there is a difference, in that the section contains a specific reference to rate-of-return regulation, no doubt reflecting the inevitability of continuing monopoly in water and sewerage provision. Secondary duties include protecting the interests of customers and potential customers in relation to charges (in particular those in rural areas, and by ensuring that no undue preference or undue discrimination is shown), protecting consumer interests in relation to the benefits of property disposals, promoting economy and efficiency by undertakers, and facilitating effective competition. The latter provision is weaker than the duty to secure effective competition contained in other regulatory legislation. The Secretary of State and Director are obliged also to take into account in particular the interests of the disabled and pensioners on quality matters.[20] Environmental and recreational duties similar to those of the environmental regulators and including a requirement to have regard to public access rights also apply to the Secretary of State and the Director, though the general environmental duty is expressly made subject to the other duties outlined above.[21] The pattern of duties as divided between the regulators is by no means a straightforward one, and should disputes reach the courts the difficulties of interpretation will be enormous.

Each company is itself made subject to a number of duties, most notably a general duty to:

---

[18] Water Industry Act, s. 2(2)(a).   [19] S. 2(2)(b).
[20] Water Industry Act, s. 2(3)–(4).   [21] Water Industry Act, s. 3.

develop and maintain an efficient and economical system of water supply within its area and to ensure that all such arrangements have been made—

(a)   for providing supplies of water to premises in that area and for making such supplies available to persons who demand them; and

(b)   for maintaining, improving and extending the water undertaker's water mains and other pipes,

as are necessary for securing that the undertaker is and continues to be able to meet its obligations.[22]

The companies are also obliged to connect domestic premises to the mains on request and to provide a sufficient supply of water;[23] similar provisions apply in relation to sewerage and were strengthened by a requirement in the 1995 Act to provide a public sewer where there are environmental or amenity problems.[24] The 1995 Act adds further duties to those applying to the companies; it inserts a duty on each water company to promote the efficient use of water by its consumers, and the Director General may impose requirements on undertakers to implement that duty.[25] The licences, in this case termed 'instruments of appointment', reinforce these duties, and contain detailed provisions on price regulation, the familiar prohibition of undue discrimination and undue preference (though this does not apply to infrastructure charges, i.e. the costs of connection to the system previously borne by all suppliers[26]) and unique provisions for the supply of information to the regulator involving an independent reporter with responsibility for certifying the accuracy of the information.[27] To this complexity has to be added, of course, the whole body of relevant European Community law. Overall, the legal scheme is far more complex, and with far more scope for conflict involving judicial resolution, than is the case for the other utilities.

The Regulator

The first, and so far only, Director General of Water Services is Ian Byatt, an economist who had previously been a Deputy Chief

---

[22] Water Industry Act, s. 37.   [23] Water Industry Act, ss. 45, 52.

[24] Water Industry Act, ss. 94, 98.

[25] Environment Act 1995, sched. 22, para. 102, inserting new ss. 93A and 101A into the Water Industry Act.

[26] See Ernst, n. 9 above, 117.

[27] Department of the Environment and Welsh Office, *Instrument of Appointment of the Water and Sewerage Undertakings* (HMSO, 1989), conds. B, E.

Economic Adviser to the Treasury after an early academic career; he was best known for having chaired the Advisory Committee on Accounting for Economic Costs and Changing Prices, which had made influential reforms to public enterprise accounting methods. Early statements by the regulator stressed his role as a surrogate for the market forces which did not exist in the water industry: '[c]onsumer sovereignty is a far cry from the water industry. . . . It remains to the regulator to provide such surrogate market forces as are possible.'[28] He also stressed the potential of 'comparative competition' permitted by the existence of several companies whose performance could be compared (also known as 'yardstick competition'), and the development of more adequate accounting methods, especially as regards the costs of capital. On charging he appeared to have a preference for a low standing charge and for the bulk of costs to be covered by metering.[29] A further element which was striking was a commitment to openness which went further than that of the other regulators; thus he stated in his first *Annual Report* that he would aim to operate an open system in order to involve users and would stimulate debate, especially through the issuing of consultation papers and would explain the reasons behind his decisions. In particular, the 'Dear Managing Director' letters conveying his views to the companies would be made available for public inspection.[30]

Later on, further information emerged when the regulator gave evidence to the Environment Select Committee. On his duties, he stated that '[m]y primary duty, under the Water Act, is to act in the manner I consider best calculated to ensure the companies can finance their functions. Subject to that, I have duties to customers to protect their interests and I also have duties to promote economic efficiency'.[31]

As we saw, whilst the universal service primary duty is differently framed from that of other regulators, it does exist, though given the near achievement of universal service it is perhaps understandable that less emphasis was placed upon it. The role of market surrogate continued to feature prominently in the regulator's public statements; thus in his first annual report he stated that his aim in relation to charges and service was to achieve through regulation the

[28] Byatt, n. 5 above, 121.   [29] *Ibid.* 129.
[30] OFWAT, *Annual Report 1989–90*, HC 458, 1989–90, 10.
[31] Environment Committee, n. 13 above, 1.

same outcome as would normally arise from a competitive market,[32] and this was to affect both his approach to environmental requirements through his concern that they be properly costed before being imposed, and to paying for water where, as we shall see, a strong preference for metering emerged where this was economically justified.

The Director General also made a statement of general principle in 1996 which is revealing of his approach.[33] Its heart was a defence of the RPI–X system of price control against alternatives such as profit sharing. He also stressed the inevitably discretionary nature of regulation; '[t]here is some uncertainty about what constitutes a regulatory contract. I am not entirely happy with the word. . . . Such a contract cannot be made for as long a period as five years.' This raised issues of regulatory legitimacy and accountability, which could be resolved through periodic governmental and Parliamentary reviews of regulatory performance; the monopoly position of companies also raised issues of company accountability, where '[t]he stakeholder approach may be able to cast some light in this area. The privatised utilities may have paid too much attention to City matters compared with other aspects of the business. . . . But the stakeholder approach does not tell us what the right balancing of interests is.' Once more the stress on openness was strong; '[r]egulation has become more transparent. Quality regulators make independent checks and publish their results—again in advance of practice in other countries. Information from OFWAT dwarfs what was provided in the past. Regulatory decisions are explained and properly documented.' Later in the same year he re-emphasized that his objectives are primarily economic but also include some social elements, including universal provision at affordable prices.[34]

This suggests an interesting set of perspectives from the regulator; his approach is fundamentally that of an economist, but is tempered by an awareness of the conflicting interests involved and the need for consumer representation and openness, with a particular concern for the proper costing of environmental objectives. What has this meant in practice?

[32] OFWAT, n. 30 above, 11.
[33] Byatt, I., *Speech at European Policy Forum on Tuesday 7 May 1996* (OFWAT, Birmingham, 1996).
[34] Byatt, I., *The Economist Conference—The Water Industry: Challenges and Opportunities* (OFWAT, Birmingham, 1996).

Regulating Monopoly: Price Control

As was the case for the other utilities examined so far, the initial setting of tariffs was a matter for the Secretary of State at privatization. The form of price control was different in one important respect, however, in that it permitted increases in prices well above the general rate of inflation; the formula adopted was, for the period until April 1995, RPI + K + U, with K representing a pass-through of certain costs, most importantly the financing of the investment needed to comply with requirements for environmental and water quality improvement under UK and European Community law. The U factor simply permitted the taking up of the amount of K not used in earlier years. The result of this system was that consumers have faced large real-term price increases each year; in the period between 1989–90 and 1994–5 domestic water and sewerage bills increased by 67 per cent on average; in the ten water and sewerage company areas the increases ranged from 54 per cent to 108 per cent for water and from 52 per cent to 122 per cent for sewerage, a period during which inflation was less than 30 per cent.[35] The initial formula was set for a ten-year period though with the power to review after five years at the request of the company or of the Director General; the latter also made it clear that companies which were not investing in such a way as to justify their K values could find these values reduced.

The real price increases, coupled with publicity for large profits for the companies, created a considerable degree of political controversy. In 1991, the Director General seemed pleased overall with the tariff arrangements: '[d]espite the imposition of new environmental obligations and contrary to many predictions at the time of privatisation, prices, with two exceptions, have generally risen by less than was permitted in the formulae set in 1989.'[36] He also promised, however, that a review of prices would take effect from April 1995 rather than at the end of the full ten-year period; he noted that little work had been done to find out how much customers were prepared to pay for quality improvements, and promised to address the rate of return on capital and the possibility

---

[35] National Consumer Council, *Water Price Controls* (National Consumer Council, London, 1994), 6.
[36] OFWAT, *Annual Report 1991*, HC 31, 1992–3, 4.

of building in efficiency targets and new environmental obligations.[37]

By 1992 the pricing problem was becoming more pressing; the Director General noted that 'I do not believe that a continuing increase in prices well above the rate of inflation, such as has taken place since 1989, will be acceptable to customers.'[38] Moreover, from 1992 capital expenditure began to run well below the planned level, and as a result the regulator negotiated a voluntary abatement by all but one of the water companies of a sixth of their K-factor allowed for 1992–3. The background to this had been stated in one of the letters to the companies:

in a situation where bills are rising rapidly, customers will not expect companies to make unnecessarily large profits and in particular to pay out excessive dividends. . . . It is up to management to decide on dividends, but if companies were to use the present position to pay out dividends above those anticipated when the K factors were set they would need to be ready to answer pointed questions from customers and from the regulator.[39]

Once more we see that a generous settlement at the time of privatization created difficulties for a regulator, exacerbated in this case by the fact that the profit formula permitted real price increases at the same time as the companies were earning large and politically controversial profits.

During this period the Director General commenced the preparations for the periodic review to be carried out in 1994 through issuing a number of consultation papers, for example on the cost of capital, suggesting that the rate of return on capital set at privatization was too high; construction costs had also declined considerably.[40] After a review of the capital investment and financial performance of the companies, in October 1992 the regulator announced that he would make a formal reduction of 2 per cent in the level of K for most companies in 1993–4. The generosity of the privatization settlement coupled with changing circumstances and political concerns about price increases and large profits thus resulted in the abandonment of an apparently fixed price formula.

---

[37] *Ibid.* 4–6.

[38] OFWAT, *Annual Report 1992*, HC 714, 1992–3, 4.

[39] OFWAT, *Profits and Dividends*, MD 55, quoted in Ernst, n. 9 above, 116.

[40] The papers were OFWAT, *The Cost of Capital* (1991), *Assessing Capital Values* (1992), *The Cost of Quality* (1992), *Paying for Quality* (1993) and *Paying for Growth* (1993).

This brings us to the periodic review process. As mentioned above, the Director General did stimulate debate effectively in this process through the issuing of consultation papers; other important consultative initiatives were taken, and the process was a unprecedentedly open one, as I shall describe towards the end of this Chapter.[41] A number of themes emerged in the review process. The first is the fact that rate of return is a central consideration; as we saw above this is actually referred to in the statutory duties applying to the regulator, and the review devotes considerable discussion to such financial issues, though it has been noted that, whilst cost of capital was an important and contentious issue early on, it was much less so in the final result due to the approach adopted by the regulator.[42] Secondly, social considerations played a role in the process; as the Director General stated to the Environment Committee:

Affordability is an important consideration in the setting of new price limits. It would not be in the interests of either customers or companies if the level of prices meant that customers, particularly those on low incomes, faced increased difficulty in paying their bills. Subject to acting in the way I consider best calculated to ensure that companies can finance their functions, I have a statutory duty to protect the interests of customers.[43]

In fact, this had been one of the major concerns in the consultative process, and in itself emphasizes the role of consumer representation; '[t]he "customer input" . . . came mainly through the Customer Service Committees and the OFWAT National Consumer Council who both emphasised affordability by the less well off. As a result, the final combination of cost and quality may not have been the one which customers wanted, nor the most economically efficient'.[44] The reference to the difference from the outcome customers wanted refers to the apparent willingness of many consumers to support additional expenditure as revealed in the industry's consultations; '[i]ncreasingly OFWAT switched the focus from "willingness to pay" to "affordability" as the criterion for

---

[41] The periodic review is OFWAT, *Future Charges for Water and Sewerage Services* (1994); for a summary of the consultative process see Smith, J., 'Water Service 1994—A Watershed Year' in Centre for the Study of Regulated Industries, *Regulatory Review 1995* (Centre for the Study of Regulated Industries, London, 1995), 105–29, 113–15.

[42] Smith, n. 41 above, 109–10.

[43] Environment Committee, n. 13 above, 19.   [44] Smith, n. 41 above, 114.

allowing discretionary improvements.'[45] Thirdly, a strong concern emerged that the environmental obligations had themselves not been properly costed and were imposing an undue burden on consumers.[46] The concern was not of course limited only to the regulator; the National Consumer Council also issued a highly critical report claiming that the price increases were not properly correlated with investment, and raised serious equity concerns. As mentioned above, this provoked a response from the Secretaries of State which set out more clearly the steps needed for the implementation of quality improvements, and legislative changes in the Environment Act 1975 go some way to implementing these. As a result, whilst '[t]he NRA was widely perceived to be the loser from the Periodic Review process . . . this is oversimplistic. . . . A further aspect of this process has been transparency—putting a price on quality improvements.'[47]

The outcome of the Periodic Review was the setting of new K factors for all the water and sewerage companies and water companies, with a weighted average K factor of 0.9, though with considerable variations between companies. Emphasizing the point about transparency, the formula became RPI–X+Q, with Q representing the cost of statutory improvements in drinking-water and environmental-quality standards.[48] This showed a marked reduction of the increases compared with those applying over the previous five years, and they were considerably lower than those implied in the companies' own plans. The efficiency savings implied in the new formulae were demanding, some 14 per cent in real terms, and except in one case the X factors were negative. The regulator decided that the companies could finance their functions at a lower rate of return on capital than that currently earned. Thus for new investment the regulator considered a return after tax of 5–6 per cent appropriate; current returns were then of some 13 per cent. The price limits were set on the expectation that real returns would fall over the ten year period to a range of 6–7 per cent after tax; he did not consider it to be part of his role to make retrospective adjustments to claw back the high returns since privatization.[49] A further aspect of the review was the proposal that where capital expenditure required to implement the Urban Waste Water

[45] *Ibid.*   [46] See OFWAT, n. 11 above, 13.
[47] Smith, n. 41 above, 112.   [48] For details see OFWAT, n. 41 above.
[49] *Ibid.* 38, 48–52.

Treatment Directive turned out to be lower than assumed, cost savings should be shared, with 40 per cent going towards further discretionary environmental improvements, 40 per cent into customer
service improvements, and the rest to shareholders. In practice
benefit-sharing occurred in other respects also; thus in 1995 North
West Water announced plans to hand over a 'social dividend' to
customers as well as a special dividend to shareholders, something
welcomed by the regulator, who wrote:

[i]f savings materialise earlier or are on a greater scale than assumed when
price limits were set, I should like to see companies bring forward sharing
of benefits with customers. Exactly how that might be achieved is a matter for the company. Customers would clearly like lower bills or cash
refunds.[50]

Voluntary rebates for customers were subsequently adopted by a
number of other companies in 1995 and 1996.[51] One water and sewerage company and one water company did not accept the outcome
of the review, and their cases were referred to the MMC, which
(after taking exactly a year to decide) broadly upheld the Director
General's price limits and his general approach, including the stress
on affordability.[52] In late 1996 it was announced that the next periodic review would take place in 1999, rather than 2004 as permitted in the licences.

In addition to the overall K factors, the regulator had to consider
domestic infrastructure charges payable in addition to direct costs
of connection when properties are connected to water and sewerage systems for the first time. On privatization these charges had
been set to enable companies to recover all the costs associated with
serving additional customers including the provision of additional
resources and treatment works; charges varied from under £200 to
over £1,000. The Director General decided that the charges should
be restricted to the costs of developing the local network, and
should be limited to £200 for each service, subsequently rising only
in line with inflation. This would avoid cross-subsidization of other
consumers by those in new properties as well as increasing opportunities for access to water supplies.[53]

[50] OFWAT, *Annual Report 1994*, HC 431, 1994–5, 6.
[51] Smith, n. 41 above, 115–19.
[52] Monopolies and Mergers Commission, *Portsmouth Water plc* and *South West
Water plc* (HMSO, London, 1995); for a summary see Smith, n. 41 above, 119–21.
[53] OFWAT, n. 41 above, 7, 42.

A number of familiar themes emerge from the periodic review process. The first is the importance of the consultation process, which will be discussed more fully towards the end of this Chapter. Moreover, distributional issues appear to have influenced the review through the involvement of consumer representatives, and to have made a real difference to outcomes. Once more the settlement adopted at privatization has been shown to have been far too generous, and review of pricing has inevitably included decisions on rate-of-return considerations, here very explicitly. It is quite clear that the price review process involved balancing of different interests rather than the application of any mechanistic formula; as OFWAT put it, '[t]he process of setting prices . . . cannot be mechanistic; the Director General had to have scope to reach his own informed judgments'.[54] Given this, he seems very skilfully to have balanced these competing interests in the review, including those represented by other regulators and by consumers. The most unpopular aspects of water charges in the form of real increases to improve quality standards and the belief that charges were being used to pay inflated remuneration to company directors were outside the Director General's control, but at least he succeeded in producing a greater degree of transparency in relation to the former. A further matter of considerable controversy has been that of the performance of the regulated companies, and it is to this that I shall now turn.

Regulating Monopoly: Quality of Service

Once more the question of service standards is complicated by the division of labour between economic and environmental regulators. Thus, as we have already seen, the European Community and the Secretary of State are the main originators of quality standards with implementation by the Environment Agency and the Drinking Water Inspectorate. Nevertheless, other aspects of quality of service have assumed great importance for the Director General, not simply because of his general duties to protect consumers but because of the role of yardstick competition comparing the performance of the various companies.

Condition J of the licences of the water and sewerage companies

---

[54] OFWAT, n. 50 above, 56.

requires them to supply information to the Director General on a number of matters relating to quality of service, and to set a number of service targets. Those to be included were identified in a letter from the Director, and level-of-service indicators include water availability, pressure, interruptions to supply, hosepipe restrictions, flooding from sewers, response to complaints, and so on; sewage collected and treated was added as a performance standard slightly later, and the information needed and operation of the targets have been reviewed in depth since. The companies must provide detailed returns on performance each year which are required to be confirmed by independent reporters approved by the Director General.[55] The companies are also required by their licences to draw up codes of practice relating to customer relations, disconnections, and leakage.[56] Moreover, arrangements were adopted for compensation for poor service, as in the case of the other utilities discussed, in the form of a guaranteed standards scheme, the normal amount of compensation being £10.[57] In 1994–5, 5,577 automatic payments were made by companies and 3,350 in response to claims by customers. Serious problems were caused however by the 1995 summer drought, during which one area, Yorkshire, threatened rota cuts. Supply failures for this reason were not covered by the compensation scheme, and the Director General issued a consultation paper which attracted wide support for including in the scheme compensation entitlement for rota cuts where the company had not acted prudently. As a result of this consultation, he recommended to the Secretaries of State that compensation be paid to domestic consumers where supply was cut off as a result of emergency restrictions, unless the circumstances were so exceptional that it would have been unreasonable for the company to have avoided the interruption; a similar but higher entitlement should apply to business customers.[58] These proposals would need legislation for their implementation.

In general the Director General has been able to report continuing improvement in the achievement of service standards. This has

[55] Department of the Environment and Welsh Office, n. 27 above, cond. J.7.
[56] *Ibid.* conds. G, H, I.
[57] Water Supply and Sewerage Service (Customer Service Standards) Regs. 1989, SI 1159.
[58] OFWAT, *Compensation for Customers: Issues Raised by the 1995 Drought* (1995); *Recommendations to the Secretary of State on Compensation Issues Raised by the 1995 Drought* (1996).

however been marred by serious problems in the quality of service offered by some particular companies; a particular problem was that of leakage, with half the companies in July 1995 reporting increased leakage between 1992–3 and 1994–5, and this exacerbated severe problems of supply during the dry summer of 1995.[59] Nevertheless, the Director General was at that stage opposed to the setting of mandatory leakage targets, as such a target could fail to take into account genuine local variations in the economic position. The Director General also examined in detail the performance of three companies in autumn 1995, North West Water, South West Water, and Yorkshire Water, in the latter case including performance during the summer drought; this was not publicized, but letters to the companies were quickly leaked to the press. In the case of Yorkshire Water the findings were highly critical; the inquiry found serious failures by the company in controlling leakage, minimizing supply interruptions, and controlling flooding from sewers, all attributable to management failures. As a result the company's licence was to be amended to reduce permissible price increases from RPI + 2.5 to RPI + zero for the year beginning in 1997, and to allow only lower price increases than allowed in existing price limits for the following two years. The Director General also required a number of management changes including the appointment of non-executive directors with experience and understanding of the interests of customers.[60]

In some ways the arrangements for monitoring quality of service are more impressive than in the other utilities already discussed; the role of the independent reporters in auditing information is extremely important, and the decision to reduce the Yorkshire price-control formula after bad performance is unprecedentedly strict. Three limitations have however affected public perceptions of the process; the lack of compensation for supply failures during the summer of 1995, the poor performance of some companies in leakage control, and the inadequacies of Yorkshire Water, also caught up in the debate about directors' pay in utilities. It remains to be seen whether further action will remedy the quality problem.

---

[59] OFWAT, *Annual Report 1995*, HC 422, 1995–6, 7.
[60] OFWAT, *News Release 28/96* (1996).

Regulation for Competition: Product and Capital Markets

For reasons stated earlier, the scope for liberalization of the product market is very limited in relation to water. The Competition and Service (Utilities) Act 1992 did attempt to provide for limited increases in competition through, amongst other changes, encouraging 'inset appointments' by which companies can supply a single large customer outside their areas.[61] Some limited progress has been made on this; and in 1995 the Director General published a paper outlining the procedure for applying.[62] By mid-1996 fifteen formal applications had been made, but only one agreed. Also in 1996, the Government announced proposals for further competition by, among other things, introducing common carriage through shared use of pipes.[63] The proposals were evolutionary and needed legislative change for their implementation, and so in the short term at least are likely to make little difference. Limitations on competition are also suggested by the difficulties in de-averaging tariffs so as to raise those for rural areas in order to compete effectively in urban areas (a familiar problem from other utilities); 'there are serious practical and political obstacles to the development of competition for domestic water supplies—not least the effects on rural areas of de-averaging tariffs'.[64] A consultation is taking place on the degree to which this should be permitted. The Director General has taken action to prevent anti-competitive practices by water companies, for example by ring-fencing to enforce separate trading within groups and dealing with complaints about preference being given to associated companies; this was supported further in the 1992 Act, which requires the regulator to secure that business with group companies is conducted at arm's length and that separate accounts are kept.[65]

Yardstick competition, on the other hand, is clearly very central to the regulator's work.[66] As he described it when outlining price control methods to the Select Committee:

[61] S. 40.
[62] OFWAT, *Competition in the Water Industry: Inset Appointments and Their Regulation* (1995).
[63] Department of the Environment, *Water: Increasing Customer Choice* (Department of the Environment, London, 1996).
[64] Smith, n. 41 above, 124.
[65] Competition and Service (Utilities) Act 1992, s. 50.
[66] See generally Burns, P., 'Yardstick Competition in UK Regulatory Processes', in Centre for the Study of Regulated Industries, n. 41 above.

I do not want it to be a cost-plus system, but on the basis of, let us not say the most efficient company in the industry, because that is not always easy to identify, but the more efficient companies. So, insofar as a company becomes more efficient, makes more money for its shareholders, gets its costs down, at the next periodic review then that low price can be applied right across the board to all companies.[67]

Examples of the use of this method can be found in a number of aspects of the periodic review. Thus the scope for lower operating expenditure was assessed comparatively, as was the delivery of cap-ital-expenditure programmes; the analysis of the potential for reductions in the cost of delivering base service levels also began with a comparison of existing costs to consumers, and companies with high unit costs were asked to explain why their costs were higher than those of other companies.[68]

The issue of yardstick competition brings us directly to the ques-tion of liberalization of the capital markets. The Littlechild Report on the economic regulation of privatized water authorities had stressed the potential role of capital market competition:

[t]he effectiveness of regulation will be enhanced by harnessing, rather than discouraging, the forces of competition in the capital market. The top man-agement of a private water authority which engages in 'empire-building', or which fails to perform adequately in other respects, will be subject to pressure from shareholders. It will become vulnerable to takeover.[69]

Considerable takeover activity has taken place and the number of water-only companies has dropped from twenty-nine in 1989 to nineteen in 1996. Although the privatized water and sewerage com-panies were initially protected by golden shares, those for the English companies expired after five years at the end of 1994, preparing the way for further takeovers. The development of the structure of the industry has thus been one of concentration since privatization, in contrast to the growth of new suppliers in telecom-munications and gas. Special provisions in the legislation, as men-tioned above, provide for an automatic reference to the Monopolies and Mergers Commission when the assets of merging water com-panies are worth more than £30 million, and these provisions were

[67] Environment Committee, n. 13 above, 7.
[68] OFWAT, n. 41 above, chs. 3 and 4.
[69] Littlechild, S., *Economic Regulation of Privatised Water Authorities* (Department of the Environment, London, 1986), para. 1.7.

amended in the 1992 Act to ensure that the MMC has regard to the need to protect the ability of the regulator to make comparisons between the companies, so preserving yardstick competition.[70] In effect this puts the onus on the bidder to justify the merger. An important role of the regulator has been to ensure that mergers do not prevent effective regulation, and so make it more difficult to protect consumers.

In fact, important guidelines had been laid down already, notably in the case of the Three Valleys Companies in 1990. This was referred to the MMC, and the Director General gave evidence, stressing the importance of preserving his ability to make proper comparisons of performance; a merger or takeover reducing that ability should only be permitted if it would bring substantial benefits to consumers, normally in the form of lower charges. The Commission found that the merger might be expected to operate against the public interest, and the Secretary of State asked the Director General to negotiate undertakings with the companies; these required abatement of the charging limits which would otherwise have applied and acceptance of the regulatory regime as if they had had a single licence.[71] The case provided a model for several future cases.

After the end of the golden shares merger activity spread to the large water and sewerage companies, and during 1995 two water merger proposals went ahead, between Lyonnaise Europe plc and Northumbrian Water Group plc, and between East Surrey Water plc and Sutton District Water plc, the first being clearly the most important. In addition, three new proposals were announced with General Utilities and SAUR Water Services proposing the purchase of Mid Kent Holdings plc, and bids for South West Water plc from both Wessex Water and Severn Trent Water. In the Northumbrian case, the MMC reported that it would operate against the public interest and asked the Director General to identify a remedy. He decided that this should take the form of water price reductions of 15 per cent by April 2001 whilst maintaining levels of service, and undertakings to this effect were written into the licence; the effect

---

[70] Water Industry Act 1991, ss. 32–5, as amended by Competition and Service (Utilities) Act 1992, s. 39.

[71] See Monopolies and Mergers Commission, *General Utilities plc.*, Cm 1029 (HMSO, London, 1990) and Department of Trade and Industry, *Press Release 90/474* (DTI, London, 1990).

was to create a new comparator at or near the most efficient level in the industry. It was also agreed that the water interests would be separately listed on the Stock Exchange to ensure the availability of information for the regulator.[72] Both the bids for South West Water were however blocked by the Secretary of State on the advice of the MMC because of the potential effects on yardstick competition and the inability of the bidders to sustain adequate price cuts to compensate.[73]

In addition to this activity within the water sector, the first mergers between water and electricity companies also took place during 1995, between North West Water and Norweb, and between Welsh Water and Swalec. The Director General worked with the Electricity Regulator and they issued joint consultation papers; the Secretary of State decided not to refer the mergers to the MMC, but made them conditional on licence amendments proposed by the two regulators. These required the water companies to act independently of their parent companies, and prohibited actions such as transfers of assets to an associated company without regulatory approval; Welsh Water was also required to appoint two non-executive directors with experience and understanding of consumer interests.[74] In 1996 Scottish Power was permitted to take over Southern Water; in this case licence amendments were agreed to the effect that average prices would be 1 per cent lower for 1997–8 and 3 per cent lower for the following two years than permitted under the periodic review, as well as providing for regulatory information and ring-fencing of the regulated business.[75]

As I suggested at the outset of this section, the Littlechild Report on the water industry, whilst accepting that competition in the product market for water and sewerage services would be limited, pointed to competition in the capital markets as providing the necessary spur to efficiency. It is clear that this also requires regulation for competition; the regulator has had a key role in advising on mergers and takeovers, both to preserve comparators and to ensure the continued provision of essential regulatory information. The Customer Service Committees also have an important role in giving evidence to the MMC, and the National Consumer Council has

[72] OFWAT, n. 59 above, 33.

[73] *Ian Lang Blocks Bids for South West Water*, Department of Trade and Industry Press Release P/96/797, 25 Oct. 1996.

[74] *Ibid.* 33–5.   [75] OFWAT, *Press Release 32/96* (1996).

proposed that cross-utility mergers should be automatically referred to the Commission so that all issues can be properly examined. In a very different sense from that in earlier chapters, competition and regulation appear not to be opposites but to be complementary in the water industry.

Social Regulation and Universal Service

The general issue of universal service will be dealt with very briefly here before I describe in more detail the questions of disconnections and metering. As already mentioned, in the case of water supply near-universal service has already been achieved; the rate is less for sewerage at 96 per cent but still greater than for telecommunications or gas. Special procedures supervised by OFGAS apply to requests for connection to the sewerage system, and the question of infrastructure charges for connection to the system has already been discussed in the context of the periodic review.[76] It should also be mentioned that differential charges are now the norm for different regions of England and Wales; in addition, some companies have introduced zonal tariffs, and there are signs of rebalancing of tariffs to the disadvantage of rural areas; the issue of rebalancing is currently under review by the Director General.[77] In view of the differential costs of environmental improvement in the areas served by different companies this is of course reflected in the periodic review, with higher K factors for areas with a long coastline.[78] Thus, although universal service has been almost completely achieved in terms of uniform coverage, there is a growing departure from the availability of broadly uniform tariffs throughout the country. There are no moves to create a universal service fund as such, although three companies have set up charitable trusts to assist customers who have difficulty paying bills.

A number of other social obligations have played some role in OFWAT decision-making. Unlike in the case of other large utilities the water companies were not required to produce a code of practice for the elderly and disabled, and an OFWAT survey of companies' practices towards these groups found them disappointing.

---

[76] See for the background Legge, D., 'OFWAT Information Note: First Time Rural Sewerage' (1992) 3 *Utilities Law Review* 117–18.

[77] Ernst, n. 9 above, 120–1; Smith, n. 41 above, 123–4.

[78] OFTEL, n. 41 above, 4; and see Environment Committee, n. 13 above, 9–10.

In response the regulator issued guidelines and recommendations to the companies on the subject in September 1991; the guidelines concerned such matters as password security systems, access to information in braille, and a company register of customers in need of special help. The implementation of the guidelines was reviewed in 1993, and it was found that, whilst there were variations between companies, most had established a register of customers with special needs and had publicized it; continuing review would take place.[79] The companies have been obliged to adopt other codes of practice on relations with customers and Customer Service Committees, on disconnection, and on leakage, which as we have already seen forms part of the more general service standard-setting process.

Social Regulation and Disconnections

The question of disconnection of water supplies has been highly controversial.[80] Before privatization, 10 to 15,000 households had their water supplies disconnected each year. There was a slight decline in the first year after privatization, and, after strong pressure from campaigning groups, the Water Industry Act prohibits disconnection where liability is disputed in the absence of a court judgment or a broken settlement,[81] and the licences require the observance of a Code of Practice on disconnection.[82] The Code, which is enforceable as a licence condition, similarly requires a court order or breach of a payment agreement before disconnection can take place. However, in 1990–1, 900,000 court summonses were issued by the water companies (about one for every twenty-three domestic and non-domestic premises in England and Wales) of which about half were brought to judgment.[83] From 1991 disconnections increased significantly, and over the year 1991–2 domestic disconnections rose from 7,673 to 21,286; very great variations also existed between individual companies, and water disconnection statistics were now higher than those for other utilities. It is thus hard

[79] Legge, D., 'Services for Elderly or Disabled Customers' (1993) 4 *Utilities Law Review* 189–90.
[80] See Herbert, A., and Kempson, E., *Water Debt and Disconnection* (Policy Studies Institute, London, 1995).
[81] Water Industry Act 1992, s. 62.
[82] Department of the Environment and Welsh Office, n. 27 above, cond. H.
[83] Ernst, n. 9 above, 147.

not to share the conclusion that '[a]s a device for protecting water consumers from disconnection, Condition H has been a singular failure'.[84] In April 1992 the Director General issued guidelines to the companies, requiring, for example, pre-disconnection visits and a greater range of payment methods, reflecting the provisions of the codes of practice for other utilities.[85] In 1993 there was a decrease of one third in the number of disconnections, although the number of summonses was up by 14 per cent and the number of judgments obtained up by 12 per cent.[86] In evidence to the Environment Committee, the Director General admitted that he was not yet satisfied that all companies were following the guidelines, and if they proved to be inadequate, a licence amendment would be considered; he also acknowledged that research had only recently begun on examining the reasons for disconnections.[87] OFWAT as well as the Policy Studies Institute, undertook such research, and in the year 1994–5 domestic disconnections were less than half their level in 1991–2, with a total figure for all disconnections of 12,832 (below pre-privatization levels), though there were considerable variations between companies. In the following year, a further large drop in disconnections took place with a total figure of 5,826; South West Water announced that it would not disconnect customers for arrears of debt unless there was clear evidence that the customer had no intention of paying the bill, though variations remained between the rates of disconnection of different companies, with three still reporting high levels.[88] The study by the Policy Studies Institute suggested that the dramatic fall in disconnections was a consequence of the changes in company policies as a result of the 1992 OFWAT guidelines.[89]

In the case of other utilities, falls in disconnection rates have been closely related to the installation of prepayment meters. Though this could not occur in the case of water for technological reasons, prepayment plans in the form of budget payment units have recently been introduced quite rapidly; by the end of March 1996 over 15,000 had been installed with four companies accounting for more than 14,000; a code of practice for their use had been

[84] *Ibid.* 149, from which the statistics are also taken.
[85] OFWAT, *Guidelines on Debt and Disconnection* (1992).
[86] OFWAT, *Annual Report 1993*, HC 416, 1993–4, 13, 40–2.
[87] Environment Committee, n. 13 above, 14–15, and qs. 94–108.
[88] OFWAT, n. 59 above, 20.   [89] Herbert and Kempson, n. 80 above, 6.

Law and the Regulators

developed by the water industry associations. The units take the form not of a metering system as in the other utilities but of a system of payment in advance through charging a smart card at a local outlet. When the period paid for expires there is an emergency credit period, normally of seven days, after which supply will temporarily cease, though before this the water company will attempt to contact the customer and tell the local authority. The use of these units has been supported by the Director General, and research has shown a favourable customer reaction, more so than in gas and electricity, apparently because most users were council tenants who had previously paid water bills with their rent.[90] Problems concern the limited range of outlets at which the cards can be recharged, and the danger of self-disconnection through credit running out, with obvious public-health implications. These concerns led a number of local authorities to question the legality of the units as amounting to disconnection in breach of the procedural protections described earlier. The response from OFWAT was that the operation of the unit by the customer did not amount to action by the water company to cut off supply, and the advantages for customers were reiterated.[91]

Paying for Water and Metering

A further issue which illustrates the interaction of social and economic considerations in regulation is that of paying for water. In the past, water charging had been based on rateable values; however the Water Industry Act requires that a different method of charging be adopted from 31 March 2000. Early on, the regulator indicated some preference for moving towards metering where this was economically justifiable; '[i]n OFWAT's view, the broad thrust of these arguments points towards tariffs where the bulk of the costs are covered by the volumetric element of the charge, and where the standing charge is relatively low. Many customers also hold this view.'[92] As this illustrates, the issue is also linked to that of the relationship between the relatively high standing charge and charging by usage. The regulator undertook consultation on different methods of paying for water, and this produced a small majority of customers in favour of metering. In 1991 he announced that

[90] *Ibid.* 69–73.
[91] OFWAT, *Press Notice 13/96* (1996).   [92] Byatt, n. 5 above, 129.

he favoured metering as the new payment method: '[i]n the long term it is the only satisfactory way of achieving payments which are well related to use. A rapid change to universal household metering would, however, be uneconomic. Instead metering should be targeted and should spread progressively.'[93] The regulator also set out a number of principles on which future charging policy should be based. These included equity or fairness, requiring that customers in similar circumstances should not pay different bills, with differentials in charging reflecting differences in circumstances and the creation of sensible incentives to customers and companies, for example to reduce consumption where costs are heavy and to ensure that demand which customers will pay for is met. The consultation paper recognized that universal compulsory metering would be uneconomic, and instead proposed selective extension where cost savings from decreased usage and reduced leakage would justify installation costs.[94]

What we see here is an essentially economic argument based on the relationship between usage and charging being used to justify metering; the effects of a change towards metering were also examined through a number of metering trials in particular areas of the country. Nevertheless, by 1992 only 3 per cent of households in England and Wales were metered, and any move to universal metering would be impracticable in the foreseeable future; moreover, metering also raises distributive questions, and half the Customer Service Committees did not support the regulator's preference for metering, particularly as evidence was found during the trials that metering led to a large fall in water consumption and in water supplied.[95] Families in properties with currently low rateable values could face large increases in bills with metering, especially if they were large families; metering has thus been opposed by groups including the National Consumer Council, the National Association of Citizens Advice Bureaux, Age Concern, and the Child Poverty Action Group; environmental groups have by contrast tended to favour metering.[96] A further measure from the regulator which facilitated the development of metering was to press for

[93] OFWAT, n. 36 above, 9.
[94] OFWAT, *Paying for Water: The Way Ahead* (1991).
[95] OFWAT, n. 38 above, 11–12.
[96] Ernst, n. 9 above, 127–8; Simpson, R., 'Water, Water Everywhere . . . ?' (1996) 94 *Poverty* 16–19.

the reduction in the difference in the standing charge between metered and unmetered customers, and this had largely been achieved by 1995.[97] In the periodic review, the regulator noted that future charges other than metering would,

> need to be fair, with charges broadly related to costs and hence to water use, and simple, so that customers understand how their bill is made up and what they can do to influence it. However, the Director has not received any proposals, other than selective metering, which meet these criteria any better than charges related to rateable value.[98]

Thus he continued to support metering on the ground that it offered greater customer choice and the ability to control bills, and because it would offer more incentive to reduce leakage.[99] In April 1995 the Secretary of State also announced that in the long term metering should be the normal basis for paying for water; in the shorter term however rateable-value based charging would continue as a crash programme of universal metering would be uneconomic.[100]

What seems to be apparent at first sight in this case is a conflict between distributive concerns based on protecting the interests of low-income families through retaining a system of charging with some relation to wealth and economic principles of charging based on usage. However, the issue is rather more complex. There are strong environmental arguments for water metering, both through providing stronger incentives for controlling leakage and more generally limiting usage, and so obviating the need for expensive and environmentally undesirable new reservoirs. In addition the economic arguments do not all point one way, given the high cost of installation of meters. Again the message is that the regulator has a difficult task of weighing different values; economic, distributive, and environmental, and that this cannot be reduced to any mechanistic formula.

Regulatory Procedures

We saw early in this Chapter that the Director General made successive pledges to be as open as possible in his decision-making; an

---

[97] OFWAT, n. 59 above, 34.   [98] OFWAT, n. 41 above, 53–4.
[99] OFWAT, n. 59 above, 36.
[100] 1994–5, 257 HC Debs., cols. 1054–5 (written answer).

example already mentioned is the publication of his letters to the companies. As with other regulators discussed in Chapters 3 and 4 above, frequent and detailed working papers have been issued for consultation purposes and a mass of information published; those papers relating to the cost of quality improvements were particularly important in focusing debate. In the case of the consultation on paying for water, 2,700 copies of a consultation paper, 6,500 copies of a statement, and over a quarter of a million leaflets were issued, eliciting some 2,000 written responses. Questionnaires were also issued with water bills, to which 290,000 responses were received, and a structured survey was carried out through the Office of Population Census and Surveys.[101]

Two particular aspects of regulatory procedures stand out. First, the direct involvement of the Customer Service Committees in the periodic review process provided a unique example of consumer input. Apart from issuing consultation papers, the Director General commissioned market research into customer views and willingness to pay for service improvements; he also asked the companies to undertake their own consultations with customers around their market plans; in some cases this was continued by companies and made a permanent feature of their business planning. In most cases the consultation was used to formulate alternative investment packages, involving different rates of price increase. The second stage of consultation involved the Customer Service Committees and the OFWAT National Consumer Council. The regulator made the confidential business plans of the companies and draft determinations available to the Chairmen of the Committees, and they were present at the formal meetings between the Director General and the companies to hear the representations from the latter on them; the Chairmen were also given a further opportunity to comment. As a result, the Committees supported the outcome of the review.[102] It also seems that the consultative process had an important effect in shaping the approach adopted by the regulator; as a source from within the industry has put it, the periodic review 'was an evolutionary process and the DG showed himself willing to change tack when necessary. Thus, while the Market Plan customer

---

[101] Ogden and Anderson, n. 8 above, 552.
[102] For fuller details see OFWAT, n. 41 above, 55–8, but for a more critical view of the consultation process see Legge, D., 'The Periodic Review: A Review of the Law' (1994) 5 *Utilities Law Review* 85–9.

consultation exercise was initially focussed on customer "willingness to pay", the DG subsequently switched to the narrower—and more subjective—criterion of "affordability" in decisions about discretionary expenditure.'[103] Thus what we see here is a process premised on openness in principle similar to that adopted by OFTEL in recent decision-making; however the form of openness is different, concentrating on the involvement of consumer representatives rather than adopting the equivalent of rule-making procedures.

The consultation process was not perfect, and was criticized by companies and consumer organizations, for example, as being used to inform the industry and consumers rather than to create a dialogue, because the results of the consultations were not published as such and because too much discretion was given to the companies as to how they undertook consultation.[104] A further problem was the lack of public availability of information which could be considered price sensitive, notably the business plans and draft determinations. Steps will be taken to meet many of these criticisms in the 1999 review; another means of doing so could be by moving closer to the OFTEL model of developmental consultation around comments submitted in earlier rounds and through further consultation being organized by OFWAT itself on that model. The direct involvement of the Committee Chairman was, however, a notable advantage which must be retained. Not only does the consultation exercise seem to have been successful in gaining support from consumer representatives for the change, but the clear reluctance to pay for uncosted quality obligations which emerged from the consultations considerably strengthened the regulator's hand in relation to the quality regulators.

Secondly, it has also been mentioned that there are particularly strong reporting requirements imposed on the companies; external reporters approved by the Director General have been appointed to oversee the information and to confirm its adequacy, accuracy, and integrity; their role is developed through workshops and individual meetings with OFWAT. Further refinement is taking place in this process, and in May 1995 a consultation paper was published by the Director General setting out his views on what future information would be needed; the manual specifying what must be con-

---

[103] Smith, n. 41 above, 110.   [104] OFWAT, n. 50 above, 56–7.

tained in returns was extensively redrafted as a result.[105] These forms of procedural innovation are different from those encountered with other regulators, suggesting that there is room for a degree of mutual learning from each other's experience.

Conclusion

It could be argued that the Water Regulator has the hardest job of all the utility regulators. He alone has had to accept the inevitability of substantial real-terms price increases as matters outside his control, he is far less able to promote competition as means of empowering consumers, and he is in an environment dominated by the decisions of other public actors; the institutions of the European Community, the Secretaries of State, and the Environment Agency.

In other ways it could be suggested that this makes his task easier; the limited degree of competition possible in the product market means that he can concentrate on regulating monopoly, and the important role of the environmental regulators means that he can concentrate on the application of economic principle in a way close to that envisaged in the original Littlechild Reports. It seems from the material in this Chapter that this is far from being the case. First, even in regulation of monopoly there is not some sort of impenetrable barrier between environmental and economic regulation; they interact, as the process of costing obligations before the periodic review showed so clearly. What is striking, however, is that the regulator has managed to secure some clarification of responsibilities through his own actions, notably the stress on public consultation and his willingness to indicate his dissatisfaction with the imposition of uncosted obligations which he is then expected to implement.

Secondly, even though product market competition has been limited, yardstick competition has been important, as has his role in relation to the market for corporate control through advice and implementation of conditions relating to mergers. Issues of disconnection and of water metering show that a complex mix of social, economic, and environmental concerns can arise even for an economic regulator. The approach adopted has been to involve the

---

[105] OFWAT, *Information for Regulation* (1995); n. 59 above, 27–8.

consumer representatives much more directly in decisions than has been the case for the other utilities discussed, and this bore fruit in the periodic review process where direct participation of the Customer Service Committee chairmen appears to have had a real effect on the outcome. The regulator has also sought to bring conflict out into the open, as was the case with the cost of environmental obligations and their consequences for prices. A further procedural advantage has been the strong reporting requirements involving an independent analysis of information provided by the companies.

6

Electricity: Regulating Through Competition

Introduction

The electricity industry shares with some other regulated industries a history of mixed private and municipal ownership, with the public corporation form having been adopted after the Second World War, the Central Electricity Generating Board being responsible for generation and transmission, while distribution and supply were in the hands of twelve regional corporations. An important characteristic here is the very long legislative history of universal service and of other regulatory duties.[1] Thus the duty to supply customers was contained in the Electric Lighting (Clauses) Act 1899 and incorporated into the Electricity Act 1947; this required the laying down of distribution mains for general supply on request (subject to certain conditions) and to supply and to continue to supply premises within fifty yards of such a main (again subject to conditions). The Electric Lighting Act 1882 made arrangements for disconnection of supplies, reinforced by the Electric Lighting Act 1909, which limited disconnection to cases where there was not a *bona fide* dispute'.[2] Even this brief account of the legislative history suggests that social obligations and universal service are central to the administration of this utility, a view reinforced by the near achievement of universal service and the extreme importance of electricity not only for fuel but for lighting purposes. Indeed, historically the creation of universal access to electric power was a key goal for the industry; we can expect universal service to play an important part in regulatory concerns.

A tension may be found, however, between such historical expectations and the structure adopted on privatization, for electricity

1 See McAuslan, P., and McEldowney, J., 'A Legal Framework for Privatised Electricity Supply' (1988) 9 *Urban Law and Policy* 165–200, 178–82.
2 1882 Act, s. 21; 1909 Act, s. 18.

was an industry in which far greater steps were taken to create a potentially competitive structure than was the case with gas or water. As we shall see below, this is apparent in the statutory duties applying to the regulator and to other industry participants; it is also reflected in the fact that liberalization of domestic supply was envisaged from the beginning and, in contrast to gas, new legislation was not necessary to implement it. Thus regulation for competition assumes particular importance, as in the case of telecommunications; moreover, the industry was broken up into a number of different companies in an attempt to provide internal competition. The considerable complexities of the privatized structures can only be hinted at here, but in brief in England and Wales two generating companies were established, National Power and PowerGen, to which has to be added nuclear generation, which was withdrawn from the sale at a late stage after proving to be unsaleable. Nuclear generation has more recently been split and the more modern stations privatized as British Energy with the older ones remaining in the public sector. As a natural monopoly the national grid was vested separately in a company initially owned by the regional supply companies but more recently floated, the National Grid Company. The supply and distribution companies (now universally known as Regional Electricity Companies or RECs) are twelve in number and have power themselves to generate electricity. In Scotland a different structure was adopted with the creation of two vertically integrated companies, Scottish Power and Hydro-Electric combining generation, transmission, and supply functions with a separate nuclear generation company. With such a fragmented structure it is not surprising that takeovers also became an important concern for the regulator.

This complexity of the structure also raises major problems of co-ordination. The basic mechanism for the purchase of electricity from the generators was envisaged as taking place through the pool, a form of spot market, though in practice most electricity is purchased under contract at a fixed price from a generating company by the RECs through contracts for differences which provide a degree of hedging against fluctuations in pool prices. A considerable degree of liberalization was envisaged from the outset, with the RECs retaining monopoly franchise powers for supplying medium-sized customers only until 1994 and losing them for all customers in 1998. New entrants were also to be encouraged into the generation business, and the emphasis on opportunities for competition led to over half of the largest companies choosing supply from a 'second tier supplier' other than their local REC by 1995–6.

However, as one commentator put it, 'within this quasi-competitive framework, the legislation and draft licences contained some distinctly non-competitive features'.[3] The most well-known feature of this kind is the 'fossil fuel levy'. The RECs were required to purchase a proportion of their electricity from non-fossil fuel sources and the costs involved can be recovered from customers through the levy. This was initially set by the Secretary of State at 10.6 per cent of consumers' bills and was later revised by the regulator to 11 per cent and then 10 per cent. The benefit of the levy went overwhelmingly to support nuclear generation; in 1993, 97 per cent of the levy was used in this way. The justification was that this would contribute to the decommissioning costs of nuclear stations, though it has been used for more general support of nuclear generation and, as one commentator has pointed out, 'the institutionalisation of this level of cross-subsidy to one sector of the industry was a highly ironic outcome for a programme designed to create a competitive electricity supply market and ostensibly operating according to economic pricing principles'.[4] In fact, the privatization of part of the nuclear industry permitted the abolition of much of the nuclear portion of the levy in 1996, the sale proceeds being earmarked for use in decommissioning. Thus the levy was reduced from 10 per cent to 3.7 per cent from November 1996.

The Secretary of State has also retained particularly strong reserve powers in addition to those of the regulator. For example, he is able to veto licence modifications by agreement and also to veto modification references to the MMC.[5] Such powers have also been retained over the industry itself; thus the Secretary of State has the power to require the maintenance of coal stocks at specified levels at power stations and to direct generators to operate, or not operate, stations at specified levels of capacity or using specified fuels, powers which have prompted one commentator to suggest that '[i]t is not too far-fetched to say that [they] would allow the Secretary of State to take over the operation of the [industry]

[3] Ernst, J., *Whose Utility? The Social Impact of Public Utility Privatization and Regulation in Britain* (Open University Press, Buckingham, 1994), 27.

[4] *Ibid.* 28.   [5] Electricity Act 1989, ss. 11(4), 12(5).

or a large part of it notwithstanding its privatisation'.[6] The pattern which thus emerges from the industry is that of the 'free economy and strong state'.[7] On the one hand the provisions for competition go further than in the case of the other utilities; yet reserve powers have been provided for government, either for use in special circumstances such as those relating to power stations (though the statute does not restrict their use to such circumstances) or as a more continuous policy tool, as illustrated by the fossil fuel levy and the continuing requirement of governmental consent for new generating capacity.[8] As we shall see, the Secretary of State has also had an important role in relation to takeovers and mergers.

Regulatory Institutions

The structure adopted for the regulatory institutions has much in common with the examples discussed earlier, though there are some differences reflecting the structure of the industry. The first characteristic to note is the fact that a separate regulator was established for the electricity industry; there was no attempt to create a more general energy regulator. As we shall see, this raised problems when the purchasing policies of the privatized industry devastated the domestic coal industry, yet this proved to be outside the jurisdiction of the Electricity Regulator. Once more the model of the industry-specific Director has been chosen, the Director General of Electricity Supply, in this case assisted by the Office of Electricity Regulation (OFFER); as already noted, the Secretary of State retains important reserve powers as well as being responsible for the initial licensing, including the setting of the initial licence conditions. These included price control, but a key aspect of the new system is that the generation prices (which in 1993–4 constituted 56 per cent of overall costs to consumers) were not initially made subject to any price control, the assumption being that competition between generators would be a more effective way of keeping charges related to costs. Price controls applied to the transmission business of the National Grid and to the distribution and supply

---

[6] Electricity Act 1989, s. 34; the comment is from the annotation in *Current Law Statutes Annotated* by John McEldowney (Sweet & Maxwell, London, 1989), 29–55.

[7] The phrase is taken from Gamble, A., *The Free Economy and the Strong State* (2nd edn., Macmillan, London, 1994).

[8] Electricity Act 1989, s. 36.

businesses of the RECs, although the supply controls permit the passing through of purchase costs from the generators. The position was complicated further by the imposition of a supplementary price cap by the Secretary of State at the time of privatization and applying up to April 1993. This supplementary cap 'was devised with the aim of limiting electricity tariff increases to the rate of inflation, and was inserted by the Secretary of State for Energy following political anxiety about the movement in prices in the early years after privatization'.[9] Moreover, in February 1994 the Director General agreed two-year voluntary undertakings with National Power and PowerGen to limit pool prices because of the limited degree of competition in generation; generation price controls in all but name. In Scotland, somewhat different arrangements were adopted involving supply price controls which explicitly limit the generation prices which may be passed through to franchise customers, thus reflecting the vertically integrated nature of the industry here.

Regulating monopoly is still an important part of the regulatory task, and the regulator retains important price-control powers; we shall see below that his use of them has proved even more controversial than in the case of the other regulators we have examined. In other respects, given the stress on competition in the system, he operates more like a competition regulator, policing competition in generation and supply including the operation of the pool. These tasks will be analysed at a later stage and have also proved highly controversial. As with gas, social regulation has been thrown into relief with liberalization of the domestic market, requiring some way to be found of continuing the effectiveness of provisions on universal service and of dealing with other access issues.

As regards consumer protection, the structures once more exhibit differences from those discussed earlier. The basic arrangements are similar to those in the water industry, with regional Consumers' Committees established and appointed by the Director General with duties to keep under review supply matters, to advise the Director General, and to resolve certain complaints.[10] As the result of an amendment to the Bill achieved largely by advocacy from the National Consumer Council, a National Consumers' Consultative Committee was added, composed of the Chairs of the Consumers'

---

[9] Ernst, n. 3 above, 30.   [10] Electricity Act 1989, ss. 2, 46, 51, and sched. 2.

Committees and chaired by the Director General. This has the wider power to 'keep under review matters affecting the interests of consumers of electricity generally'.[11] It has been subjected to unfavourable criticism by the more independent Gas Consumers Council, although the Trade and Industry Committee has rather grudgingly accepted that its structure has evolved and that the National Committee has achieved greater independence from the Director General.[12] A non-statutory Electricity Consumers' Committees Chairmen's Group was also established in 1993 to provide a national view in a more independent way.

Finally, the European Community is also a potentially important actor in electricity. As mentioned in earlier chapters, rules for a common electricity market were delayed for several years after serious disagreements between Member States; however, a compromise agreement was reached in June 1996. This will permit a two-speed approach to market liberalization, and important questions remain to be resolved before implementation, so the immediate effect on UK arrangements is likely to be minimal.[13] Nevertheless, as the example of telecommunications has shown, once liberalization moves have commenced they can have considerable influence on the regulatory environment.

The Legislation

It has already been mentioned that the legislation applying to electricity is more competition-oriented than is the case for other utilities. Thus the primary duties applying to the Secretary of State and the regulator are three in number: to secure that all reasonable demands for electricity are satisfied, to secure that licence holders are able to finance the carrying on of the activities which they are authorized by their licences to carry on, and to promote competition in the generation and supply of electricity.[14] Thus when compared to the original legislation for gas regulation after

[11] Electricity Act 1989, s. 53(2)(a).
[12] Trade and Industry Committee, HC 185, 1993–4, *Minutes of Evidence*, 17–18; Trade and Industry Committee, *Aspects of the Electricity Supply Industry*, HC 481, 1994–5, paras. 97–9.
[13] EC Commission, *Press Release: Results of the Extraordinary Meeting of the Energy Council*, 20 June 1996; Hancher, L., 'The New Rules for the Community Electricity Market' (1996) 7 *Utilities Law Review* 217–20.
[14] Electricity Act 1989, s. 3(1).

privatization, the most striking contrast is the promotion of competition into a primary duty (although in the case of gas such a duty has been incorporated by later legislation[15]). The universal service duty is, on the other hand, wider in potential scope given the absence of any qualification of the meeting of reasonable demands by the phrase 'so far as it is economical to meet them'.[16] The Energy Committee of the House of Commons has criticized the absence of consumer protection amongst the primary duties.[17]

The competition duty applying to the Secretary of State and regulator is explicitly made subject to another duty applying only to the North of Scotland and requiring that there is no distinction between tariffs for urban and rural areas and that public electricity suppliers are not subject to a competitive disadvantage because of this.[18] The range of secondary duties includes some more familiar matters; thus Secretary of State and Director are under a duty to exercise their functions in the manner considered best calculated to protect the interests of consumers in relation to prices and other terms of supply, continuity of supply, and quality of supply, to promote efficiency and economy by electricity suppliers and the efficient use of electricity supplied to consumers, and to take into account the effect of activities on the physical environment.[19] The Secretary of State and Director are also required to take into account in particular the protection of the interests of consumers in rural areas in pricing matters and the interests of those who are disabled or of pensionable age in quality matters.[20]

Apart from the duties applying to the minister and regulator, a number of important duties apply directly to the RECs. Thus they are required to develop and maintain an efficient, co-ordinated, and economical system of electricity supply.[21] More specifically, the companies are required to give a supply of electricity to premises on request; it is made explicit that this includes a requirement to continue to provide supply, but the requirement is of course

---

[15] Competition and Service (Utilities) Act 1992, s. 38(1); Gas Act 1995, s. 1.
[16] Gas Act 1986, s. 4(1)(a).
[17] Energy Committee, *Consequences of Electricity Privatisation*, HC 113, 1991–2, para. 134.
[18] Electricity Act 1989, s. 3(2); and see Industry Department for Scotland, *Scottish Hydro-Electric plc: Generation, Transmission and Public Electricity Supply Licence Document* (HMSO, London, 1990), Pt. V, cond. 4(4).
[19] Electricity Act 1989, s. 3(3).   [20] Electricity Act 1989, s. 3(4)–(5).
[21] Electricity Act 1989, s. 9(1).

subject to a number of exceptions.[22] This requirement has recently been the subject of litigation, in a stated case against a conviction for unlawfully harassing a debtor. It was argued that the supply of electricity was non-contractual, and so there was no contractual basis for debt recovery by the supplier. This argument was upheld on the ground that supply could not be regarded as contractual because of the element of compulsion in the obligation to supply; the court considered the exceptions to this to be very limited, though statutory provisions provided an alternative means of debt recovery for the supplier. As Dyson J put it, '[d]iscretion does not come into play. Thus save in certain narrowly defined circumstances, if a customer requests the supply of electricity, the supplier is obliged to supply.'[23] The Act also obliges the RECs to provide a minimum period of notice before disconnecting a tariff customer and does not permit this in the case of an amount which is genuinely in dispute.[24] There is an obligation to resume supply promptly after the payment has been settled.[25] The REC is also prohibited from charging for changing a disabled customer's meter position.[26]

The RECs are not permitted to show undue preference to any person or class of persons, nor to exercise any undue discrimination against any person or class of persons.[27] As was seen in Chapter 1, this is not a new provision on privatization, and its predecessors had also resulted in litigation; in the most important of the cases the courts adopted an approach which was concerned not simply with whether preference had taken place but with whether it could be reasonably justified.[28]

In addition to the duties outlined, a number of provisions of the statute provide for service standards, provisions which we saw above were later extended to other utilities by the 1992 legislation. Thus the Act provides for the setting of standards in individual cases and of overall standards by the Director; he may also set stan-

---

[22] Electricity Act 1989, ss. 16, 17.
[23] *Norweb plc* v. *Dixon* [1995] 3 All ER 952, at 959 (QBD DC).
[24] Electricity Act 1989, sched. 6, para. 1(6)–(10).
[25] Electricity Act 1989, sched. 6, para. 2.
[26] Electricity Act 1989, sched. 6, para. 1(2).   [27] Electricity Act 1989, s. 18(4).
[28] *South of Scotland Electricity Board* v. *British Oxygen Co.* [1956] 3 All ER 199 (HL); and see the other cases discussed in Ch. 1 above.

dards for the promotion of the efficient use of electricity; these provisions are further elaborated by the 1992 Act.[29]

Finally, further duties are included in the supply licences. These include provisions requiring the publication of and compliance with codes of practice approved by the regulator relating to payment of electricity bills, treatment of defaulting customers, provision of services for elderly and disabled customers, providing advice on the efficient use of electricity and on complaint handling procedures.[30]

We can see then that even this most competition-oriented legislative model does not simply confer on the regulator a straightforward duty to maximize competition, but contains a number of important duties with other rationales; we saw in Chapter 1 that in the European Union notions of universal service have also loomed large in reform proposals. More litigation has occurred in the past around statutory provisions than in the case of the other utilities; the regulator has also been subject to successful challenge by judicial review on the ground that he had misinterpreted his statutory powers to resolve disputes, so the legal environment of regulation is important.[31] Nevertheless, much also depends on the implementation of the various provisions by the Director, and it is to him that I shall now turn.

The Regulator

The first Director General of Electricity Supply was Professor Stephen Littlechild. He had been Professor of Commerce at the University of Birmingham and previously Professor of Applied Economics at the University of Aston. He will of course already be familiar to readers as the author of the two Littlechild Reports on the regulation of BT's profitability and on the regulation of the privatized water companies. He, more than anyone, was the architect of the regulatory system envisaged on privatization of the utilities.

It will not be surprising that his initial interpretation of his

---

[29] Electricity Act 1989, ss. 39–41; Competition and Service (Utilities) Act 1992, ss. 20–5.

[30] Department of Energy, *Public Electricity Supply Licence* (HMSO, London, 1990), conds. 18–23; Industry Department for Scotland, n. 18 above, conds. 12–17 and *Scottish Power plc: Generation, Transmission and Public Electricity Supply Licence* (HMSO, London, 1990), conds. 12–17.

[31] *R.* v. *Director General of Electricity Supply, ex parte Redrow Homes, The Times*, 21 Feb. 1995.

statutory duties was '[i]f one had to summarise all these duties in a few words it would probably be protection of customers and promotion of competition. To a greater or lesser extent, this theme runs through all the regulatory bodies.'[32] He continued:

[m]y job is to promote competition where it is feasible and sensible to do so, bearing in mind that it was not possible at the time of privatisation to move in a single step from a state-owned monopoly to a privately owned, fully competitive industry. My task in part is therefore to help to complete the transition: not merely to monitor competition but actively to promote it.[33]

Regulation was thus understood as essentially transitional, a first step leading to its own eventual demise with the arrival of effective competition. This pro-competition attitude pervaded all his work, and is the key to an apparently surprising attitude which he expressed early on:

I am sometimes asked whether there is not a conflict between all these objectives [i.e. the statutory duties] and if so how I go about resolving it. Which of all these duties has priority? I answer that I do not see it that way at present. In my experience so far, there has not been a conflict between these objectives. This is not to say that the duties are irrelevant: far from it. Rather, the more immediate problems so far have been to trace through the full implications of the available actions for the statutory duties, and to assess what types of arrangements would be relevant in a competitive market.[34]

Partly as a result of this strongly pro-competition attitude, the Director General has also faced criticism that his regulatory style has been too 'hands-off'. This emerged particularly in an investigation by the Trade and Industry Committee into the effects on the coal industry of the shift to gas generation of electricity.[35] The conclusions of the Committee are worth quoting at length:

There has been much criticism of the Director General during our inquiry. Dr Helm, for example, noted 'the very narrow interpretation of consumer interests by the Director General, in practice equating these interests almost exclusively with the advancement of a particular concept of com-

[32] Littlechild, S., 'Office of Electricity Regulation: The New Regulatory Framework for Electricity', in Veljanovski, C., *Regulators and the Market* (Institute of Economic Affairs, London, 1991), 107–18, 108.
[33] *Ibid.*   [34] *Ibid.*
[35] *British Energy Policy and the Market for Coal*, HC 237, 1992–3.

petition'. The view of the Major Energy Users Council was that 'he has been inclined to be too reactive and has waited for things to happen rather than taking an initiative and anticipating irregularities and flaws in the electricity market and the regulation and implementation of that market.' . . . we do not regard the way the Director General has discharged his duties as satisfactory. Our concerns are encapsulated in the remarks just quoted.[36]

Part of the explanation for this lies in the limiting of his remit to electricity regulation rather than regulation of energy more generally, as the Committee noted, but some of the points made by the regulator particularly surprised the Committee, for example, his admission that he had never met the President of the Board of Trade, let alone discussed energy policy with him, more than a year after he had taken office.[37] The Committee recommended changes to the statutory duties and a review of the powers of the energy regulators in order to secure greater government and parliamentary control.[38] This raises issues of the relationship between regulators and government which will be addressed in my concluding chapter.

We shall see later in this Chapter whether a hands-off or proactive approach has actually proved possible in electricity regulation. The point to be stressed here is that the regulator has, even more than in the case of the other utilities, conceived his role not as providing surrogate competition for a monopoly but as essentially transitional through developing liberalization to create real competition as much as possible. The similarity is thus with telecommunications rather than with gas and water; however, this perception of the regulatory role has been considerably more controversial than in telecommunications.

Regulating Monopoly: Price Control

Price control is unusually complex in the electricity industry due to the number of components making up electricity charges, each requiring separate controls. In 1995–6 the proportions of each component in pricing for consumers as a whole in England and Wales were generation 52 per cent, distribution 29 per cent, transmission 4 per cent, supply 6 per cent and the Fossil Fuel Levy

---

[36] *Ibid.* paras. 290–1 (references omitted).   [37] *Ibid. Minutes of Evidence*, 72.
[38] *Ibid.* paras. 292–3.

nearly 9 per cent.[39] As was mentioned earlier, generation was not formally subject to price controls in England and Wales, and the RECs were permitted to pass through the costs of purchase of electricity from the generating companies, although they are under an obligation under their licences to purchase electricity economically.[40] However, a generation price cap in all but name was imposed for two years from February 1994 after the Director General had concluded that the extent of competition in generation was not sufficient to restrain National Power and PowerGen if they wished to increase prices. This took the form of agreement by the companies that they would bid into the pool in such a way that the average pool purchase price would not exceed specified sums per kilowatt hour.[41] After some difficulties in enforcement, the Director General decided that the undertakings would not be extended beyond two years because of agreements to dispose of generating plant and emerging competition in the market.[42] Transmission by the National Grid was subject to a price control, originally set at RPI and then tightened by the Director General to RPI–3 from April 1993–7; in 1995–6 he issued four consultation papers on a new formula from 1997 and engaged consultants to examine the company's business plan and proposed capital expenditure; proposals were then issued for a new control involving a 20 per cent cut in prices followed by RPI–4 for three years, which the company accepted.[43]

Supply was capped initially for three years to March 1993 by a formula of RPI + F, F representing the Fossil Fuel Levy. This control was the 'supplementary price cap' referred to above and introduced by the Secretary of State to avoid increases above the rate of inflation in the years immediately following privatization. The supply cap from March 1993 became RPI + Y, Y representing electricity purchase costs, distribution charges, the fossil fuel levy, transmission charges, and administration charges for the pool; this was revised from 1 April 1994 by the regulator to RPI – 2 + Y; the

[39] OFFER, *The Competitive Electricity Market from 1998: Price Constraints* (1996), 6.

[40] Department of Energy, n. 30 above, cond. 5; Industry Department for Scotland, n. 30 above, cond. 6.

[41] OFFER, *Annual Report 1994*, HC 432, 1994–5, 22–3.

[42] OFFER, *Annual Report 1995*, HC 348, 1995–6, 23–5.

[43] OFFER, *The Transmission Price Control Review of the National Grid Company: Proposals* (1996).

supply controls apply only to customers who do not have a peak demand exceeding 100kw. Finally, and as we shall see most controversially, the distribution controls were initially set at different figures for different companies, ranging from RPI + 0 to RPI + 2. In August 1994 the regulator attempted to reset the distribution controls at an average of RPI − 2, but was forced to withdraw the proposals at a late stage after acquiring more information about the companies; instead a control of RPI − 3 was set. In Scotland the initial supply price controls took the form of RPI − 0.3 and 0.5 with an RPI control on electricity purchasing costs; this changed from 1994 to RPI − 2, with the generation costs derived from the costs of electricity purchases in England and Wales; distribution controls were also tightened. Transmission price controls in Scotland were RPI − 1 and RPI − 0.5, and from 1994 RPI − 1 and RPI − 1.5.

This overview considerably understates the complexity of the issues involved. It is thus hard to disagree with the view of the regulator that the controls are 'not easy to understand, nor is it straightforward to check whether or not a licensee is complying with them'.[44] The position was not made any easier by difficulties in applying the supplementary price cap which in fact coincided with increases in prices above the rate of inflation and led the Regulator to write to companies, warning them of a potential breach of price control; refunds were eventually made to customers.[45] The very existence of the supplementary price cap shows the importance of the political environment in which the regulator was undertaking his work; the *de facto* generation price cap also illustrates the limits to competition in the industry; these had been seriously overestimated at the time of privatization.

In his first Annual Report the Director General set out his general approach:

In reviewing the operation of price controls at the end of the relevant periods specified in the licences, I shall have regard, inter alia, to the actual and prospective cash flows of the companies, including the savings achievable through greater efficiency and where appropriate any additional costs arising from changes in the environment or wider regulatory regime. I shall also have regard to the rate of return which the markets will require.[46]

[44] OFFER, *Annual Report 1991*, HC 289, 1991–2, 7.
[45] Ernst, n. 3 above, 128–30.
[46] OFFER, *Annual Report 1989*, HC 367, 1989–90, 5–6.

He also emphasized the need for stability: 'I recognise the importance of stability in the new regime and would require a continuing
case to be made before proposing any radical change'.[47] The same
considerations applied more particularly to the distribution price
controls; as the Director General put it in his 1992 Report:

[w]ork is also under way on the review of the REC distribution price controls. Some commentators observing high profits earned by the regional
companies have suggested that I should bring forward this review. While I
understand their argument, I am not convinced that a change to the specified timetable would in fact be helpful to customers. It would introduce
additional uncertainty about regulation. This would increase the companies' cost of capital and reduce their incentive to cut other costs.
Ultimately, higher costs mean higher prices to customers. I believe that
these higher costs and prices, which would continue into the future, would
more than offset any short-term gain from lower prices for a year or two.[48]

This seems to reflect very much the sort of view one would expect
from the author of the first Littlechild Report; a regime of stability
with periodic revisions of price controls only at stated intervals and
with an expectation that they would be left in place to run their full
duration.

The impracticality of this model eventually became clear with the
attempt in 1994 to establish a revised set of distribution price controls. The original price controls set by the Government and permitting price increase at or above inflation were described by the
Trade and Industry Committee as permitting 'indisputably excessive profits', and it considered that they 'had clearly been wrongly
set' and should have been reset within the initial five-year period.[49]
The proposals made by the Director in August 1994 for the next
period were based on the assumption that the companies could cut
their costs by an average of 3 per cent per year and had a cost of
capital of 7 per cent. He decided to retain the RPI–X form of control, though the stress was more on the scope for incentives to efficiency saving that it offered than on stability:

I consider that an RPI–X price control, rather than a profit control, is
likely to be in the best interests of customers who are not protected by a
competitive market. It gives better incentives to greater efficiency, and the

[47] *Ibid.* 4.
[48] OFFER, *Annual Report 1992*, HC 646, 1992–3, 6.
[49] Trade and Industry Committee, *Aspects of the Electricity Supply Industry*, HC
481, 1994–5, para. 82.

achieved improvements in productivity during one price control period can be reflected in revised price controls for the next, along with the estimated scope for improvements in future.[50]

Nevertheless, the stability theme emerged in the decision to set the new control for a five-year period:

> If the distribution price control were set for only three years, work on a new control would need to begin less than two years from now, and there would be little time for any incentive effects to be felt. On the other hand, it is also important that price controls be left to run their full period in other than exceptional circumstances. This provides a full incentive to companies to reduce costs, minimises uncertainty amongst investors and avoids increasing the cost of capital. Frequent adjustment of price controls also invites interference in the day to day operation of companies. This would create the very confusion and inefficiency which privatisation and arm's length regulation were designed to reduce.[51]

As part of the review the Director undertook a detailed examination of operating costs and the asset base, although there is relatively little on the cost of capital or gearing.[52] The proposals varied from company to company, but were designed to secure initial price reductions equal to 11 per cent, 14 per cent and 15 per cent for the companies (for this purpose grouped together in three categories) with further reductions of 2 per cent per year in real terms for the following four years.[53] Similar but more complex proposals were made for the Scottish companies as regards both distribution and supply.[54] All the English companies accepted the outcome (although it was harsher than their own proposals); one Scottish company, Hydro-Electric, with special circumstances, referred the proposed controls to the MMC. The reaction suggested that the English companies had done remarkably well:

> [t]he Financial Times headed its report 'Review starts champagne corks popping'. Privately, many electricity companies executives [*sic*] were prepared to admit that they had been playing a game of bluff with the regulator over the true size of their costs—and had won. This was certainly the view of the stock market, where electricity shares promptly powered ahead.

---

[50] OFFER, *The Distribution Price Control Proposals* (1994), para. 3.1.
[51] *Ibid.*, para. 3.19.   [52] See *ibid.* paras. 5.46–5.65.
[53] See *ibid.* 79–82.
[54] OFFER, *The Scottish Distribution and Supply Price Proposals* (1994).

But Prof. Littlechild stuck to his view that the new formula was firm and fair.[55]

The English proposals were announced in August 1994, those for Scotland in September 1994. In December, Trafalgar House launched a takeover bid for Northern Electric, and the company mounted a defence including a promise of £563 million worth of financial incentives for loyal shareholders and cuts in capital expenditure; a dividend increase of 33 per cent was forecast for the year. The formal period for consultation on the licence amendment for the English companies was due to end by 11 March 1995. On 7 March the regulator announced that in view of information which had emerged, especially in the bid for Northern Electric, and 'what appears to be widespread public concern about whether the price control proposals are sufficiently demanding on the RECs and whether they represent an appropriate balance between the interests of customers and shareholders', he was prepared to consider a further tightening of controls from 1 April 1996.[56] The result was widespread outrage and confusion, particularly as the announcement was made one day after the government had sold its 40 per cent residual stake in the generating companies; whilst they were not directly affected by the distribution controls, their shares fell sharply and institutional holdings began trading below the offer price. Many calls were made for both reform of the regulatory system and Professor Littlechild's resignation. The decision was also enough to sink the takeover bid. The explanation given by the regulator noted that public concern was increasing that the proposed controls were not sufficiently demanding on companies, and 'if I had ignored it, this could have led to increasing loss of confidence in the price controls and in the regulatory regime generally'. He noted that share prices of RECs had risen after his proposals and had continued to rise, and that Northern Electric's defence document had envisaged big cuts in capital spending, a dramatic increase in gearing, special payments to shareholders, and a forecast of substantially rising dividends. All these new circumstances

[55] Lascelles, D., 'The Electricity Industry 1994–5', in Centre for the Study of Regulated Industries, *Regulatory Review 1995* (Centre for the Study of Regulated Industries, London, 1995), 19–31, 22.
[56] The statement is reproduced in full as 'Widespread Public Concern Over Planned Price Controls', *Financial Times*, 8 Mar. 1995.

constituted reasons for considering further controls.[57] Over the following three months the Director General re-examined all aspects of his original proposal, by now aided by the Monopolies and Mergers Commission decision relating to Hydro-Electric, which had eased the formula slightly, but had confirmed his decision on cost of capital.[58] Through making relatively small changes to the valuation of existing assets and other adjustments, the Director General was able to announce new controls imposing further reductions in distribution charges of 10–13 per cent from April 1996, and a tougher formula of RPI – 3 for the following three years to 2000.

A number of conclusions can be drawn from these events. First, the widespread outrage at the decision of the Director General to change proposals before the end of the consultation period illustrates just how much of a formality the consultation process was assumed to have become; decisions are assumed to be firm before the start of the statutory consultation.[59] Secondly, none of the circumstances referred to were exactly new and they should have been ascertainable at the time of the original proposals; it is ironic that early on Professor Littlechild had claimed that:

[t]he nature and powers provided in the Act and in the licences reflect a learning experience on the part of government. For example, there are more extensive and more explicit powers for the DGES to obtain information from licensees than there are for some other Directors. I suspect there has also been a learning experience on the part of industry.[60]

Not only did his faith in his powers to obtain accurate information from the industry appear misplaced, the events illustrated vividly that the power to require information is not enough; there must be some forum in which the information can be properly tested through searching criticism and debate. Publishing consultation papers is not adequate for this and some form of hearing would seem to be the only adequate response. Apart from these procedural matters, the process shows very clearly how it is impossible to separate tariff setting from a wider context of social and political concern, and how a regime of stability interrupted by occasional

[57] Littlechild, S., 'Better to Grasp the Nettle Now', *Financial Times*, 9 Mar. 1995.
[58] Monopolies and Mergers Commission, *Scottish Hydro-Electric plc.* (HMSO, London, 1995).
[59] But cf. 'Littlechild May Alter Price Caps', *Financial Times*, 23 Feb. 1995, noting the possibility of the proposals being reopened.
[60] Littlechild, n. 32 above, 114.

technical resetting of prices is quite unrealistic in the politically charged arena of utility prices. Moreover, price control is not a temporary phenomenon; distribution and transmission controls will continue indefinitely. Even supply price controls are likely to remain for a period after supply liberalization in 1998.[61]

Regulating Monopoly: Quality of Service

This can be dealt with more briefly as there has not been such controversy here as in price setting, or indeed as in water services. The companies are subject to service standards, in the form of ten guaranteed service standards in individual cases for which compensation is payable if they are not met, and also eight overall service standards and performance standards for the efficient use of electricity. The guaranteed standards include, for example, the speed of restoration of supply after faults, the provision of supply and of a meter, notice of supply interruptions, and the keeping of appointments. Overall standards include the minimum percentage of supplies to be reconnected following faults in three hours and in twenty-four hours, the minimum percentage of customers for whom a firm meter reading must be obtained at least once a year, and response to customer correspondence within ten days. The standards have been revised as part of the setting of the distribution price controls, during which the Director also asked for statements of services in relation to prepayment meter customers.[62] As a result, the standards were reviewed and tightened in 1995. The companies are also required to meet standards of performance on electricity efficiency, and to comply with codes of practice on the payment of bills by domestic customers, services for customers with prepayment meters, services for the elderly and the disabled, advice on efficient use of electricity, and complaint handling; revised codes were approved in Autumn 1996.

The major question remaining about such standards and other social obligations is that of their role in a liberalized tariff market. Of course, standards relating to distribution will remain, as this will not be liberalized. In supply, standards will be retained for the RECs' tariff customers; for others, there is no power to set guar-

---

[61] OFFER, *The Competitive Electricity Market From 1998: Price Restraints* (1996).
[62] OFFER, n. 50 above, paras. 8.31–35.

anteed standards, however it is intended that other suppliers should be required to report the level of service they provide in areas covered by overall service standards. Licences will include provisions requiring all suppliers to offer a range of payment methods and requiring the production of the codes of practice referred to above.

Regulation for Competition: Generation

Increasing competition has been at the heart of electricity regulation, and has occurred in a number of different parts of the industry. The first is that of generation. As we have seen, generation was established as an allegedly competitive regime, free of price controls in England and Wales, and with a complex pool mechanism established to facilitate this; the regulator was also under a primary duty to promote competition here. This has not, however, proved to be without problems, particularly because of the large market shares of National Power and PowerGen, which have dominated the mid-merit supply which effectively fixes the pool price.[63] Much concern has been expressed about anti-competitive practices in relation to the pool, not least by large electricity users such as ICI, and the Director General in 1994 was forced to obtain undertakings from the two large generating companies in the form first of the unofficial price cap discussed above, and secondly to dispose of 6000 MW of generating plant by the end of 1995; this would amount to just under 10 per cent of capacity in England and Wales.[64] It was made clear that the alternative to such sales would be a reference to the MMC. Sales were delayed after difficulties in agreeing a price, and at the end of 1995, although PowerGen had arranged for disposals to a REC, discussions in the case of National Power were still continuing. However, in 1996 a sale was agreed to the same REC, and this was considered to comply with the undertakings.

Although this was the most important action to increase competition in generation, concern in fact dates back much earlier; in the special case of Scotland, in 1990 the Director General noted that '[a]s yet there has been no new entry into generation on a significant scale, and there is little prospect of it for the foreseeable

---

[63] For a detailed discussion of this issue see Trade and Industry Committee, (1994–5) n. 12 above, paras. 32–46.
[64] See OFFER, n. 41 above, 22–5.

future'.[65] South of the Border, in the pool there was an unexpected rise in prices in 1991 which led to the Director General contemplating a reference to the MMC; in fact he undertook his own pool price inquiry that led to more information being made available on forecast capacity and changes were made to the rules to prevent the manipulation of availability payments to the generators.[66] Nevertheless, problems of high and unpredictable pool prices continued and the operation of the pool was heavily criticized by the Trade and Industry Committee in 1995 as lacking in transparency.[67]

The Director General has thus had a major role in attempting to increase competition in electricity generation. This had been a difficult task, particularly as the complex system of the pool exaggerates the effect of dominance by the two largest generators, and competition seems a delicate flower; it needs constant support and policing from a specialist regulator who understands the industry in depth to permit its survival. A further concern is however that this competition has had considerable effects outside the scope of the Regulator's remit, notably through the licensing of new gas generators resulting in the near destruction of the domestic coal industry.[68] However, the extensive criticism made of the Director General here rather neglects the point that it was the lack of a more general framework of energy policy on the part of the Government which was at issue; after all, licensing of new generating plant remains a task for government rather than for the regulator.[69] The latter's role was to ensure that the RECs were not in breach of their duty to purchase electricity at the best effective price, and such a breach was not established.[70] I shall return to the question of relations between regulators and government and broader policy frameworks in the conclusion to this book.

[65] OFFER, *Annual Report 1990*, HC 355, 1990–1, 6.
[66] OFFER, n. 48 above, 7.
[67] Trade and Industry Committee (1994–5), n. 12 above, paras. 47–72.
[68] Trade and Industry Committee, *British Energy Policy and the Market for Coal*, HC 237, 1992–3.
[69] Electricity Act 1989, s. 36.
[70] See OFFER, *Review of Economic Purchasing* (1992); but cf. Corry, D., Hewett, C., and Tindale, S. (eds.), *Energy '98: Competing for Power* (Institute for Public Policy Research, London, 1996), 52.

Regulation for Competition: Capital Markets

We discovered in the previous chapter that a somewhat unexpected role of the Water Regulator was to offer advice concerning the regulatory and consumer implications of mergers and takeovers. This has been even more important in electricity. The Government ended its golden shares in the RECs in March 1995; already, as we have seen, Trafalgar House had launched a bid for Northern Electric, though this fell in the aftermath of the price control reopening. It was the first example of many; during 1995 the regulator was faced with no fewer than nine more takeover bids for RECs, with more to follow in 1996. In electricity there is no compulsory reference to the MMC, though a concordat has been reached with the Office of Fair Trading that the regulator's views are sought at an early stage; he has stated that his concern is that customers are properly protected and that he has continued access to information and the ability to regulate effectively the companies concerned. When the hitherto independent RECs become subsidiaries within a wider group, licence conditions are put into place to secure continued provision of information and to ring-fence their assets and secure that they have adequate financial resources.[71] The role of the regulator is thus central to scrutiny of proposed mergers and takeovers; as one commentator has put it, '[i]n a nutshell, it is all down to the regulators'.[72]

This sounds reasonably straightforward, but the practice has once more been controversial, with a complex division of labour between the Regulator, the Director General of Fair Trading, the MMC, and the Secretary of State. Thus in the case of the successful bid by Scottish Power for MANWEB, the Electricity Regulator was concerned about the reduction of comparators for yardstick competition that this would cause and advised that it be referred to the MMC; the Secretary of State refused to do so.[73] The Secretary of State did, however, state the main considerations he would take into account in deciding whether to make a reference; he would decide primarily on grounds of competition, with concerns about foreign ownership and management efficiency unlikely to be a

[71] OFFER, n. 42 above, 10.
[72] Bailey, K., 'A Bid Too Far?' (1996) 7 *Utilities Law Review* 134–6, 135.
[73] OFFER, n. 42 above, 10–11.

sufficient justification for a reference; he would also consider the effect on the ability of the regulator to perform his duties and the potential loss of comparators.[74] These issues came to a head with bids by generators for RECs, raising the question of vertical integration and threatening the deliberately vertically disintegrated industry structure adopted at privatization. The first such bid was the successful one mentioned above by Scottish Power for MAN-WEB; however, the issue arose much more strongly with bids by PowerGen for Midlands Electricity and National Power for Southern Electricity. On the advice of the regulator, these were referred to the MMC, which reported that the mergers would operate against the public interest but, by a majority, that if undertakings were imposed giving further power to the regulator the adverse effects would not justify prohibition.[75] The Secretary of State, however, decided not to follow the recommendations of the MMC and blocked the bids on the ground that they would create significant detriments to competition in the current state of the market, a decision welcomed by the Director General.[76] Fears that this would open up National Power to an American bid were countered by a decision to retain the golden shares in the generators, giving government a veto on takeovers.

The decision to block the takeovers may have been justified, given regulatory concerns, but according to a commentator who supported it, '[a]ccording to the analysts, the decision defied the logic of the market place. To be sure, in some respects at least, it was inconsistent with the Secretary of State's own criteria. The more widely held view was that it was dictated by political motives.'[77] Whilst the regulator, as in water, had a reasonably clear set of criteria for advising on mergers (and consulted effectively before offering his advice), the other institutions involved, especially the Government, did not have consistent criteria; as a PowerGen executive put it, '[t]his is a game that doesn't have any rules; you get the feeling that they are making it up as they go along.'[78]

[74] Department of Trade and Industry, *Press Releases*, 31 Aug. 1995 and 2 Nov. 1995; see Bailey, n. 72 above, 134–5.

[75] Monopolies and Mergers Commission, *National Power plc and Southern Electric plc*, Cm 3230, and *PowerGen plc and Midlands Electricity plc*, Cm 3231 (1996).

[76] DTI, *Press Release*, 24 Apr. 1996.   [77] Bailey, n. 72 above, 135.

[78] Quoted in 'UK to Block Bid for Generators with "Golden Share"', *Financial Times*, 3 May 1996.

Regulation for Competition: Product Markets

A further area in which the Director General has acted to enhance competition is that of electricity supply. Considerable competition for large users has already developed; by 1995–6 over half of customers with a maximum use of over one megawatt (large industry or hospitals) had chosen a 'second tier' supplier, i.e. a supplier other than their local REC. From April 1994 (1995 in Scotland) the opportunity to choose such a supplier was extended to customers with a maximum demand over 100 kilowatts (medium sized industry, department stores, and large shops) and by 1995–6 33 per cent had chosen a second-tier supplier.[79] The extension of competition in these markets was thus a great success. From 1998 competition is to be extended to all consumers, however small, but this raises more problems.[80]

We have seen already that a similar process of liberalization for domestic consumers is being undertaken for gas, and that this has involved new legislation. This is not required in electricity, though the process raises some fearsome technical problems, notably in relation to metering and the licensing arrangements needed to protect customer interests; this latter theme will be considered in the following section. The general process of preparation for domestic liberalization was heavily criticized by the Trade and Industry Committee in 1995.[81] The Committee noted that it was 'a vast enterprise without precedent anywhere in the world, bringing 22 million consumers into the competitive market', yet there had been remarkably little analysis of the potential benefits or costs. There was no clear allocation of responsibility for seeing the changes through, alternatives to costly new metering had not been properly thought through, and there were no firm proposals for genuine trials; overall, 'we were astonished by what we learned in this inquiry about the preparations for liberalisation'. In response the Director General agreed to take a more proactive stance and appointed a Competitive Supply Code Executive of industry and consumer representatives, appointed consultants, drew up a clear timetable, and

---

[79] OFFER, n. 42 above, 2.

[80] For an excellent general discussion of the issues see Corry, Hewett, and Tindale, n. 70 above.

[81] Trade and Industry Committee, 1995, n. 12 above, paras. 7–31.

published a number of consultative papers on the subject.[82] He continued to be concerned about foot-dragging by RECs in the process, however, especially when the pool's advisers estimated that it had a less than 50 per cent chance of implementation on schedule in April 1988.[83] Draft licences published in August 1996 included contingency arrangements for competitive supply for customers even where companies had not completed all the preparatory steps, and it was later decided to phase in competition over six months from April 1998.[84]

Liberalization of the industrial market has thus proved highly successful. Liberalization of the domestic and small-business market will however be a much more complex task, and to carry it through successfully detailed planning and co-ordination are required by the Director General. The same will no doubt be true of policing the liberalized domestic market, and this raises the issue of the continuance of social obligations after liberalization.

Social Regulation and Universal Service

As in the case of other utilities, there are a number of social obligations which apply to the electricity suppliers and are enforceable by the regulator; he has summarized them as, in particular, the duty to develop and maintain an efficient, co-ordinated, and economical system of supply, to act in accordance with the distribution code and meet technical standards, to supply any person on request, and to produce codes of practice referred to earlier.[85]

On disconnections, considerable progress has been made by the Director General. Before privatization disconnections of customers' supply were running at the rate of 70,000 *per annum* (although there had been a gradual decline since 1986, apparently due to new technology[86]), and the Director General stated at the outset that '[o]ne of my priorities will be to secure a continued and significant reduction in the number of customers disconnected for non-payment of

---

[82] See, e.g., OFFER, *The Competitive Electricity Market from 1998* (1995); *The Competitive Electricity Market from 1998: Supply Code, Trading Arrangements and Costs* (1996).

[83] OFFER, n. 42 above, 43.

[84] OFFER, *The Competitive Electricity Market from 1998: Overview of Draft Electricity Supply Licences and Codes*, n. 82 above, paras. 7.14–24.

[85] OFFER, *The Competitive Electricity Market from 1998* (1995), para. 5.3.

[86] Ernst, n. 3 above, 140.

bills'.[87] He was assisted in this by provisions in the Act and licences preventing disconnection where there is a genuine dispute and requiring the issuing of a code of practice incorporating specified provisions which largely preclude disconnection unless a prepayment meter has been offered as an alternative.[88] As a result, disconnections dropped dramatically to 19,266 in the year ending 31 March 1990. In 1991 there was a further large fall of 30 per cent in the number of disconnections (and this extended to Scotland, where disconnections by the two companies fell by 44 per cent and 35 per cent), and the Director General was able to state as his objective 'I believe it is now feasible for all companies . . . to end the practice of disconnecting domestic customers. I will be actively promoting this objective.'[89] By 1992 the number of disconnections in England and Wales was 75 per cent lower than pre-privatization and 82 per cent lower in Scotland. By 1993, the number of disconnections was less than 5 per cent of the 1989–90 level, and in 1995–6 only 674 domestic customers were disconnected for non-payment of bills.[90] This is a remarkable record, but some qualifications have to be entered here. First, different companies have had different records in reducing disconnections; even on the very low figures for 1995–6, London Electricity had no disconnections at all whilst Eastern showed an increase to over 238.[91] Secondly, the shift away from disconnection has been mainly the result of a shift to prepayment meters, but these may impose costs both through higher standing charges and 'self-disconnection'.[92]

The Trade and Industry Committee was concerned about some of the social implications of the ending of cross-subsidy with the liberalization of the domestic market, echoing its concerns in its study of liberalization of the domestic gas market.[93] In electricity more had been done already to dismantle cross-subsidy, and large regional price variations already existed; nevertheless, 'cherry-picking' might still take place, and there was a danger that the host

[87] OFFER, n. 46 above, 10.

[88] Electricity Act 1989, sched. 6, para. 1(6)–(10); Department of Energy, n. 30 above, cond. 19; Industry Department for Scotland, nn. 18 and 30 above, cond. 13; Ernst, n. 3 above, 131.

[89] OFFER, n. 44 above, 2–3.

[90] OFFER, n. 48 above, 13; *Annual Report 1993*, HC 352, 1993–4, 8; *Report on Customer Services 1995–6* (1996), 31.

[91] Ernst, n. 3 above, 143–4; OFFER, *Report on Customer Services 1995–6*, n. 90 above.   [92] See Ernst, n. 3 above, 145–6.

[93] Trade and Industry Committee (1994–5), n. 12 above, second item, paras. 13–19.

RECs would be left with a disproportionate share of customers such as the elderly and disabled requiring special services. The Committee recommended that there should be a thorough examination of the standards needed in a competitive market, and that there should be equal obligations on all suppliers in respect of customers with special needs.

Initially, the Director General had expressed himself reluctant to impose social obligations on new entrants. Thus, in a consultation paper published at the beginning of 1995 he noted that no new primary legislation was needed for liberalization, and that the existing social (or 'customer protection') obligations would continue to apply to the RECs, but, at least for a transitional period, it seemed that they would not be applied to competitors; '[i]mposing inappropriate conditions on competitors could deter or hamper new entry, reduce the extent or variety of competitive terms on offer and reinforce the existing monopolies of the [RECs], all to the potential detriment of customers'.[94] Nor should the market work to the disadvantage of customers paying through prepayment meters; 'in a fully competitive market all customers are potentially attractive to suppliers'.[95] However, a consultative process then took place, and the outcome was that broadly similar obligations to those of the RECs were to apply to second-tier (i.e. competing) suppliers who wished to supply domestic consumers. Thus a consultation paper in November 1995 suggested that second-tier suppliers should be obliged to supply on request on published terms; although there is no obligation of the type which exists in gas to refuse licence applications framed to discriminate against particular types of consumers, in fact such discrimination would only be permitted on technical grounds. Price control of RECs would continue as a transitional measure after 1998 in respect of smaller customers; the same requirements to draw up codes of practice should apply to second-tier suppliers as to the RECs, and they would be required to publish information about performance against their own standards. Consumers' Committees would continue to represent the interests of consumers in their areas, irrespective of supplier.[96] These obligations are incorporated into the draft supply licences for the competitive market, though no provision is made for a levy to

---

[94] OFFER, (1995), n. 82 above, para. 5.6.   [95] *Ibid.* para. 5.9.

[96] OFFER, *The Competitive Electricity Market from 1998: Customer Protection, Competition and Regulation* (1995).

compensate RECs for an undue number of unprofitable customers as was made in gas.[97] The consultative process also produced other minor changes in the proposed conditions, for example extending the scope of the code on energy efficiency and that on customers with special needs.

Maintaining social obligations, including the duty to supply, has thus been an important concern in the process of liberalizing the domestic market; although the absence of the possibility of a levy means that the protections are in one way weaker than in gas, in other ways they are very similar. The extent of the protections in relation to second-tier suppliers expanded during the consultation process, and indeed the example of gas influenced the development of the complex consumer protections now proposed; some Consumers' Committees even considered that these protections had gone too far. The strong competition orientation of the Director General of Electricity Supply has rather tended to disguise the existence of social obligations amongst his responsibilities. Nevertheless, he has achieved substantial improvements in disconnection rates, and the onset of the competitive market for small consumers from 1998 has highlighted the importance of other social obligations. It is now clear that substantial social obligations will continue after that date, both for the RECs themselves and for second-tier suppliers, and the consultation process reinforced their importance. Electricity is in this respect no different from the other utilities studied in this book; as with gas, only time will show how effective these protections will be.

Energy Efficiency

The Electricity Act contains as one of the secondary duties the promotion of the efficient use of electricity supplied to consumers; [98] the Director General is also empowered to set standards to promote efficient electricity use,[99] and the supply licences require the RECs to publish codes of practice on the provision of advice on the efficient use of electricity.[100] Apart from encouraging the provision

---

[97] OFFER, *The Competitive Electricity Market from 1998: Overview of Draft Electricity Supply Licences and Codes* (1996). Support for a levy can be found in Corry, Hewett, and Tindale, n. 70 above, 136.

[98] Electricity Act 1989, s. 3(3)(b).   [99] Electricity Act 1989, s. 41.

[100] Department of Energy, n. 30 above, cond. 22; Industry Department for Scotland, nn. 18 and 30 above, cond. 16.

of advice, steps have been taken to encourage the companies to adopt increasingly energy-efficient policies. In the review of the supply price control in 1992 they were allowed to have the costs incurred in supporting energy-efficiency projects taken into account in the setting of the control.[101] The new control provided that less than one-fifth of the revenue covered by the price control would be directly related to the number of units sold, thus reducing the incentive to maximize sales, and the companies were also permitted to attach a special revenue allowance onto charges of up to £1 per customer to fund energy-efficiency projects.[102] The distribution price review also reduced the link between the price control formula and volume of sales.

The special revenue allowance of course raises the question which was so controversial in the case of gas; whether it is legitimate for a regulator to support a levy on customers for energy efficiency purposes. Professor Littlechild has adopted the McKinnon rather than the Spottiswoode approach to this; the revised supply price controls provided for customers to be charged an additional £100 million over four years to finance energy demand-side management schemes; standards of performance on energy efficiency set criteria for the selection of projects as well as specifying the level of energy savings which the companies must aim to achieve for consumers.[103] Following discussion with the Consumers' Committees and with the Energy Saving Trust a number of particular schemes had been put forward, and by the end of 1995 255 projects had been approved; each company was required to publish annual reports on progress in meeting the targets.[104] The Director General does however have some reservations:

I am also conscious that whilst all customers would contribute to the funding of such projects not all would share in the benefits. As I made clear in making my supply price control proposals, if the required level of expenditure were to be substantially greater than the £100 million allowed for in that control, it would raise issues more appropriately dealt with through general fiscal policy rather than through price control mechanisms proposed by a regulator. I have concluded therefore that it would not be appropriate for me to propose any further allowance for specific expendi-

[101] OFFER, n. 48 above, 72.   [102] OFFER, n. 90 above, 6–7.
[103] OFFER, *Energy Efficiency: Standards of Performance* (1994).
[104] OFFER, n. 42 above, 76–9.

ture on energy efficiency projects beyond the £100 million already provided.[105]

This view has been endorsed by the Trade and Industry
Committee,[106] but the progress made in funding schemes is substantially greater than the minimal provision agreed in gas.

Regulatory Procedures

There has been a substantial amount of criticism of the procedures
adopted by OFFER; more so, it would appear, than in the case of
the other utility regulators. This has come both from the industry
and consumer groups; the Chief Executive of Yorkshire Electricity
publicly criticized lack of explanation of the calculations used in the
distribution price review, whilst, according to the National
Consumer Council, 'the process of decision-making in electricity
price regulation has been distinctly less open than for the other
industries.'[107] Nor have the consumer committee chairs been used
directly in price reviews in the way that occurred in water; rather
they have been expected to respond after the publication of proposals by the regulator.

One example of the problems created was illustrated earlier in
discussing the distribution price control review, and it was suggested there that what was needed was some forum in which there
could be challenge and criticism of evidence submitted by others,
either in the form of double notice and comment or of a competitive hearing, or indeed both. The criticisms were echoed by the
Trade and Industry Committee, which considered that accountability required that the regulator be given more precise duties and
less discretion in order to separate his role more clearly from that
of government; that he should be required to give reasons for his
decisions; that he should engage in more effective consultation,
including giving contributors to consultation exercises the ability to
comment on and challenge each others' evidence; that a forum be
created in which he be required to explain his activities; and that
an appeals or arbitration procedure be set up. The Committee

---

[105] OFFER, n. 50 above, para. 4.8.
[106] Trade and Industry Committee (1994–5), n. 12 above, para. 96.
[107] Chatwin, M., 'The Companies' Interest' in Corry, D. (ed.), *Profiting from the
Utilities* (Institute for Public Policy Research, London, 1995), 44–7, 45; National
Consumer Council, *Paying the Price* (HMSO, London, 1993), 76–7.

recommended that he be placed under a statutory duty to give reasons, and that ways of improving the consultation process be considered.[108] This echoed some of the evidence given to it; for example, National Power stated that:

> the Regulator would have a better opportunity to weigh the evidence being put forward if contributors were able to comment in advance of a decision being taken on other parties' submissions. . . . [i]n some cases, consultation exercises based on written submissions will not be enough. Some public hearings may be necessary—although for some this may be moving too close to the US system.[109]

In response, the Government rejected the proposal of a duty to give reasons on the curious ground that ministers eschew unnecessary regulation and that reasons were fully explained in practice anyway. The Director General noted that he frequently issued consultation papers, and was proposing to improve the conduct of price control reviews through publishing more information in the course of a review rather than merely publishing a consultation paper at the beginning.[110] This bore fruit in the case of the transmission price control review during 1995–6 as he issued four consultation papers; the final one, as well as setting out his thinking, summarized responses which were also made available in the OFFER library unless confidentiality had been requested. Consultants' reports on operating costs and on capital expenditure were discussed with the National Grid Company and published in summary form; however the full report on operating costs including projected staff reductions was not made available to the trade unions, despite a request for it.[111] The publication of several consultation papers setting out the regulator's developing thinking and summarizing responses has of course been common practice for other regulators. No public hearings were organized, and there is no regular process of double notice and comment so, despite the welcome increase in openness during recent price-control consultation, procedures still fall short of those adopted in telecommunications and water.

[108] Trade and Industry Committee (1994–5), n. 12 above, paras. 103–4.

[109] *Ibid. Minutes of Evidence*, 76–7.

[110] *Government Observations on the Eleventh Report from the Trade and Industry Committee (Session 1994–5) on Aspects of the Electricity Supply Industry*, HC 774, 1994–5, ix, xii–xiii.

[111] OFFER, *The Transmission Price Control Review of the National Grid Company: Second Consultation Document* (1996); *The Transmission Price Control Review of the National Grid Company: Proposals* (1996), para. 2.10.

Conclusion

Both in terms of the industry structure adopted and in the intellectual predispositions of the regulator, electricity is the area of regulation where the greatest stress has been placed on the development of competition as the best means of maximizing consumer advantage. It is quite clear, however, from the problems of lack of effective competition in generation and from the difficulties in implementing the 1998 liberalization that this has not removed the necessity for regulation but has given to the regulator the key role of developing and policing competition in a situation where there is a natural tendency for anti-competitive behaviour. This could be left to a general competition regulator, but given the immense complexity of the industry there must be strong arguments for specialist scrutiny of a continuing kind which the Office of Fair Trading and MMC could not offer, at least in their present form. Regulation for competition will remain a key concern for the regulator.

On price setting, what has become absolutely clear is that it is not a science but an art and is dependent on a number of factors not envisaged at the time of the design of the basic price-control system. It has been demonstrated above that the hoped-for degree of stability has not been obtainable, and the late amendment of the distribution price-control proposals was such as to create a real crisis of regulatory legitimacy. This is not to say that the RPI–X formula does not have advantages, but rather that they lie in efficiency incentives rather than in the promise of stability; no formula can be immune from public and political pressure where the providers of basic services are seen to be making excessive profits. The circumstances of the amendment of the proposals illustrate vividly two problems concerning regulatory procedures. First, statutory consultation on licence amendments has not been treated as offering any serious possibility of affecting outcomes, and secondly even wide statutory powers to gain information from companies are not sufficient in themselves to prevent regulators from being seriously misled; what is additionally needed is some forum for competitive debate and analysis of information offered, and here OFTEL procedures offer important lessons. It is hoped that the development of competition will reduce the need for this type of regulation of monopoly; however we have seen that some price control is envisaged for domestic supply even after liberalization, and of course distribution and transmission are just as likely to remain monopolies as is water supply. Price control will not wither away. Moreover, just as in gas, the question of the asset base is becoming extremely controversial, as shown in the transmission price review.

On social regulation, the big current question has been how social obligations will be dealt with after complete liberalization of the tariff market. In gas, political and social concerns have led to a sharing of social obligations amongst all new suppliers, and this has required a considerable degree of legal change to support it; after a slower start the Director General has implemented a similar process for electricity, though without the use of fresh legislation. It remains to be seen how effective the protections will be, although considerable success has been achieved already in reducing disconnections.

A further question, not fully addressed in this Chapter as it has been referred to in Chapter 2 and will be discussed in Chapter 10, is the relationship between the Electricity Regulator and the rest of the energy market. The limitations on the regulator's power led to serious concern at the time of the shift in purchasing away from coal, and a number of solutions could be offered to the problems in terms of the creation of an energy regulator and of a clearer policy framework by government. More recently, the Government appears to have left the way open for a possible merger with OFGAS after 1998, and this is the most likely form of structural change in the foreseeable future.[112] Setting this aside for the moment, however, we may see in electricity, as in gas and telecommunications, a divergence in regulatory tasks towards two future poles. The first is acting as specialist competition authority policing competitive conduct, for example in relation to the pool. The second is policing a rump of monopoly price controls and of social obligations. Neither corresponds to the vision set out in the reports on which the current regulatory structures were based.

---

[112] *Government Observations on the Eleventh Report from the Trade and Industry Committee*, n. 110 above, viii.

7

Transport: Regulation and Franchising, and Competition Without Regulation

PART ONE: RAILWAYS: REGULATION AND FRANCHISING

Historical Introduction

This Chapter will cover two very different regulatory regimes introduced as a result of, or accompanying, the privatizations of the 1980s and 1990s. It omits civil aviation and airports, which will be dealt with separately in considering the role of the Civil Aviation Authority in Chapter 8 below. In the case of rail, more historical detail will be provided in the introduction because of the long history of regulation, the models offered for other regulatory regimes, and the opportunity to evaluate different types of regulatory institution, expanding on the discussion in Chapter 2 above.

Railways are of course a product of the nineteenth century, and it was then that the regulatory regimes also developed. The first stage has been characterized by Foster as 'regulation by Parliament'; it involved the use of Private Acts of Parliament authorizing railway construction and incorporating a variety of regulatory provisions, thus providing the equivalent of the modern licence.[1] There is no doubt that this was not an effective means of regulation; as he documents:

the first period of railway regulation was a failure. It did not meet the complaints that customers of monopolies had against them on price and quality. It did not promote competition—indeed, arguably it encouraged collusion and entrenched the practice of collusion for a century to come, a practice which was copied outside the railways. And it did not secure a reasonable return on capital in the long run, so that further investment was discouraged. The chief financial beneficiaries of its failure were the

[1] Foster, C. D., *Privatization, Public Ownership and the Regulation of Natural Monopoly* (Blackwell, Oxford, 1992), ch. 1.

promoters of railways and their allies. . . . And there was no review procedure to ensure that even the inadequate terms of the statutes were being observed . . . enforcement of railway legislation including the private acts was ordinarily left to local justices of the peace, which meant that it was hardly enforced at all.[2]

Despite the serious deficiency of the regulatory institutions, however, a number of familiar modern regulatory provisions can be found in an embryonic state in very early railway regulation; for example, as early as 1854 the Canal and Railway Traffic Regulation Act required that every railway and canal company was to 'afford all reasonable facilities for the receiving and forwarding and delivering of traffic' on its system and to grant reasonable facilities for receiving and forwarding traffic on continuous lines (an early form of interconnection), and no company was to 'make or give any undue or unreasonable preferences or advantage' to any person or firm or class of traffic, or to show 'any undue or unreasonable prejudice or disadvantage'.[3] Moreover, some degree of social regulation also took place, especially on matters of safety, but also through a form of universal service requirement in the 1844 Railways Act to the effect that a 'Parliamentary Train' be provided by every railway at an average speed of at least twelve mph for third-class passengers at a fare of a penny a mile.[4]

Under the 1854 Act enforcement was by the Court of Common Pleas; this is universally perceived as having failed just as seriously as regulation through Parliament. In the twenty years of its jurisdiction the Court dealt with only about forty cases; as the promoters of later legislation put it, it was:

a cumbrous and unfitting body for putting such an Act in force . . . from the very fact of its being a Court of Law, it deterred many from coming to it who would otherwise be most anxious to avail themselves of the powers and protection of the Act; and it was of itself most reluctant to undertake the duties imposed on it by Parliament.[5]

---

[2] *Ibid.* 35.
[3] See Robson, W., *Justice and Administrative Law* (3rd edn., Stevens, London, 1951), 91–2.
[4] Foster, n. 1 above, 33.
[5] The President of the Board of Trade, Mr Chichester Fortescue (1873) 214 Hansard (3rd series) 235, quoted in Arthurs, H., *'Without the Law': Administrative Justice and Legal Pluralism in Nineteenth-Century England* (University of Toronto Press, Toronto, 1985), 128.

The problems had in fact been anticipated in the debates on the 1854 Act by the then Lord Chief Justice, who:

had spent a great part of his life in studying law, but he confessed he was wholly unacquainted with railway management. . . . He knew not how to determine what was a reasonable fare, what was undue delay or within what time trucks or boats should be returned. . . . But Parliament preferred to listen to the interested demands of the railway companies rather than to the self-confessed limitations of the judges.[6]

It is difficult to imagine an approach more likely to make regulation ineffective than to entrust it to the unreformed courts of common law. The next stage of regulation has been characterized by Foster as 'regulation by commission';[7] this may seem to be much closer to the modern regulatory regimes described in this book, but in practice it inherited many of the characteristics of earlier regulation by Parliament and by the court. The first such Commission was the Railway Commission established by the Regulation of Railways Act 1873. It was intended to avoid the inappropriateness exhibited by the Court of Common Pleas and instead would 'be well adapted for the duties which it had to perform, and would decide the questions which came before it promptly, efficiently and cheaply'.[8] The new Commission consisted of three full-time commissioners including one lawyer and one member with expertise in railway business; they were to conduct their proceedings 'in such manner as may seem to them most convenient for the speedy despatch of business'.[9] In 1888, however, the Railway and Canal Traffic Act re-established it as the Railway and Canal Commission, now requiring that a judge of the High Court should be a member *ex officio* and should preside over deliberations, his opinion prevailing on any point of law; appeal lay to the Court of Appeal, and the Commission was made a court of record. As Robson noted, 'the Railway Commission, after 1888, bore a far closer resemblance to a court of justice than to an administrative tribunal',[10] and Foster quotes an American commentator as describing this as the only period in Britain during which the form of regulation became as legalistic as it has remained in the United

---

[6] Robson, n. 3 above, 569.　　　　　　[7] Foster, n. 1 above, 2.

[8] The President of the Board of Trade, quoted in Arthurs, n. 5 above, 128.

[9] Regulation of Railways Act 1873, s. 27; and see Arthurs, n. 5 above.

[10] Robson, n. 3 above, 95.

States.[11] In brief, the task of the Commission involved reviewing all railway rates to eliminate those which were discriminatory; with the burden of proof lying on the objector this was quite ineffective, and the Commission was in effect outmanœuvred by the companies. After severe criticism, the Railway and Canal Traffic Act in effect froze charges from 1884 by shifting the burden or proof to the railway company to justify changes; the result was rigidity which seriously affected both labour relations and safety.[12] Further regulation relating to safety took place by the Railway Regulation Act 1893, which gave the Railways Inspectorate power to impose safety requirements at the railways' own cost. In 1913 'the Government had to pass a further Act to allow railways to raise their rates . . . by 4 per cent in a totally arbitrary manner, cutting across the machinery of the Railway and Canal Commission and the courts. Railway policy was in complete disarray.'[13]

The railways were under state control during the First World War and the following two years; this was followed by a forced amalgamation into the 'big four' companies by the Railways Act 1921. The Act set up the Railway Rates Tribunal, intended to be less judicial in character, with for example a lawyer rather than a judge in the Chair. It remained a court of record with appeal to the Court of Appeal, however, and remained strikingly like a court of justice.[14] The principle to which it had to give effect was similar to more modern examples of profit control, but this failed to anticipate growing competition from road transport, and remained in effect a dead letter.[15] After direct government control once more during the Second World War the system was nationalized by the Transport Act 1947. Railway charges remained subject to the confirmation of the Transport Tribunal as the latest descendent of the Commissions discussed above; procedure followed that of the Railway Rates Tribunal closely and the rules 'are legalistic and smack of High Court terminology and style. They also show signs

---

[11] Foster, n. 1 above, 48 quoting Keller, M., 'The Pluralist State: American Economic Regulation, 1900–1930' in McCraw, T. K. (ed.), *Regulation in Perspective* (Harvard, Cambridge, Mass., 1981), 56–94, 67.

[12] Parris, H., *Government and the Railways in Nineteenth-Century Britain* (Routledge, London, 1965), 225–6; Foster, n. 1 above, 48–52.

[13] Foster, n. 1 above, 57.

[14] Foster, n. 1 above, 59–60; Robson, n. 3 above, 96–8.

[15] Kahn-Freund, O., *Law of Carriage by Inland Transport* (4th edn., Stevens, London, 1965), 782.

of that tendency towards the over-elaboration of procedural or adjectival law which is so beloved of the English judicial system.'[16] Perhaps not surprisingly in view of its legalistic procedures, the Tribunal's first review of charges was seriously delayed.[17] The Transport Act 1953 removed detailed regulation of such matters as undue preference, leaving matters instead to the discretion of the tribunal, but the scheme of charges introduced under it in 1955 after discussions with users was subject to an inquiry before the Tribunal lasting forty-four days and involving twenty-one counsel for the British Transport Commission alone; the new scheme could not be put into effect until July 1957.[18] The Transport Act 1962 finally abolished the jurisdiction of the Tribunal over rail charges outside London.

This sorry tale makes it clear that the adjudicative model of regulation based closely on the procedures of a court of law is totally unsuitable for a regulatory institution deciding matters of general principle such as price control; reasons for this include delay. Nevertheless, the avoidance of adjudicatory models does not mean avoiding law; as we have already seen, there is inevitably a vast body of law applying to any utility regulator. Nor does it necessarily mean avoiding participation by lawyers; the Monopolies and Mergers Commission and the Civil Aviation Authority, which will be examined later, both assume such participation in key decisions. The task is to assess the best means of avoiding such primitive problems of regulatory procedure as are revealed by the story of railway regulation whilst avoiding the alternative of extreme regulatory discretion. It should also be added that the failures of railway regulation were not due solely to legalistic procedures; the substantive tools available for regulation were also seriously defective. Are matters likely to be improved in the next stage of development, the regulation of the railway industry after privatization under the Railways Act 1993?

Regulatory Institutions

The privatization of rail is radically different from the other utility privatizations discussed so far, incorporating, through the use of

---

[16] Robson, n. 3 above, 102.
[17] Bagwell, P. S., *The Transport Revolution, 1770–1985* (Routledge, London, 1988), 305.　　　　　　　　　　　　　　　　　　[18] *Ibid.* 320–1.

franchising, disciplines more similar to compulsory competitive tendering and involving an unprecedented fragmentation of the former nationalized enterprise; there will be almost a hundred new companies formed, with about half of them being of major importance. This is reflected in considerable regulatory complexity.[19] The closest to the other regulators discussed in this book is the Rail Regulator (who is given this title rather than that of Director General by the Act); he is assisted by the Office of the Rail Regulator or ORR. However other regulatory tasks are carried out by the Franchising Director, who is much more closely linked to the Secretary of State, having for example, a permanent duty to comply with objectives issued by the minister on such matters as levels and quality of service, fare control, and the budget for services.[20] Nevertheless, the Franchising Director will undertake a number of tasks associated with the regulators we have discussed elsewhere, such as determining service standards and monitoring and enforcing them, and (in circumstances determined late on in the privatization process) limiting fare increases. The Director is given statutory enforcement powers for breach of a franchise agreement setting out the conditions on which services are to be provided; the regulator is given corresponding powers for breach of a condition in a licence, licences being required for all operators of railway assets.[21] The Secretary of State remains a major regulatory actor apart from his role in relation to the Franchising Director; for example, he issued the licence of Railtrack, the operator of track and signalling. It could also be argued that the now privatized Railtrack has some regulatory powers in relation to the validation of safety cases and allocation of train paths. This Chapter will concentrate on the Rail Regulator, though discussion of other actors will inevitably have to be included to give a complete picture.

What are the Rail Regulator's functions? He listed the following in his first Annual Report:

approval of all access agreements by which operators acquire the right to use track, stations and light maintenance depots;
granting, modifying and enforcing licences, without which no track, train, station or such depot may be operated unless exempt;

[19] For a good summary of the new arrangements see Glaister, S., 'The New Rail Industry, 1994–5' in Centre for the Study of Regulated Industries, *Regulatory Review 1995* (Centre for the Study of Regulated Industries, London, 1995), 59–91.
[20] Railways Act 1993, s. 5.   [21] Railways Act 1993, ss. 55–8.

funding and generally sponsoring the Consultative Committees;
deciding on proposals to close passenger services (subject to appeal to the
Secretary of State);
enforcement of certain aspects of competition law (concurrently with the
Director General of Fair Trading); and more generally,
keeping under review the provision of railway services in Great Britain and
elsewhere.[22]

It should be immediately apparent that his work is radically different from that of the other utility regulators. The task of approval
of access agreements could be seen as the equivalent of interconnection, but the context is radically different, as the agreements are
not necessarily part of a process of developing competition; as we
shall see, competition is to be radically limited in important
respects. The licences are much simpler than in the case of the other
utilities, and key economic decisions, in particular the control of
prices, is a function of access agreements rather than licences.[23]

The system of consumer representation appears at first sight similar to that in water and electricity, with Consultative Committees
appointed as part of the regulator's advisory institutions. However,
the Committees have a particularly important role in relation to
passenger rail closures, as we shall see, as did their predecessors
under public ownership, and the system adopted reflects that existing previously, with a national Central Rail Users' Consultative
Committee and regional Rail Users' Consultative Committees.
Members are now appointed by the regulator after consulting the
Secretary of State, Chairmen by the Secretary of State after consulting the Regulator.[24] The most important procedural difference
from the role of their predecessors is that the Committees are
required to meet in public, subject to exceptions concerning, for
example, information furnished in confidence;[25] they are also now
able to consider fares and reductions in service, as their predecessors could not. Especially given the split between the regulator and
the Franchising Director, and the potential involvement of the
MMC as in other regulatory regimes, there is considerable scope
for regulatory conflict; as we shall see initial guidance binding the
regulator also aims at facilitating the Franchise Director's initial
franchise allocation, and the restrictions on the licensing powers of

---

[22] ORR, *Report of the Rail Regulator, 1993–4*, HC 662, 1993–4, 7.
[23] Glaister, n. 19 above, 62.   [24] Railways Act 1993, ss. 2–3.
[25] Railways Act 1993, sched. 2, para. 6; sched. 3, para. 6.

the regulator under authority delegated from the Secretary of State prevent, for example, his attaching conditions to licences relating to the level or quality of franchised passenger services, and so coming into conflict with the Franchising Director's 'Citizens' Charter'-type responsibilities.[26]

The Legislation

Despite the very different structure of the regulatory regime, the structure of the relevant provisions of the Railways Act is broadly similar to that of the other privatization statutes already discussed. The duties applying to the Secretary of State and the regulator are to protect the interests of users of railway services (in particular the disabled), to promote the use of the network and its development to the greatest extent that he considers economically practicable, to promote efficiency and economy and competition, and to promote measures to facilitate journeys involving more than one operator.[27] Provisions with no counterparts in earlier legislation are the duties 'to impose on the operators of railway services the minimum restrictions which are consistent with the performance of his functions under this part' and 'to enable persons providing railway services to plan the future of their businesses with a reasonable degree of assurance'.[28] There are no financing or universal service primary duties of the type found in the other statutes; however, the regulator is also under duties not to render it unduly difficult for network operators to finance their activities and to have regard to the financial position of the Franchising Director.[29] Without prejudice to these general duties there is a duty to protect the interests of passengers in monopoly services and the interests of operators in relation to using facilities.[30] The regulator and Secretary of State are also required to take into account the need to protect all persons from dangers arising from the operation of the railways and to have regard to the effect of the provision of railway services on the environment.[31] The regulator is obliged to prepare and publish a code of practice for the protection of disabled rail users after consulting the Disabled Persons Transport Advisory Committee established

---

[26] For the guidance and the General Authority see ORR, n. 22 above, apps. 2, 3.
[27] Railways Act 1993, s. 4(1).　　　　[28] Railways Act 1993, s. 4(1)(f)–(g).
[29] Railways Act 1993, s. 4(5).　　　　[30] Railways Act 1993, s. 4(2).
[31] Railways Act 1993, s. 4(3).

by the Transport Act 1985; he can, however, merely encourage its adoption.[32]

As we shall see in more detail below, the position of the Rail Regulator also differs from that of the other utility regulators in that he commenced work before privatization; to reflect this, he is required until 31 December 1996 to take into account guidance issued by the Secretary of State.[33] The effect of the guidance is most importantly to require the regulator to facilitate the achievement of the Secretary of State's objective of the private-sector provision of rail services and that of the Franchising Director of franchising services; competition is to be moderated to ensure the successful launch of the first generation of franchises. He is also during the period of the guidance obliged to adopt the access charging principles established by the Government and to avoid interfering with the franchising process or with Railtrack's achievement of its financial regime as agreed with the Secretary of State.[34] As mentioned above, this is supplemented by restrictions contained in the general authority to issue licences delegated by the Secretary of State; these are of permanent application, and include prohibitions on including licence conditions relating to fares (except in very limited circumstances on competition grounds) or service quality.[35] Most remarkably, the hybrid Channel Tunnel Rail Link Act contains a clause which imposes an overriding duty on the regulator not to impede performance of the contract between the Secretary of State and the promoter of the new railway.[36] Finally, it should be mentioned that there are a number of provisions of European Community law of relevance, and these are likely to increase; the most important for the present is Directive 91/440, making provision for rights of access to railway infrastructure by international services; it also requires railways to keep separate accounts for infrastructure and for train operations; charges for the use of infrastructure are to be non-discriminatory. More recently, directives have also been enacted relating to the licensing of railway undertakings, and on the allocation of railway infrastructure capacity

---

[32] Railways Act 1993, s. 70.   [33] Railways Act 1993, s. 4(5).
[34] The guidance is set out in ORR, n. 22 above, app. 2.
[35] *Ibid.* app. 3.
[36] s. 21; for discussion see Windsor, T., 'Rail Regulation 1995–6' in Centre for the Study of Regulated Industries, *Regulatory Review 1996* (Centre for the Study of Regulated Industries, London, 1996), 73–86 at 80.

and the charging of infrastructure fees.[37] A White Paper has also been issued making a number of proposals, including extending access rights, requiring full separation of infrastructure management and transport operation, generalizing the use of public-service contracts and requiring independent bodies to supervise access rights, perhaps in the form of a European Railways Agency.[38] The complex division of labour in the industry has thus led to an equally complex set of legal duties.

The Regulator

Perhaps in part reflecting the complexity noted above, it is interesting to see that for the first time the regulator is a lawyer, John Swift QC. This may also reflect the particularly great role of legal involvement in the interrelationship of the companies comprising the new rail system which will be co-ordinated through contractual techniques. In his first annual report he stressed his independence from government, his accountability to the courts, to Railtrack and to users, and to Parliament, and his guiding principle that his decisions should promote the public interest. He also stressed his commitment to openness and wide consultation; and indeed in the decisions taken so far he has consulted effectively through the issuing of consultation papers.[39] In press interviews he has stressed the need for flexibility and innovation, and his intention to concentrate on 'pockets of monopoly' in the new system; in general efficiency and economy will be implemented by the market. The duty to enable service providers to plan has been interpreted as a concern that regulation be not over-zealous, something which he intends to fulfil by listening carefully before making decisions.[40] The third annual report contained a refined statement of objectives; these were at a high level of generality, but a process of more detailed refinement of objectives was taking place.[41] The overall role of the

---

[37] Dirs. 91/440/EEC [1991] OJ L237/25; 95/18/EC [1995] OJ L143/70; 95/19/EC [1995] OJ L143/75.

[38] EC Commission, COM(96)421 final; *A Strategy for Revitalising Europe's Railways* (1996).

[39] ORR, *Annual Report 1993–4*, n. 22 above, 8–11.

[40] Ford, R., 'Regulating the Privatised Railway—John Swift QC' (1994) 51 *Modern Railways* 458–9.

[41] ORR, *Annual Report 1995–6* (1996), app. 1.

regulator was summarized in ways reminiscent of the types of regulation analysed in this book:

I do not seek confrontation with those upon whom passengers and users will continue to rely for safe and effective railway services. At the same time they must understand that where there is monopoly it will be controlled in the public interest; where there is a need for cooperation the Regulator will expect it to be forthcoming; where competition can be made to work it will be promoted.[42]

More detailed definitions of the consumer interest were adopted from consumer principles developed by the National Consumer Council, including access to goods and services, choice, information, redress, equity, value for money, and representation.[43] Finally, in his statement for the Railtrack Prospectus the regulator listed as his key objectives commercial freedom as a means of promoting the public interest, the achievement of a stable regulatory framework for the industry, not making it unduly difficult for Railtrack to finance its activities, stimulating both competition and effective co-operation within the industry, and finally safeguarding the infrastructure and essential facilities. One more there is a strong emphasis on clarity and accountability in regulatory decision-making; to what extent these have been achieved will be discussed in the section on procedures below.[44] Once again, the objectives are complex and potentially contradictory; however, steps have been taken to clarify them and develop more detailed principles to guide their application in practice. How implementation takes place will now be examined through discussion of some key areas of importance.

Regulating Monopoly: Price Control

As mentioned earlier the price-control system is radically different from those we have discussed earlier, as consumer prices are subject to extensive control by the Franchising Director and the Rail Regulator has no direct power to control them. However, the regulator has an extremely important power over Railtrack prices through the requirement that he approve Railtrack's track access charges to be payable by operators; this is part of his role in relation to access agreements which dominated the first phase of his

---

[42] *Ibid.* 6–7.   [43] *Ibid.* 22–4.   [44] *Ibid.* app. 2.

work. These form the backbone of the privatized rail system through giving operators permission to use track, stations, or depots owned by other operators; agreements between operators, including Railtrack, need the Rail Regulator's approval, and a code of standard conditions is provided as the Railtrack Track Access Conditions. As part of the process it was necessary to determine the future structure and level of Railtrack charges to other operators; the regulator noted that this was 'the first time that an independent regulator has been involved in determining the future structure and level of charges for a utility *before* it has been privatised'.[45] For freight services, reflecting the policy of the Government,[46] his framework for approving charges was based around the key principle that charges should be greater than or equal to avoidable costs, with a negotiated approach to the covering of other costs based on the concept of a notionally efficient operator and the avoidance of distorting competition.[47]

As regards franchised passenger services, the task is particularly difficult in view of the fact that only 9 per cent of track access charges vary directly with use; the rest are in the form of fixed charges. In considering the structure of charges, the regulator concluded that, in comparison with the initial structure reached on reorganization of the railways, it should be more transparent, that there should be risk-sharing arrangements between operators and Railtrack where revenue falls, and that greater variability of charges be permitted during the period of the access agreement as it becomes possible to apportion costs more accurately.[48] In considering the level of charges, the regulator, once more after a consultation process, concluded that the initial access charges agreed on reorganization were too generous; Railtrack had scope to reduce costs by 3 per cent a year in real terms, and the figure of 8 per cent return on capital was too high. He thus decided that charges should be rebased from 1995–6 with a real reduction of 8 per cent in that year, thereafter falling under an RPI–2 formula, with a further

[45] ORR, *Railtrack's Track Access Charges for Franchised Passenger Services—Developing the Structure of Charges: A Policy Statement* (1994), 1. For a detailed description of the issues involved, see Glaister, n. 19 above, 70–7.

[46] See Department of Transport, *Gaining Access to the Railway Network* (Department of Transport, London, 1993).

[47] ORR, *Framework for the Approval of Railtrack's Track Access Charges for Freight Services* (1995).

[48] ORR, n. 45 above.

review in the year 2000.[49] This of course repeats a familiar pattern; an initial setting of prices at a level too favourable to the utility followed by regulatory intervention to reduce it, although this case is unique in that the regulator's actions precede privatization. Related questions have continued to be dealt with by the Rail Regulator through his consultation procedures; for example, setting access charges so as to facilitate investment in the enhancement of the rail network.[50]

In earlier chapters of this book, a key aspect of monopoly regulation was the setting and monitoring of quality standards. As mentioned above, rail customer standards are for the Franchising Director rather than for the Rail Regulator. Nevertheless, some of the other responsibilities of the regulator may impinge indirectly on customer standards; for example, in approving the new National Conditions of Carriage he required the establishment of a new minimum entitlement to compensation for delayed services of 10 per cent of the price paid in the case of delays of over an hour; operators may offer more but not less.

Regulation for Competition

The main area of controversy here is that of open-access passenger services; i.e. those provided other than under a franchise agreement. In this respect, the initial guidance from the Secretary of State imposes important constraints on the regulator as it states:

you should facilitate the achievement by the Franchising Director of his objective of securing that railway passenger services in Great Britain . . . are provided under franchise agreements as soon as reasonably practicable. It is the policy of the Government that competition on routes to be franchised should be moderated to the extent necessary to ensure the successful launch of the first generation of franchises.[51]

This was reflected in the policy statement of the regulator on competition; as he put it:

the railway industry is still at an early stage of a period of fundamental restructuring. Before that process is complete, it is difficult to predict with

[49] ORR, *Railtrack's Access Charges for Franchised Passenger Services: The Future Level of Charges; A Policy Statement* (1995).
[50] ORR, *Investment in the Enhancement of the Rail Network* (1996).
[51] ORR, n. 22 above, app. 2, para. 3.

confidence the effects of allowing unrestricted—or uncontrolled—competition on train operators, the Franchising Director and the passengers. I do not believe it would be wise to expose these parties to the risks of such an experiment. In particular, any adverse effects on the privatisation process could negate many of the expected benefits of the restructuring of the industry for consumers.[52]

Thus (to summarize a complex decision) the regulator determined that no significant competitive new entry be allowed before 31 March 1999, and that substantial restrictions should remain for at least a further three years. Any changes after 2002 would be incremental.[53]

Despite the relatively low degree of passenger competition made inevitable by the Secretary of State's guidance, the Rail Regulator has had a number of responsibilities in which he has had to protect and maximize competitive opportunities. Open access is more fully developed in freight, and at the end of 1995 two large new freight operators commenced operation. As regards more specific regulatory powers, for example, the Act gives the Rail Regulator power to compel a facility owner to grant access to any applicant, such as another operator; this is an application of the 'essential facilities' doctrine familiar from much competition law, including that of the European Community and discussed briefly in Chapter 1 above.[54] Although he has no formal powers in relation to mergers, he may make representations to the Director General of Fair Trading on competition issues arising in the railway industry, and has issued criteria and procedures to be used in relation to competition and other regulatory issues raised by change of control.[55] The Transport Committee of the House of Commons recommended that the regulator's powers be extended to cover contracts between franchisees and rolling-stock leasing companies, but this was rejected by the Government; it is likely to assume greater importance with the purchase of one of the latter by a franchise holder and bidder for further franchises.[56] Finally, in 1996 the regulator

---

[52] ORR, *Competition for Railway Passenger Services: A Policy Statement* (1994).
[53] For a detailed analysis see Glaister, n. 19 above, 80–4.
[54] Railways Act 1993, s. 17.
[55] ORR, *Change of Control of Passenger Train Operators: Criteria and Procedures* (1996).
[56] Transport Committee, *Railway Finances*, HC 206, 1994–5, para. 154; *Government Observations on the Fourth Report of the Committee*, HC 71, 1995–6, xiv.

commenced a wide-ranging inquiry into accurate and impartial retailing of tickets.[57]

Universal Service

This section will examine questions of the ensuring of availability of services, the railway equivalent to universal service obligations and including questions such as access in rural areas familiar from telecommunications regulation. Obligations of this kind figure in a number of places in the new scheme, for example in the duty of the Franchising Director to secure the provision of services where a franchise has ended but not been replaced, and the power to make a Railway Administration Order to ensure the continued provision of services where an operator has become insolvent.[58] There are also special requirements relating to the disabled, for example the publication of a code of practice and the preparation by operators of Disabled People's Protection Policies.[59] The most important of such provisions are however those imposing demanding procedures before the withdrawal of passenger services.[60] Such provisions have a long history in relation to the nationalized operator, and closure hearings have been prolonged and controversial.[61] The new structure retains many elements of the old system, with proposed service withdrawals having to be advertised, with the opportunity of lodging objections with the regulator. Objections are then sent to the relevant Consultative Committee which investigates whether the closure will cause hardship, reporting to the regulator who decides whether the closure will take effect; he may impose conditions in doing so. The fact that it is the regulator, rather than the Secretary of State, who takes the decision is the major difference from the previous arrangements, although any person aggrieved may appeal to the Secretary of State, and this is likely to happen in controversial cases. There are also a number of improvements in the coverage of the procedure through including parts of stations and light maintenance depots; the provisions on closures were subject to considerable amendment to reflect the concerns of the consultative

[57] ORR, *Accurate and Impartial Retailing: A Consultation Document* (1996).
[58] Railways Act 1993, ss. 30, 59, 63.
[59] See ORR, *Annual Report 1994–5*, (1995), 41–2.
[60] Railways Act 1993, ss. 37–44, 55.
[61] See Prosser, T., *Nationalised Industries and Public Control* (Blackwell, Oxford, 1986), 65–8.

committees, which were broadly successful in preserving the pre-privatization protections.

Soon after the new procedures came into effect, important clarification was given to their scope by the Court of Session. It had been the practice for some time to avoid the procedure in cases where infrastructure was to be retained but passenger services effectively withdrawn by running 'ghost trains' symbolic services of minimal use to the public. The sleeper service between London and Fort William was not included in the services to be provided under a franchise agreement; it was withdrawn and, to avoid the closure proceedings, three new services were introduced over short stretches of line previously used only by the sleeper. British Rail admitted that there was no proven need for these services and that they were unlikely to benefit the travelling public. The Inner House upheld the decision of the Lord Ordinary that this was unlawful, as the new services were a mere device to obviate the closure procedures, and interdict was issued to prevent the withdrawal of the sleeper until the closure procedures had been implemented.[62] In the event a revised sleeper service was continued as part of the passenger service requirement to be franchised; the judicial review proceedings had led to a proper reassessment of how the service could continue at a much reduced cost. The overall effect of the decision of the court is to strengthen considerably the practical effect of the protections afforded by the closure procedures; so far proposed closures considered by the regulator have been of very limited importance.[63]

Apart from question of the total withdrawal of passenger services, a matter of great concern even before privatization was the reduction of services on a line; this fell outside the scope of the formal closure procedures, and now falls within the competence of the Franchising Director rather than that of the Rail Regulator. As part of the franchising process, the Director had to specify minimum levels of service on lines to be franchised; the 1993 Act requires that he acts in accordance with instructions, guidance, and objectives given him by the Secretary of State.[64] The guidance issued required that the minimum service levels be based on the BR timetable immediately before franchising; however, the levels in some cases were substantially below this. Once again the courts

---

[62] *Highland Regional Council* v. *British Railways Board*, 1996 SLT 274 (1st Div.).
[63] ORR, n. 41 above, app. 5.   [64] Railways Act 1993, s. 5(1)(a).

became involved, and the Court of Appeal held that, although 'based on' did not require exact reproduction of the British Rail specification, changes must be only marginal and not significant or substantial, and so the Director had acted beyond his powers in specifying reduced minimum services for a number of lines.[65] In this case the Government reaction was simply to amend the instructions and guidance to give the Director greater flexibility in setting minimum service levels.[66]

A further universal service question which was highly controversial was that of the availability of tickets. The question arose early on with the publication of a Rail Regulator's consultation paper on ticket retailing. This set out three options, one of which envisaged that tickets be sold only at a number of core stations, the number being much smaller than those currently retailing. The proposal produced an outcry in the press and in Parliament; the responses strongly supported the other option of retaining the present system. In his policy statement after the consultation this was the solution the regulator adopted. His reasons for doing so are interesting:

public opinion does not necessarily sympathise with arguments that railway services are part of broader competitive markets and that competition in those broader markets is the best guarantee of better value for money. In the short-term, at least, passengers want assurances as to what they know operators must provide them with, rather than what competitive market analysis suggests should be made available to them. But public opinion can be quite different from the public interest—that collection of statutory objectives which Parliament requires me to pursue and which includes the promotion of efficiency and economy. So the strength of public opinion in favour of the current system and change for the better, while relevant, would not be decisive if I considered that the public interest would be better served by new and radically different arrangements which I was satisfied would provide better value for money and a better railway. . . . *I have concluded that, on this issue, public opinion and the public interest are at one.*[67]

Thus we have a clear moderation of 'competitive market analysis' in favour of a balancing role for the Rail Regulator here, again

[65] *R. v. Director of Passenger Rail Franchising, ex parte Save Our Railways and Others, The Times*, 18 Dec. 1995.

[66] See 268 HC Debs., cols. 1236–7, (18 Dec. 1995) and Goh, J., 'Privatisation of the Railways and Judicial Review' (1996) 7 *Utilities Law Review* 42–3.

[67] ORR, *Ticket Retailing: A Policy Statement* (1995) (emphasis retained).

making the procedures adopted for decision-making of key importance.

It should be added that on environmental grounds certain measures have also been taken to encourage railway freight traffic. Thus the Act empowers the Secretary of State to make payments towards freight access charges to produce social or environmental benefits, and to make grants towards the provision of freight facilities, though there were considerable delays in making grants available.[68]

As with other examples of utility regulation we have considerable evidence of concern with universal service which goes beyond economic principle. The procedures applying to passenger closures have been strengthened both by the 1993 Act and by the decision of the Court of Session; although the Franchising Director's minimum service levels were successfully challenged by judicial review, this had little lasting effect owing to Governmental amendment of the instructions and guidance issued. Nevertheless, it should be remembered that before the 1993 Act there were no minimum service requirements applying to the publicly owned operator. Although there is considerable public concern about the effect of privatization on marginal services, the legal protections for them have actually increased.

Regulatory Procedures

We saw earlier that the Rail Regulator has placed transparency of procedures high amongst his objectives from the beginning. The closure procedures already discussed of course provide a public forum unique in regulatory affairs; considerable effort has been made also to open up procedures in other areas. This has taken the familiar form of the issue of consultation papers and other documents such as guidance to operators; by April 1996, thirty-eight such publications had been issued. In some cases, as in the case of Railtrack access charges, several documents have been published at different stages of the decision-making process, although the OFTEL model of double notice and comment has not formally been adopted. A World Wide Web page is currently under consideration as a means of further dissemination of publications. The

---

[68] Railways Act 1993, ss. 137, 139, and see National Audit Office, *Freight Facilities Grants in England*, HC 632, 1995–6.

regulator has also adopted a policy of giving full reasons for his decisions.

An innovation has been the use of formal hearings where major issues are raised in consultation relating to passenger service access. Four such hearings were held in 1994–5 and included a number of interested participants:

[t]hese hearings allow the Regulator to ask questions of the parties to a contract in the presence of consultees—other operators whose services are affected by the terms of the proposed contract and those responsible for providing financial support for services, for example representatives of affected Passenger Transport Executives (PTEs). Prior to the hearings detailed written questions to the parties are sent out. These, and the answers received, are made available to consultees, who are also given the opportunity to make representations. Those present at hearings are always encouraged to comment on any aspect of the process and the Regulator provides written reasons for his decisions.[69]

Although the hearings are held in private, they represent a significant move towards a formal mechanism for competitive debate going beyond anything adopted by other utility regulators.

Conclusion

The Rail Regulator has commenced work relatively recently and, as I have noted, there are important differences between his work and that of the other utility regulators, notably, his ability to examine Railtrack charges before privatization, the lack of direct power in relation to consumer service standards, and the limited role of competition as a determinant of general industry structure. Nevertheless, many of the themes in this section reflect those in relation to other utilities. These include revision of an initially generous pricing arrangement set by the Government, and concern with universal service issues through the closure procedures. Indeed, the closure procedures give an example of an unusually formal means of participation in regulatory decision-making, and one which has been significantly strengthened rather than weakened with the creation of the new regulatory arrangements. The regulator has also made very explicit his concern with due process as one of his key objectives, and has made an interesting use of

[69] ORR, n. 59 above, 22; see also Glaister, n. 19 above, 65–6.

hearings in which a number of interests are represented as part of the consultative process. It is interesting to note also that, in the event of a change of government, the role of the Rail Regulator will become even more important. According to the then opposition transport spokeswoman, 'the powers of the Rail Regulator are central to the achievement of the objectives of a Labour Government', though these would be amended to create a closer and more permanent relationship with the Secretary of State.[70] This is an important illustration of how widely accepted the idea of regulatory agencies has become; I will now turn to a very different area of transport in which policy has been to avoid creating any specialist regulator.

PART TWO: BUSES: COMPETITION WITHOUT REGULATION

The example of buses is radically different from that of railways, as it is the nearest we have to 'pure' deregulation. As we shall see, the effects have not been precisely as envisaged, though they have some striking similarities to the experiences after airline deregulation in the United States.[71] A further advantage of the bus experience is that it gives an opportunity to assess the role of the ordinary competition authorities as regulators, a model sometimes suggested for other areas of utility regulation; as we shall see, it has hardly been free of problems. To understand the present position it is necessary to begin with some brief history.

Historical Introduction

After the initial development of bus transport subject to very limited regulation early in this century, concern was expressed about two particular problems. These were 'the unscheduled and irregular intervention by "pirate" operators at peak times—when returns were highest—on some routes, thus removing the "cream" from the regular operators', and 'concern with wasteful duplication caused by inter-modal competition between the motor bus and both the

[70] Short, C., *The Future for Rail*, Speech at Swindon, 29 Mar. 1996 (The Labour Party, London, 1996).
[71] For a brief account see Kahn, A., 'Surprises of Airline Deregulation' (1988) 78(2) *American Economic Review* 316–22.

tram/trolley bus systems, and the railways'.[72] A Royal Commission recommended a statutory monopoly on each route controlled by independent commissioners, and this was implemented by the Road Traffic Act 1930. The Act established regional Traffic Commissioners with responsibility for licensing. Operators of stage and express services required two licences. The first was a public service vehicle (PSV) licence personal to the holder; it was a means of controlling safety and fitness of the operator. Secondly, a route licence was required for any service; this was the means of implementing the statutory monopoly. Criteria for the grant of this licence included the extent to which the service was necessary or desirable in the public interest and 'the needs of the area as a whole in relation to traffic (including the provision of adequate, suitable and efficient services, the elimination of unnecessary services and the provision of unremunerative services) and the co-ordination of all forms of passenger transport, including transport by rail'.[73] The Commissioners were empowered to attach conditions to licences, most importantly on fares which were in effect completely regulated to support cross-subsidy. Procedures before the Commissioners took the form of a public hearing; objections to licence applications could be, and normally were, made by rival operators and local authorities. Appeal lay to the minister, who would invariably appoint an inspector to hold an inquiry before the decision; appeal could be made by objectors as well as by a disappointed applicant.

We have here a relatively formal means of regulation resembling the examples of monopoly regulation discussed earlier; however, the industry was not a natural monopoly and the aim was rather to support a network of services through cross-subsidy. Regulation incorporated a number of important procedural protections; thus the Commissioners' hearings were required to be in public, and they were required to give reasons and were later to come within the jurisdiction of the Council on Tribunals. The report of the inspector on appeal would be made publicly available, and the minister would give reasons, though not required to do so by statute.[74] The criteria in the statute and the extensive provision for objections to licences were clearly designed to create a restrictive regime, and this is precisely what occurred. The major principles adopted in

---

[72] Savage, I., *The Deregulation of Bus Services* (Gower, Aldershot, 1985), 3–4.
[73] Road Traffic Act 1930, s. 72.
[74] Kahn-Freund, n. 15 above, 159–63, 188–90.

allocating route licences have been characterized as giving priority to existing operators over challengers, protecting operators against potentially competing services (for example through imposing setting down restrictions on express services) and maintaining a network based on cross-subsidy of unremunerative activities from profits earned on profitable activities; '[o]verall the 1930 Road Traffic Act led to a system of territorial monopoly franchises with preference for, and hence protection to, well established operators. This protection against casual intervention by other operators was given in return for running unremunerative services and maintaining a network.'[75]

Deregulation

The system remained remarkably unchanged until legislation in 1980, despite radical changes in bus patronage, which rose to a peak of 16.7 billion journeys in 1950 and then fell with the growth in car ownership; the number of journeys was 6.2 billion in 1980 and 4.4 billion in 1993–4. The first major attempt at deregulation was the Transport Act 1980. The Act firstly deregulated express coaching by removing the requirement of a route licence for express services, newly defined as those with thirty miles or more between stops.[76] Secondly, the route licensing provisions for local services were altered, mainly through reversing the burden of proof so that a licence now had to be issued unless the objectors could prove that this would be against the public interest.[77] The general power to attach conditions relating to fares was removed, with instead only a reserve power for use in limited circumstances.[78] Thirdly, provision was made for the establishment of 'trial areas' in which the effects of total route deregulation could be assessed.[79] Quality licensing was however strengthened with the requirement of a PSV operator's licence before trading could commence and of annual vehicle inspections.[80]

Trials of full route deregulation were carried out in areas of Norfolk, Herefordshire, and Devon, and in 1984 the Government issued a White Paper proposing the total abolition of route licens-

---

[75] Savage, n. 72 above, 5–7.　　　　　[76] Transport Act 1980, ss. 3–4.
[77] Ss. 4–5, and see, e.g., *R.* v. *Secretary of State for Transport, ex parte Cumbria County Council* [1983] RTR 129 (CA).
[78] S. 7.　　　　　[79] Ss. 12–15.　　　　　[80] Ss. 17, 19.

ing outside London.[81] The proposals were implemented in the Transport Act 1985, effective from 1 October 1986. It did indeed abolish such licensing, and so gave operators outside London the opportunity to run services according to their commercial judgement, subject to the requirement of giving forty-two days' notice of the proposed service to the Traffic Commissioners, although the Commissioners now had no power to reject registration by reference to public demand or existing services and no objections could be made by other operators or local authorities.[82] The Commissioners were re-established in the form of single-area Commissioners rather than the previous tribunal, and retained responsibility for quality regulation through the issuing of PSV operators' licences. Indeed, new powers to impose conditions on PSV operators' licences were provided.[83] The Commissioners were also given the power to impose traffic regulation conditions at the request of traffic authorities; these powers have more recently been extended to permit the regulation of the number of buses permitted to run on a particular route and to prevent the use of duplicate buses where passenger demand cannot be demonstrated.[84] In the cases of such conditions appeals still lay to the Secretary of State, although other appeals now lay to the Transport Tribunal.[85] A further, extremely important, change was that local authorities were permitted to subsidize services only through a process of competitive tendering;[86] not only did this encourage efficiency savings, but for the first time it required a clear distinction to be drawn between the commercial and the subsidized (or 'tendered') network. The Act lifted exemptions for bus services from ordinary competition law, with consequences which will be described in detail below.[87] Finally, the Act also made provision for the breaking up and privatization of the National Bus Company.[88]

This revolutionary change did not extend to London, although the Government announced its intention of deregulating London services, and this was included as a commitment in its 1992 general election manifesto. However, after a highly critical report from the Transport Select Committee, the Government abandoned its plans

[81] *Buses*, Cmnd. 9300 (HMSO, London, 1994).
[82] Transport Act 1985, ss. 1, 6.   [83] Ss. 24–31.
[84] S. 7, and see the Public Service Vehicles (Registration of Local Services) (Amendment) Regs., SI 1994/3271, and the Public Service Vehicles (Traffic Regulation Conditions) (Amendment) Regs., SI 1994/3272.
[85] Ss. 7, 31.   [86] S. 89.   [87] Ss. 114–15.   [88] Pt. III.

to do so at least for that Parliament, instead planning the extension of the tendering programme to all London bus routes and the privatization of London Buses subsidiaries.[89]

Effects of Deregulation

It will be most useful to start with a discussion of the deregulation of express coaching, as this commenced earlier and there is extensive literature available on it. For example, an early study documented entry by a number of operators grouped in the British Coachways consortium. In most cases they failed, and the consortium broke up in 1981–3. Reasons for the failure included intense price competition from the incumbent National Express, difficulties in gaining access to bus stations and marketing advantages of the incumbent; those few who succeeded did so by exploiting niche markets or by entering into joint agreements with National Express. The latter was forced by the competition to reorient its activities by reducing cross-subsidy and reducing fares, however, and patronage grew spectacularly. Services were withdrawn from smaller settlements. The study concludes that customers had gained considerably on trunk routes.[90] A more recent study has confirmed that there have been substantial customer benefits, although the major surprise has been the degree to which National Express has been able to fight entry and maintain its share of the market; since 1982 real price levels have risen after earlier falls. The continued dominance of National Express has occurred despite its privatization and the use of competition law and legislative change to require non-discriminatory access to bus stations.[91] The study found that consumers except for those on very minor provincial routes, have benefited significantly from deregulation but that National Express has continued to exercise market power and that remaining barriers to entry have enabled prices to be maintained above competitive levels.[92] The market has recently become more

---

[89] See Transport Committee, *The Government's Proposals for the Deregulation of Buses in London*, HC 623, 1992–3, and *Government Observations on the Fourth Report of the Transport Committee, Session 1992–3*, HC 136, 1993–4.

[90] Kilvington, R., and Cross, A., *Deregulation of Express Coach Services in Britain* (Gower, Aldershot, 1986).

[91] Transport Act 1985, ss. 82, 116.

[92] Thompson, D., and Whitfield, A., 'Express Coaching; Privatization, Incumbent Advantage, and the Competitive Process', in Bishop, M., Kay, J., and Mayer, C., *The Regulatory Challenge* (OUP, Oxford, 1995), 18–42.

highly concentrated, notably with the decision of Stagecoach, the most successful new entrant, to withdraw in 1989 to concentrate on local bus services, and the acquisition in 1994 by National Express of Saltire Holdings, the rival Anglo-Scottish competitor, giving National Express four-fifths of the scheduled coach services in Great Britain, the remainder being run by a small number of operators each with only a handful of point-to-point routes.[93]

Moving now to local bus services, the pattern has been similar in some respects, though with much greater initial entry and greater problems of co-ordination and congestion.[94] When the Transport Committee of the House of Commons examined the prospects for deregulation in London in 1993, the evidence given by its specialist adviser on the effects of deregulation elsewhere suggested that:

[t]he number of bus miles has increased overall, especially by smaller buses, on the more heavily used routes and times of day. Competition for these services started at a modest level, grew for about two years, and then levelled off. Costs, and especially wages, have gone down substantially, and fares have increased substantially. The initial period of confusion and disruption was deeper, and lasted longer, than had been expected.[95]

In some cities, serious problems of congestion were experienced and co-ordination of timetabling has proved particularly difficult; frequent and serious accusations were made of predatory and anti-competitive conduct.[96] Compulsory tendering did however produce substantial savings; thus in the case of Strathclyde bus revenue support fell by no less than 63 per cent between 1985 and 1987; in Great Britain as a whole it decreased by 56 per cent between 1985–6 and 1991–2, although of course factors other than tendering may have had an important effect here, for example general reductions in public expenditure.[97]

The first phase of deregulation was thus one of considerable new entry and intense competition on the most heavily used routes. The second phase is, however, one of consolidation as operators fail and

[93] Monopolies and Mergers Commission, *National Express Group plc and Saltire Holdings*, Cm 2468 (1994), para. 1.2.

[94] A synthesis of the evidence on local bus deregulation is provided by the Transport Committee, *The Consequences of Bus Deregulation*, HC 54, 1995–6.

[95] Transport Committee, 1992–3, n. 89 above, *Minutes of Evidence*, 2.

[96] For a summary see Transport Committee, 1995–6, n. 94 above, paras. 25–46.

[97] See Scottish Office Central Research Unit, *Bus Deregulation in Scotland* (Scottish Office, 1988), Table 9; Transport Committee, 1992–3, n. 89 above, para. 20.

acquisitions and mergers take place. Thus by 1995 the seven largest companies had over 40 per cent of the bus market with only 35 per cent in the hands of small operators; in a number of areas closed markets had been created, controlled by large companies. While creating concerns about the contestability of markets, the consolidation of the industry also had some beneficial effects, particularly through increasing investment in new vehicles and providing service stability. On these grounds consolidation had been supported by a number of consumer groups.[98] Both anti-competitive conduct and consolidation of course raise the question of the role of the competition authorities, and it is to this that I shall now turn.

Regulation for Competition: The Competition Authorities

The regulation of buses is fundamentally different from the other cases discussed in this book. As mentioned above, deregulation has not been total, for the requirement of a PSV operator's licence remains in relation to quality and safety matters; indeed the role of such licences has actually been strengthened. Decision-making remains in the hands of the re-constituted Traffic Commissioners, providing a more formal and open set of procedures than those applying to other regulators discussed so far. Competition matters, however, have been the subject of pure deregulation through the abolition of route licensing, and this is policed by the competition authorities under ordinary competition law, the previous exclusions of such law in relation to bus services having been lifted by the 1985 Act.[99]

This is not the place for a detailed analysis of UK competition law; the role of the competition authorities will be analysed in general terms in Chapter 10 below, so this Chapter will simply mention some of the aspects most relevant to buses and to regulatory comparison with other utilities.[100] It is interesting to note that the regulation of competition shares several of the most criticized characteristics of other regulators; indeed, some of the problems are even greater. The first striking characteristic is, in the words of Paul Craig:

---

[98] Transport Committee, 1995–6, n. 94 above, paras. 21–4, 51, 139–40.

[99] Transport Act 1985, ss. 114–15.

[100] For a comprehensive account of UK competition law see Whish, R., and Sufrin, B., *Competition Law* (3rd edn., Butterworths, London, 1993).

that the structure of our antitrust legislation vividly demonstrates the retention of ultimate control by the political arm of government. This is apparent in the role played by the Secretary of State in the initiation of monopoly and merger references, and more particularly at the remedial level. A second theme is to be found in the preference for public enforcement of competition policy and the correlatively small role accorded to the individual.[101]

Although buses have not proved as politically charged a subject as some other areas of competition law, we shall see in a moment that the arrangements are seriously defective in terms of direct remedies for undertakings affected by anti-competitive conduct. Secondly, one might expect competition law to be more rule-based than other examples of regulation; after all, one of the themes in much economic literature is the need for a clear framework of rules within which businesses can plan with a degree of certainty. In fact, to quote the same author, even setting aside ministerial discretion, 'the MMC at present operates an essentially discretionary system: provided that the monopoly or merger qualifies for a reference to the MMC, the outcome of the reference is determined by the MMC's view as to what the public interest is in that particular instance'.[102] Nor is maximization of competition a straightforward guide to decision-making; although the policy of the Government is that the main consideration in evaluating a merger for reference to the MMC should be the potential effect on competition in the United Kingdom, other objectives are also present in the law. In the context of bus regulation, the MMC has stated that it has no set formula for assessing the public interest and decides on a case-to-case basis; it cannot provide any such formula, as that would amount to unlawfully fettering its discretion.[103] Finally, it is a mistake to assume that, by avoiding the creation of a regulatory agency, legal complexity and litigation can be minimized, for there has been a considerable amount of recent litigation concerning decision-making and procedures of the competition authorities. The most obviously relevant example was a challenge to the MMC's investigation of a bus company acquisition on the ground that the area

---

[101] Craig, P., 'The Monopolies and Mergers Commission' in Baldwin, R., and McCrudden, C., *Regulation and Public Law* (Weidenfeld and Nicolson, London, 1987), 201–26, 217–18.

[102] *Ibid.* at 214.

[103] Transport Committee, 1995–6, n. 94 above, *Minutes of Evidence*, 125–6.

affected was not 'a substantial part of the United Kingdom' as required in the Fair Trading Act. The reference was made in March 1990 and the adverse report challenged by judicial review; the Divisional Court held that the interpretation adopted by the Commission was unlawful, an interpretation which would have effectively prevented investigation of the vast majority of bus mergers. The Court of Appeal dismissed the appeal by a majority, but the Commission's interpretation was upheld at the end of 1992 in the House of Lords.[104] In no other area of regulation so far examined has litigation played so great a recent role.[105]

The policing of competition in the bus industry has formed one of the chief tasks of the Director General of Fair Trading (DGFT) and of the Monopolies and Mergers Commission (MMC) since the 1985 Act; between 1987 and the end of 1994 the Office of Fair Trading received 541 complaints alleging anti-competitive conduct by bus operators and fifteen references were made to the MMC, again far more than in the other areas of regulation we have examined.[106] I shall now briefly describe the three major types of MMC investigation; it should be noted that the DGFT has also had to devote considerable resources to the industry, and he has stated that his office 'gets a lot more cases in buses than in everything else put together'.[107] Given the increasing degree of concentration through acquisition in the industry, merger references are of particular current importance.[108] As Whish has stated, '[t]he system of control is benign and is essentially predisposed in favour of mergers.'[109] The discretion to refer a merger to the MMC lies in the hands of the Secretary of State, acting on the advice of the DGFT. He may refer to the Commission mergers which create or strengthen a monopoly situation in a substantial part of the United Kingdom or involve the takeover of assets above a threshold figure of £70 million. The MMC must then report on whether the merger qualifies for investigation and whether it operates against the

---

[104] *South Yorkshire Transport* v. *Monopolies and Mergers Commission* [1993] 1 All ER 23 (HL).

[105] For a further challenge in which the approach to be taken to review on procedural grounds was set out see *R.* v. *Monopolies and Mergers Commission, ex parte Stagecoach Holdings plc, The Times*, 23 July 1996 (QBD).

[106] Transport Committee, 1995–6, n. 94 above, para. 62.

[107] *Ibid.* para. 142.

[108] The control of mergers is governed by the Fair Trading Act 1973.

[109] Whish and Sufrin, n. 100 above, 679.

public interest. The criteria for assessing the public-interest element are contained in the Act; the Commission is to take into account all matters appearing to it in the particular circumstances to be relevant, and among other things shall have regard to the desirability of maintaining and promoting effective competition, promoting the interests of consumers, the reduction of costs and the entry of new competitors, maintaining and promoting the balanced distribution of industry in the United Kingdom, and promoting competitive activity by UK producers overseas.[110] If the Commission finds the merger not to be against the public interest it may not be blocked; if it finds that it is, the Secretary of State may at his discretion prevent the merger, although in practice the DGFT is usually asked instead to enter into negotiations with the companies to secure undertakings from them; more recent provisions have permitted the Secretary of State to accept undertakings in lieu of a merger reference to the MMC.[111]

One of many examples in the bus industry was the report on the acquisition by Stagecoach of a 20 per cent stake in Mainline, the former municipal operator in South Yorkshire, now employee-owned. The MMC considered that this was a merger covered by the Act, as the acquisition was such as to enable Stagecoach materially to influence the policy of Mainline. The public-interest issues considered were the effects on actual and potential competition between the two operators and from other operators; it considered that the former would be extinguished or sharply reduced, and that in relation to the latter that Stagecoach's aggressive reputation would be significant deterrent to potential competitors. Against this it was argued that the merger would produce cost savings and increase investment, and indeed the Commission accepted that a high level of competition from small operators 'has not been an unmixed blessing for Sheffield'. Despite strong support for the merger locally, the MMC considered that, especially because of the effect on potential new entry, the merger would operate against the public interest; however, to require divestment would be disproportionate to the adverse effects and would put at risk the benefits, so the holding should be capped at 20 per cent.[112] The

---

[110] Fair Trading Act 1973, s. 84.
[111] Deregulation and Contracting Out Act 1994, s. 9.
[112] MMC, *Stagecoach Holdings and Mainline Partnership*, Cm 2728 (HMSO, London, 1995). The quotation is from para. 2.101.

Secretary of State, however, ordered divestment, but in the resulting judicial review proceedings agreed that he would take no action based on the report.[113]

Secondly, the competition authorities may also investigate certain monopolies.[114] In this case reference may be made either by the Secretary of State or by the DGFT; the usual form of reference once more involves the assessment of the consequences for the public interest by the MMC applying the same criteria as above, and the Secretary of State retains discretion on implementation. The first example in relation to the bus industry involved a DGFT reference relating to the supply of bus services in Mid and West Kent.[115] The Commission found that the dominant operator had a two-thirds share of services, thus constituting a scale monopoly, and that the operation of additional journeys timed immediately before those of competitors and at fares not covering costs operated against the public interest. This was to be remedied by undertakings to be implemented by the DGFT on the registration of services.

Thirdly, the Competition Act 1980 provides for the investigation of anti-competitive practices, initially by the DGFT, who may then refer the matter to the MMC, which once more reports to the Secretary of State. Thus, for example, the Commission examined a reference relating to Southdown Motor Services to the effect that it had set uneconomic fares on two routes with the intention of undermining the viability of an incoming competitor; as a result the competitor had to sell out to Southdown. The company denied that this action was against the public interest as it would avoid the proliferation of low-quality operators engaging in 'cream-skimming'. Nevertheless, the Commission found that the setting of such fares operated against the public interest, and should be remedied by undertakings.[116]

A number of these themes came together in what is probably the most important of the MMC references, that relating to the north-

---

[113] Department of Transport Press Notice P/95/171, *Stagecoach to be Required to Divest its 20 per cent Shareholding in Mainline*, 9 Mar. 1995; *R.* v. *Monopolies and Mergers Commission, ex parte Stagecoach Holdings plc*, The Times, 23 July 1996 (QBD).
[114] The law is once more contained in the Fair Trading Act 1973.
[115] MMC, *The Supply of Bus Services in Mid and West Kent*, Cm 2309 (HMSO, London, 1993).
[116] MMC, *Southdown Motor Services Limited*, Cm 2248 (HMSO, London, 1993).

east of England.[117] This was a monopoly reference following complaints of anti-competitive conduct, most importantly in Darlington, where over 90 per cent of services were supplied by the subsidiaries of four large groups. The local authority put up for sale its operation, DTC. A preferred bidder was announced, whilst Busways, a Stagecoach subsidiary, had made an unsuccessful bid. Busways then recruited the great majority of DTC drivers, offering bonuses of £1,000 per head and a guarantee of three years' employment. It registered services on all DTC's commercial routes and commenced a free service on them. The preferred bidder withdrew, no other buyer could be found, and DTC went into liquidation. According to the MMC, '[i]t was the combination of Busways' actions in recruiting so many of DTC's drivers so quickly, registering services on all its routes and running free services which caused DTC's final collapse. We find these actions to be predatory, deplorable and against the public interest.'[118] The Commission noted that it had no power to impose a penalty in relation to past conduct and that to demand divestment by Stagecoach at this late stage would be 'a disservice to the long-suffering townspeople'.[119] It did however recommend that there should be a moratorium on registration of competing services during the sale of local-authority bus companies and that action be considered to prevent the running of unregistered services, though these met with only a partial response from government.[120]

These few cases merely give the flavour of the many cases investigated by the competition authorities in considerable detail. It is now clear that the authorities do not consider themselves to be appropriate institutions for this task.[121] Thus the DGFT stated that the continuing high volume of complaints against bus operators points to a continuing problem of securing effective and sustained competition in the bus industry.[122] The MMC has also expressed concern in a number of reports. Thus in a 1990 report it called for a more general review of the bus industry and the introduction of interim relief pending investigations (currently not available, a

---

[117] MMC, *The Supply of Bus Services in the North-East of England*, Cm 2933 (HMSO, London, 1995).

[118] *Ibid.* para. 1.6.   [119] *Ibid.* para. 1.7.

[120] See Transport Committee, *Government Observations on the First Report of the Committee, Session 1995–6*, HC 392, 1995–6, vii, xi.

[121] And see Foster, n. 1 above, 122 for a similar conclusion.

[122] Director General of Fair Trading, *Annual Report 1993*, HC 551, 1993–4.

considerable limitation on the ability of competitors to survive anti-competitive behaviour).[123] In the monopoly inquiry on services in Kent discussed above it noted the difficulties in framing suitable remedies, and repeated the request for a searching review of the industry, examining the possibility of introducing effective competition through franchising and the establishment of an 'OFBUS' Regulator.[124] Finally, in the *Mainline* case the Commission repeated its plea for a general review of the industry; this was rejected by the Minister.[125]

The most developed proposal for change came however from the Transport Committee of the House of Commons. After hearing extensive evidence critical of current procedures, it recommended the creation of a specialist regulator for the bus industry, though on a smaller scale than the utility regulators. The new regulator would have a general duty to promote bus travel as well as fair competition, and would have power to prevent the registration of services which are clearly predatory, to prohibit anti-competitive behaviour pending investigation, to issue class licences to large operators with power to revoke these for repeated breaches, to impose penalties and to award compensation to victims of predation, and to apply a general price cap on fares in areas of *de facto* monopoly.[126] The Government rejected this, preferring to continue the existing system of using ordinary competition law; powers to award interim relief may however be granted as part of a general reform of competition law, although the Bill to do so was omitted from the 1996 Queen's Speech. The Committee described the Government response as disappointing and a misrepresentation of its recommendations; its conclusion can act as an appropriate summary of this section; '[w]e believe that competitive challenges to the large companies now dominating the market would be more likely to be sustained if entrants offering high quality services, possibly with lower fares, were effectively protected from predatory responses. This requires more effective regulation and enforcement.'[127]

---

[123] MMC, *Stagecoach (Holdings) Ltd. and Portsmouth Citybus Ltd*, Cm 1130 (HMSO, London, 1990).

[124] MMC, n. 115 above, paras. 6.85–7.

[125] MMC, n. 112 above, para. 2.115; Department of Transport Press Release P/95/171, n. 113 above.

[126] Transport Committee, n. 94 above, paras. 142–6.

[127] Transport Committee, n. 120 above, paras. 2–8, vii–ix.

Conclusions

In my discussion of rail we found that there was a plethora of specialist regulators and minimal competition; indeed, it had been made explicit that successful franchising was more important than maximizing competitive opportunities, at least initially. Nevertheless, the Rail Regulator had a number of important roles, including indirect price control and the enforcement of certain universal service requirements, and his involvement had led to a real increase in the transparency of the rail industry. The importance of the regulator has been recognized by the Parliamentary Opposition and will continue even in the event of a change of government. Buses fall at the other extreme; although the well-established regulators of safety have been retained, economic deregulation has taken place without the establishment of any specialist regulator. It seems quite clear that this is unsatisfactory. There have been many problems of anti-competitive practices and now of concentration; existing competition law has proved unequal to the task of successful regulation, not least because of the limitations of the existing authorities and the lack of effective remedies. Nor has the use of competition law provided a clearer and more rational framework within which businesses can plan with the maximum of certainty, for the system remains highly discretionary and one of the major criticisms made has been the absence of any clear principles which can provide a guide to companies on what is acceptable practice and what is not. Indeed, given the extensive ministerial discretion involved, the management of competition is more politicized than the other examples of regulation discussed earlier. Clearly pure deregulation subject to the general competition authorities is not an answer to the problems of the bus industry, a theme which will be addressed in general terms in Chapter 10 below.

8

Aviation: Deregulation and Hearings

The areas of regulation to be examined in this Chapter are substantially different from those in the rest of the book. Thus even though the most important British airports were privatized in the 1980s they are not regarded as public utilities as they do not provide the same essentials of life as those discussed in earlier chapters, though, as we shall see, the structure adopted on privatization raises some similar concerns about competition. In addition, private individuals are consumers of basic airport services only at second remove; such matters as airport charges primarily concern the airlines, which are far more able to protect their own interests. In the regulation of civil aviation itself, no natural monopoly arguments exist, there is a considerable degree of competition already in some areas, and the regulation that remains is more the result of government-negotiated treaty rights than of a concern to protect vulnerable consumers through cross-subsidy or other social goals. Because of these differences it will not longer be possible to follow the common structure of regulation of monopoly, regulation for competition, and universal service adopted in earlier chapters as not all these types of regulation apply in civil aviation.

Nevertheless, there are a number of similarities to the themes in the earlier chapters. Some airports are regulated as partial monopolies, and this raises familiar problems of price control. In civil aviation itself we can examine the effects of deregulation carried out on a scale larger than that for other utilities. This is not to say that we have seen anything on the scale of the heroic airline deregulation of civil aviation in the United States, but on domestic and European routes deregulation has been substantial and some lessons can be drawn from it. Most importantly of all, we can assess the experience of a more long-established regulator in UK civil aviation, and one that has been characterized by greater openness and a use of public hearings in a way not shared by any other of the regulators examined in this book; this will give us some important evidence on the use of such techniques and problems which may result. Another important difference is that it takes the form of a regulatory commission rather than of an individual Director General. Thirdly, it is striking that a number of possible solutions suggested for perceived crises in regulatory operations in other fields have previously been adopted in civil aviation; not only public hearings but also policy guidance from government. This will make it easier for us to assess whether such innovations offer a general answer to deficits in regulatory responsibility.

This Chapter will be relatively narrowly focused on economic regulation, and will exclude the important activity of safety regulation. I shall commence with the regulation of airports, as that is most closely compatible with the regulation of the public utilities discussed in earlier chapters, and then continue with examination of some other aspects of the work of the key regulator, the Civil Aviation Authority. This will exclude its operational activities, such as the provision of air traffic control, and some regulatory activities, such as safety and consumer protection through the Air Travel Organisers' Licensing Scheme, as these have no direct counterparts in the regulatory activities discussed in the earlier chapters.

PART ONE: THE REGULATION OF AIRPORTS

Regulatory Institutions

For reasons which will become clear later, airport regulation falls squarely within the category of regulating monopoly rather than regulation for competition or universal service.[1] The regulatory authority for the major British airports is the Civil Aviation Authority (CAA). As we shall see in the second part of this Chapter, it has had a relatively long history in the regulation of civil aviation.[2] The structure and constitution of the CAA will be fully discussed later on; it should just be noted here that it differs in important ways from the regulators discussed earlier. It takes the form, not of an individual Director General on whom powers are

[1] For fuller details see Shawcross, C., and Beaumont, K., *Air Law* (4th edn., Butterworths, London, 1995), chs. 7–9.
[2] A detailed history of the Authority is Baldwin, R., *Regulating the Airlines* (Clarendon Press, Oxford, 1985).

personally conferred, but of a commission of six to twelve members. In relation to certain of its functions it also has a more quasi-judicial form than the regulators already discussed, indeed it has for long fallen, as a tribunal, under the jurisdiction of the Council on Tribunals.[3]

For the moment I will concentrate on the CAA's regulatory powers relating specifically to airports. The most important examples are set out in Part IV of the Airports Act 1986. To summarize some highly complex provisions, two tiers of regulation operate. Airports with a turnover of £1 million or more must seek permission from the CAA to levy charges on airlines and comply with special accounting requirements. Airports designated under the second, more demanding, tier are subject to a quinquennial review by the CAA and the Monopolies and Mergers Commission; these airports are Heathrow, Gatwick, and Stansted in the South East and Manchester in the North West. The CAA will set a five-year price cap after the review; it also has powers to investigate complaints against unfair trading practices at all airports.[4] For the first six months after the Act came into effect these powers were exercisable by the Secretary of State, who used them to set the initial formulae for the seven privatized airports; this dispensed with the need for a reference to the MMC and for the observance of other procedural safeguards.[5]

All this may appear very similar to the price-setting procedures adopted by the other regulators, but there are some important differences. The most striking is the mandatory nature of the reference to the MMC; in the other cases the Commission is involved only in the absence of agreement between regulator and company, but here reference is obligatory before the setting of a price formula unless the Secretary of State directs otherwise, though there are plans to

---

[3] Tribunals and Inquiries Act 1992, sched. 1.

[4] For a summary of the current position see Department of Transport, *Review of the Airports Act 1986 System of Economic Regulation: Consultation Paper* (Department of Transport, London, 1994), and for recent developments Jones, I., and Willis, C., 'Airport Regulation 1994/5' in Centre for the Study of Regulated Industries, *Regulatory Review 1995* (Centre for the Study of Regulated Industries, London, 1995), 5–18, and Condie, S., 'Airport Regulation 1995/6' in Centre for the Study of Regulated Industries, *Regulatory Review 1996* (Centre for the Study of Regulated Industries, London, 1996), 5–20.

[5] Airports Act 1986, s. 53; Civil Aviation Authority (Economic Regulation of Airports) Regs. 1986, SI 1986/1544, Reg. 7(1).

change this.[6] Secondly, uniquely to the case of airports the reviews must take place every five years, and a mid-term review may take place only with the agreement of the airport concerned and not as a response to complaints.[7] Again this is proposed for reform; further details of the charges review process will be given below.

Even more than in the case of the utilities discussed in earlier chapters, substantial powers remain in the hands of the Secretary of State which directly affect airport regulation. These are particularly relevant to the highly congested airports at Heathrow and Gatwick. The Secretary of State has thus the power to issue traffic distribution rules, and this was done with the aim of building up Gatwick as an international airport, although in 1991 the rules were changed and their use in distributing demand amongst the South East airports was ended; the Secretary of State may also limit aircraft movements and may require the CAA to prepare a scheme to restrict access to airports.[8] The Government has in fact been criticized for its lack of any clear strategic framework for airports policy, and the issue of a new White Paper has been recommended by the Transport Committee of the House of Commons.[9] It should be added here also that the controversial and, from the competition viewpoint, essential matter of the distribution of landing slots at airports is delegated to Airport Scheduling Committees following procedures established by IATA, the airlines' own association. This is now subject to European Community rules, though their effectiveness has been heavily criticized and a consultation process is taking place around them as there needs to be a decision by July 1997 whether they are to be continued or revised.[10]

As will be evident from the discussion above, the regulatory complexity of this area is increased by the mandatory reference to the MMC for the quinquennial price reviews. A recent governmental review of airport regulation considered that this system could be slow and expensive (with the review of the Manchester formula taking almost a year and costs to the MMC alone approaching £0.5

---

[6] Airports Act 1986, s. 40(9).   [7] Airports Act 1986, s. 4(4), (6).

[8] Airports Act 1986, ss. 31–3; and see Department of Transport, *Traffic Distribution Rules 1991* (Department of Transport, London, 1991); for the advisory role of the CAA in relation to the Rules see its *Annual Report 1989–90*, 44.

[9] Transport Committee, *UK Airport Capacity*, HC 67, 1995–6, paras. 25, 37.

[10] Council Reg. 95/93 [1993] OJ L14/1; and see The Airports Slot Allocation Regs. 1993, SI 1993/1067. For criticism see Jones and Willis, n. 4 above, 13–15 and CAA, *Slot Allocation: A Proposal for Europe's Airports*, CAP 644 (1995).

million) and involved duplication of effort. It thus recommended that the most attractive option for the future is that of reference to the MMC only in cases of dispute, although this would require a broadening of CAA expertise in the non-aviation area. However, problems in finding legislative time for the necessary change meant that this could take effect only after the next quinquennial reviews of the South East airports and of Manchester, to which the existing system would apply. The option of establishing a new, 'more pro-active' regulator in the form of an OFAIR was rejected, as airports differ from the utilities in that the direct users—the airlines—are in a much stronger position than are individual consumers.[11] More details of the working of the price control system in practice will be given below.

The system is further complicated by the fact that, while the price formula applies to airport charges paid by user airlines, more income is generated through commercial activities; thus for the three South East airports in 1993–4 airport charges provided 34 per cent of income whilst income from rents and concessions accounted for 64 per cent, and this is increasing. The price reviews adopt a 'single till' approach, however, in which they take into account virtually all airport revenue in setting the price cap for landing charges, thus the X figure has to be higher and higher to have a given effect on profits.[12] The MMC may also investigate as part of the quinquennial review whether an airport operator has pursued a course of conduct against the public interest in relation to charges or other matters carried out for the benefit of airport users.[13] The CAA as well has a direct role in considering complaints about trading practices or pricing policies; examples of the kinds of complaints considered by the CAA are a complaint by Sabena about preferred treatment for British Airways in gate access at Heathrow, a complaint by freight operators at Heathrow about the acquisition of a cargo shed by a BAA subsidiary, and a complaint by Luton Airport about low charges at Stansted.[14] The Office of Fair Trading can investigate anti-competitive conduct, and for example in 1989–90 examined car-parking charges, duty-free prices, and

---

[11] Department of Transport, *Review of the Framework for Economic Regulation of Airports* (Department of Transport, London, 1995), paras. 7–19.

[12] See Condie, n. 4 above, 5; and Baldwin, R., *Regulation in Question: The Growing Agenda* (London School of Economics, London, 1995), 67, 69.

[13] Airports Act 1986, s. 43.   [14] CAA, *Annual Review 1994* (1995), 31.

restrictions on competition, abandoning plans for an MMC investigation when BAA agreed not to increase car-parking charges faster than inflation.[15] The OFT and the CAA have agreed that their principle interests can be broadly defined as 'landside' and 'airside' respectively.[16] The 1995 review rejected fundamental reform of the regulatory structure, but recommended that the CAA and OFT jointly clarify their responsibilities and that the CAA more effectively explain its procedures and its approach to complaints.[17] Finally, the European Community plays an increasing role in the economic regulation of airports, for example in relation to discriminatory landing charges, abuse of a dominant position in ground handling services, and predatory pricing.[18] The familiar problem of regulatory complexity thus applies strongly to the case of airports.

The Legislation

The most important duties applying to the CAA in its regulation of airports are set out in the 1986 Act which provides that in the setting of conditions it shall perform its functions in the manner it considers best calculated:

(a)   to further the reasonable interests of users of airports within the United Kingdom;
(b)   to promote the efficient, economic and profitable operation of such airports;
(c)   to encourage investment in new facilities at airports in time to satisfy anticipated demands by the users of such airports; and
(d)   to impose the minimum restrictions that are consistent with the performance by the CAA of its functions under those sections.

The general duties of the CAA, to be discussed below, are disapplied from the economic regulation of airports.[19] The first point to note is the absence of any duty to promote competition, such as that which applies to other regulators created in the latter phase of the privatization programme. This absence reflects the fact that '[t]he privatisation of BAA demonstrated the Government's preference for a regulated private monopoly over public monopoly and

[15] Baldwin (1995), n. 12 above, 71.
[16] Department of Transport, n. 4 above, para. 5.4.1.
[17] Department of Transport, n. 11 above, para. 19.
[18] Condie, n. 4 above, 7–8.   [19] Airports Act 1986, s. 39(1).

has been said to have had "virtually nothing to do with competition"'.[20] The possibility of adding such a duty was considered in the 1995 Review, but rejected by the Government as:

the promotion of greater competition between airports could work against interests of passengers and airport efficiency if it encouraged a more dispersed pattern of airport provision. A more concentrated pattern of larger airports can bring benefits to passengers through greater choice of routes and higher frequency of services, and to airlines through the encouragement of interlining traffic.[21]

As in the case of railways, the value of competition, whilst used as a major justification for privatization, is heavily qualified in practice.

Some other familiar regulatory duties are also absent, for example a duty on BAA to meet all reasonable demand or a duty on the regulator to ensure that such demand is met, or prohibitions on undue discrimination (although unreasonable discrimination against classes of user is a course of conduct which may result in action by the CAA[22]). The pattern of duties is complicated, however, by the fact that the Act also obliges the CAA to take into account the United Kingdom's international obligations as notified by the Secretary of State.[23] Examples of relevant international agreements are those of the International Civil Aviation Organisation requiring that airports be open to all overseas users and that there is no discrimination in charging; others impose as a constraint on airport income a 'reasonable return' based on costs.[24] Such international obligations would prevent the United Kingdom from raising prices at Heathrow to a level that would drive airlines to use other airports.[25]

Given the inevitably central role of the MMC in this area of regulation and the wide-ranging activities of the CAA in other areas of regulation, it would not be helpful to attempt here to assess the CAA's regulatory philosophy; more usefully, I will examine

---

[20] Baldwin, n. 12 above, 67, quoting Vickers, J., and Yarrow, G., *Privatisation, an Economic Analysis* (MIT Press, Boston, Mass., 1988), 354.

[21] Department of Transport, n. 11 above, para. 17.

[22] Airports Act 1986, s. 41(3).   [23] Airports Act 1986, s. 39(3).

[24] Shawcross and Beaumont, n. 1 above, III(1); for further details see Doganis, R., *The Airport Business* (Routledge, London, 1992), 71–5, 78–80.

[25] Transport Committee, n. 9 above, para. 195.

some of the most important airport matters in relation to which regulatory decisions have had to be made.

Regulating Monopoly: Price Control

It may appear curious that airports are regulated by the CAA 'as an effective monopoly on a similar basis to the newly privatised utilities to prevent them from exploiting a monopoly through over-charging'.[26] There are none of the natural monopoly elements of an integrated system which justify such regulation in, for example, gas transportation. Nevertheless, the system of airport regulation has strong similarities to that for the utilities discussed above, although, as has already been established, it has some marked peculiarities, notably the fixed period for price control each five years and the obligatory involvement of the MMC in the process. Initial formulae were set by the Secretary of State; by the end of 1996 there had been two reviews of the price formula for Manchester and two for the South East airports. The Act requires two things to be assessed in the reviews: the maximum charges to be levied in the following five-year period, and whether the operator has carried out a course of conduct against the public interest since the last review, and, if so, remedies to prevent such conduct. The pricing proposals from the MMC do not have to be followed by the CAA, although public-interest findings are binding unless vetoed by the Secretary of State.[27] It will be of interest to give an account of a couple of the reviews.[28]

The first review for the South East airports shows that the CAA retains an important role despite the mandatory MMC report; on charging matters the latter can only make recommendations. Thus the Commission found that airport charges accounted for only about 40 per cent of income and took into account projections of income from other commercial activities. It concluded that it would be reasonable for BAA to earn a current-cost rate of return of about 8 per cent, to be achieved by imposing a formula of RPI–4 per cent.[29] The CAA proposed instead that a 7 per cent rate of

---

[26] Transport Committee, n. 9 above, para. 180 and *Minutes of Evidence*, 2.

[27] Airports Act 1986, ss. 43(1)–(2), 45–6.

[28] For a more general discussion of them see Jones and Willis, n. 4 above, 16–18; Condie, n. 4 above, 9–14; Transport Committee, n. 9 above, paras. 180–8, 206–7.

[29] MMC, *BAA plc: South East Airports* (CAA, London, 1991).

return was appropriate with a formula of RPI–8; extensive discussion followed on the funding of investment and price caps were finally set at RPI–8 in the first two years, RPI–4 in the third, and RPI–1 in the fourth and fifth years; cost pass-through was also allowed of 95 per cent of government-imposed security costs.[30]

Considerable controversy concerns the review of prices for the South East airports from April 1997, especially concerning the combined ownership of Heathrow, Gatwick, and Stansted by BAA, making it the monopoly provider of airport services in the South East, and their regulation as a single entity. The CAA identified key issues for the review for consultation before the MMC report; these included whether the three airports should be regulated together or separately, the valuation of BAA's assets (described as 'the single most important quantitative issue in the setting of the price formula'), and its capital expenditure programme; these are familiar questions from other utility regulation.[31] The CAA did not however believe that the MMC could investigate the BAA monopoly as such, although it had done so in its earlier review and a minority report had recommended reassessment of BAA's structure. The Transport Committee of the House of Commons recommended that during the review the CAA and MMC re-examine whether ownership of the airports in the South East should be split up.[32] However, the MMC in its report on the price control did not do so as it did not find the existing arrangements to be against the public interest, though certain aspects of BAA policies were; it recommended a price control of RPI–3 for Heathrow and Gatwick and a separate price formula for Stansted of RPI–1, provoking further calls for consideration of a break up of the South East airports and for the legislation to be amended to include a duty for the regulator to promote competition.[33] The CAA implemented the MMC proposals. It should also be mentioned, for the sake of completeness in discussing price control that BAA has agreed a voluntary price cap for Glasgow and Edinburgh airports of RPI–3 after the

---

[30] CAA, *Annual Report 1991–2*, 23; see also Baldwin, n. 12 above, 69.

[31] Transport Committee, n. 9 above, para. 181 and *Appendices to the Minutes of Evidence*, 1.

[32] *Ibid.* para. 207.

[33] MMC, *BAA plc. A Report on the Economic Regulation of the London Airports Companies* (CAA, London, 1996); 'Regulating BAA', *Financial Times*, 17 July 1996 (leader). For further discussion see Condie, n. 4 above, 9–14.

Department had considered, but rejected, the case for designating them for full price control.[34]

The relationship between price control and the extent of monopoly ownership is of course familiar from earlier chapters, for example when considering gas regulation. Moreover, despite the central and obligatory role of the MMC, the discretionary decision-making of the CAA is important, as it retains the discretion to depart from the MMC proposals if it gives reasons for doing so.[35] This is likely to become stronger, of course, when the new regulatory model proposed in the review is implemented. Secondly, both the rate of return and the asset base have become central to revision of the price formula, as has ensuring that planned capital investment is actually implemented; this may be made easier by the proposed eventual introduction of the power for the CAA to initiate a mid-term review in response to complaints or on its own initiative without the consent of the airport concerned as one situation which might trigger such a review would be a shortfall in investment.[36]

Regulating Monopoly: Quality of Service

In this case the role of the CAA is radically different from that of other utility regulators. Quality of service, and of course investment, can be taken into account in the setting of the price caps; indeed, the trade-off between quality standards and pricing was identified as one of the key issues for the 1996 review of prices in the South East airports. However, the CAA has no specific responsibilities for setting and monitoring service standards, and complaints are considered by the OFT instead. In the consultative paper preceding the 1995 Departmental Review, it was suggested that the CAA might be given a more specific obligation regarding service standards to bring it into line with other regulators, either in its present form or as a new OFAIR. In the Review, the Government noted that there had been some support for such a model, especially from airlines, but it did not believe that this would represent a good use of resources given the stronger position of the airlines when compared to small consumers of the other

---

[34] Jones and Willis, n. 4 above, 10.   [35] Airports Act 1986, s. 46(5).
[36] Department of Transport, n. 11 above, para. 23; for sanctions currently available see Condie, n. 4 above, 11–12.

utilities. Instead, responsibilities as between the CAA and the Office of Fair Trading should be clarified, and the CAA should more effectively explain its procedures and its approach to complaints.[37] In this respect the CAA is much closer to the Rail Regulator than to the others discussed in earlier chapters. Nevertheless, in the 1996 price review the MMC accepted undertakings from BAA that service level agreements would be introduced, in some cases incorporating penalties.[38]

Regulation for Competition

It has been noted above that the encouragement of competition plays a much smaller role here than in the case of most other regulators; moreover, the Government retains a golden share in BAA and takeovers have not become an issue. The possible addition of a duty to promote competition to the CAA's airport duties was canvassed in the Department's Consultation Paper but rejected in the review, as it might work against the interests of passengers if it encouraged a more dispersed pattern of airport provision.[39] Instead the CAA should work through the consideration of individual cases of alleged anti-competitive conduct; as we saw above, it does receive and deal with complaints of this nature, and such issues can be examined by the MMC on quinquennial review and by the OFT; recent controversy about the lack of competition between the three BAA airports in the South East suggests, however, that the debate is unlikely to end here.

A further means of recourse in relation to complaints of anti-competitive conduct is the European Commission, of course, though we shall see in the second part of this Chapter that it does not provide the most effective grievance mechanism imaginable. It was used by Luton Airport, which complained that BAA was abusing a dominant position and so in breach of Article 86 of the EC Treaty through setting predatory prices at Stansted and offering special terms to attract airlines there and away from Luton. The CAA had already rejected the complaint. The investigation is a slow one and has not yet been completed.

---

[37] Department of Transport, n. 4 above, para. 6.1; n. 11 above, paras. 13–15.

[38] See Condie, n. 4 above, 14–16.

[39] Department of Transport, n. 11 above, paras. 16–18.

Regulatory Procedures

We shall see later in this Chapter that in other aviation matters the CAA has developed a distinctive role for public hearings which has made its procedures quite distinct from those of other regulators in the United Kingdom. This does not extend to airport regulation, however, where procedures broadly follow those of the utility regulators. The CAA (though not the minister acting within the first six months) is obliged to give notice and to receive representations on refusing permission to levy charges or imposing conditions; where the Authority diverges from recommendations of the MMC in a price review it must give reasons for doing so.[40] If a complaint has been made that a licence condition has been broken, the complainant may require a private hearing to be held on the record with a right to legal representation.[41] This has no counterpart in the case of the utility regulators, where all that is required is notice and an opportunity to make representations where it is alleged that a licence condition has been breached; it is closer to the usual procedures of the CAA in other civil aviation matters.

The 1995 departmental review considered a number of questions concerning procedure. The consultation paper noted that airlines have suggested that they should have additional opportunities to make representations during the quinquennial review, particularly to the MMC before the latter makes recommendations to the CAA. At present practice is normally to allow only the airport operator a second hearing after evidence has been collected and the main issues of public interest identified. This also raised the question of the amount of commercially sensitive evidence from the airport which could be made available to the airlines before publication of the MMC report. In addition, the question which had attracted the most criticism was the amount of information removed from the published reports on grounds of commercial sensitivity.[42] The review itself determined that a further stage of consultation before the MMC makes recommendations to the CAA would prolong the process and introduce an undesirable adversarial element to it; in

---

[40] Airports Act 1986, s. 46(5)(b); Civil Aviation Authority (Economic Regulation of Airports) Regs. SI 1544/1986, regs. 7–12.
[41] Civil Aviation Authority (Economic Regulation of Airports) Regs., n. 40 above, reg. 13.
[42] Department of Transport, n. 4 above, paras. 7.1, 7.3.

other words, any equivalent of a second round of notice and comment would take place only informally without a formal commitment to such a stage of consultation. Instead further access should be granted to the airport's evidence (subject to commercial sensitivity) when it is submitted to the MMC, and discussions will be held with the airports designed to implement the principle that excisions should be kept to the minimum.[43]

Conclusion on Airport Regulation

The economic regulation of airports is thus a rather interesting hybrid of procedures derived from utility regulation and those existing in the rest of civil aviation. In some ways it has proved unsatisfactory, as the Government's review has suggested, and some of the general problems of regulation, such as the difficulties of price review and the policing of capital expenditure, are apparent also. The most controversial issue in the near future is likely to be the lack of a duty to promote competition and the treatment of regulation as essentially monopoly regulation when the airports structure is very different from natural monopolies discussed in earlier chapters. A number of weaknesses in regulatory procedures have also been identified. For an examination of a radically different set of procedures however we must turn to the established regulatory activities of the CAA in the field of civil aviation.

PART TWO: THE REGULATION OF CIVIL AVIATION

Institutions

We can now examine a field of regulatory activity with a long history; that of civil aviation.[44] In this case some types of regulation resemble the monopoly regulation described earlier; for example price control. Yet here, even more clearly than in the case of airports, there is no suggestion that natural monopoly is present, and this type of regulation owes more to the protection of national flag-carrying airlines than any real argument from monopoly. In recent years regulation for competition has become much more important,

---

[43] Department of Transport, n. 11 above, paras. 35-9.
[44] See generally Shawcross and Beaumont, n. 1 above, chs. 10–15.

culminating in liberalization of European markets. Universal service has had very limited application, but the British practice of regulation has raised interesting procedural issues, as it differs markedly from the procedures adopted by other regulators. The history will not be repeated here, as there is an excellent account available elsewhere.[45] In brief, the early history of regulation was not a happy one. In part this was due to an extreme example of regulatory complexity; the provision of air transport was subject to the requirement of a dual process of authorization, first a licence from the Civil Aviation Authority or its predecessor, the Air Transport Licensing Board created in 1960, and secondly designation by the minister under air-service agreements agreed between governments. In addition to the requirement of ministerial designation, appeal lay to the Minister against the licensing decisions of the Board, and this became the chief way in which he was able to impose his policy; in the period 1962–71 about 100 issues were appealed, and in 30 per cent the Board's decision was overturned, with a further 10 per cent referred back to it for rehearing.[46]

The creation of the Civil Aviation Authority by the Civil Aviation Act 1971 was intended to alleviate these problems. The most important means of doing so was the provision of a system of policy guidance issued by the Secretary of State for Trade and Industry to provide a framework in which the CAA was to operate; this guidance was to be in writing, to be published, and to be approved in draft by a resolution of each House of Parliament.[47] The intention was that a broad policy framework be established within which the Authority would have a considerable degree of autonomy in deciding particular cases. In view of more recent suggestions for the creation of a similar system of ministerial guidance for the utility regulators this is of considerable current interest.

The system of policy guidance was however short-lived. A second guidance document was issued as a White Paper in early 1976 after a change of government. While it attempted to co-ordinate the availability of traffic rights under air service agreements with the licensing process more effectively than previously and encouraged the Authority to engage in a more open process of rule-making and to publish its licensing criteria, the most controversial part of the guidance provided that the CAA should not license more than one

---

[45] See Baldwin, n. 2 above.   [46] *Ibid.* 41–7.
[47] Civil Aviation Act 1971, s. 3.

British airline for long-haul routes. Thus the Government would cancel the traffic rights designation for the Laker 'Skytrain' on the North Atlantic route, and the CAA was, in effect, instructed to withdraw Laker's licence.

This use of guidance was successfully challenged in the Court of Appeal.[48] The Court held that the minister's action was unlawful as his power to issue guidance did not permit him to overrule the Authority's exercise of its quasi-judicial functions, nor could the guidance contradict the statutory objectives under which it operated. Moreover, withdrawal of traffic-rights designation could not be used by the minister to circumvent the procedures and protections set out for licensing decisions in the statute by rendering a licence useless. The case was interpreted as severely limiting the use of the guidance system, and after a further change of government in 1979 the system was withdrawn and replaced with new statutory objectives combined with a duty on the CAA itself to draw up statements of policy; both of these will be discussed below.

Does this failure discredit the use of government policy guidance for regulators? There are several reasons for suggesting that it does not. First, the international character of civil aviation offers opportunities for ministers to overrule regulators in individual cases through appeals or withdrawal of traffic-rights designation which do not exist in other areas of regulation. Thus in the other areas we have examined the minister has fewer sanctions to back up a misuse of guidance to determine individual decisions. Secondly, there is evidence to suggest that the system of guidance had had considerable success. Baldwin concludes:

[w]hat can be said at this stage is that, simply in term of the relationship between the agency and the Government, the policy guidance system did, between 1972 and 1979, succeed in placing control on a public basis in a manner that had never before been achieved. Whether or not the 'Skytrain' decision was to destroy the policy-making system, it could not be doubted that until 1979 affairs had been conducted with a new openness.[49]

When one turns now from the constitutional status of the CAA to its tasks, they are varied in the extreme. The CAA provides air

---

[48] *Laker Airways* v. *Department of Trade* [1977] 2 WLR 234; for a more recent decision in which the High Court held that the Secretary of State had acted unlawfully in designating British Airways whilst an appeal against its route licence was still pending see *R. v. Secretary of State for Transport, ex parte Dan Air Services Ltd.*, CO/524/90 (QBD), 11 Apr. 1990.

[49] N. 2 above, 116; see also 250.

traffic control services (though since April 1996 these have been placed in the hands of a separate, wholly-owned company, National Air Traffic Services), it is responsible for air-safety matters including airworthiness of aircraft and licensing of flight crew, advising the government on aviation issues, and conducting research, as well as the economic regulation considered here. For our purposes its most important function is that of licensing airlines; this has traditionally been termed air-transport licensing, but now there is an important distinction to be made between three types of licence.[50] All operators based in the United Kingdom must have an operating licence granted by the CAA; the conditions for granting such a licence are laid down in Community law, and for most flights in the European Union no further licence is needed, either from the CAA or from the authorities of another Member State.[51] For flights by UK-registered aircraft outside the European Union and for flights on a few remaining routes within it, the airline also needs route licenses from the CAA which may cover an area or an individual route. The combination of the two forms of licence replaces the need to hold air transport licences which existed up to 1 January 1993. Air transport licences are still required, however, for airlines based or registered outside the European Union which operate UK-registered aircraft; i.e. those based in the Channel Islands or the Isle of Man. As we shall see later, the distinction between different types of licence is crucial in determining the procedures which the CAA must follow in licensing decisions. A further point of importance is that conditions attached to air transport licences have been used extensively in the past as a means of regulating frequency, capacity, fares, and competition matters; although this is still possible for route licences, operating licences cannot be used in this way.

It will already be apparent that the European Community institutions also have a very important role in civil aviation; more important than in any other of the regulatory areas discussed, including telecommunications. The move to operating licences reflects a more general package which liberalized fares within the Union from 1993 as well as providing open access to most routes

[50] For the relevant provisions see the Civil Aviation Act 1982, ss. 64–8, 69A (all as amended).
[51] Council Reg. 2407/92 of 23 July 1992 on licensing of air carriers [1992] OJ L240/1; and see the Licensing of Air Carriers Regs. SI 1992/2992.

within the Union for all European Union-based airlines. The Community also has other functions in relation to procedures for the allocation of take-off and landing slots, the control of computer reservation systems, the control of mergers and the harmonization of air traffic control systems, though the adequacy of current responses on these matters has been heavily criticized; on the other hand, the route and fare liberalization package seems to have worked reasonably well.[52]

Finally in considering the question of the division of regulatory responsibilities, it should be added that the CAA established in 1973 a non-statutory Air Transport Users' Committee, now renamed the Air Transport Users' Council. This is responsible for making recommendations to the CAA for fulfilling the needs of transport users, and also handles complaints.

The Legislation

The general objectives of the CAA are set out in the Civil Aviation Act 1982.[53] The Authority is thus to perform its functions in the manner it considers best calculated:

(a) to secure that British airlines provide air transport services which satisfy all substantial categories of public demand (so far as British airlines may reasonably be expected to provide such services) at the lowest charges consistent with a high standard of safety in operating the services and an economic return to efficient operators on the sums invested in providing the industry of the United Kingdom; and
(b) to further the reasonable interests of users of air transport services.

These are supplemented by general duties which apply in relation to its air transport licensing functions and these are 'to perform its air transport licensing functions in the manner which it considers is best calculated to ensure that British airlines compete as effectively as possible with other airlines in providing air transport services on international routes', taking into account advice from the Secretary of State on the likely outcome of negotiations with other govern-

---

[52] For a summary see Prosser, T., 'Legal and Administrative Problems of Airline Deregulation in the United Kingdom' in Bridge, J., Banakas, W., *et al.* (eds.), *United Kingdom Law in the Mid-1990s* (The UK National Committee of Comparative Law, London, 1994), 315–38, at 327–37; and for more detailed criticism, CAA, *The Single European Aviation Market: Progress So Far*, CAP 654, (1995).

[53] Civil Aviation Act 1982, s. 4(1).

ments over traffic rights and the need to secure the most effective use of UK airports.[54] The CAA must also take into account environmental factors in exercising these functions;[55] there are also duties relating to competition. Thus the CAA in licensing must:

> have regard to the effect on existing air transport services provided by British airlines of authorising any new services the applicant proposes to provide under the licence, and in any case where those existing services are similar (in terms of route) to the proposed new services or where two or more applicants have applied for licences under which each proposes to provide similar services, the CAA shall have regard in particular to any benefits which may arise from enabling two or more airlines to provide the services in question.[56]

These are very different from the competition provisions of the utilities legislation, and owe more to the history of detailed route regulation to prevent competition through dividing up routes between countries by means of bilateral capacity-sharing agreements. Finally, 'it shall be the duty of the CAA to perform its air transport licensing functions in the manner which it considers is best calculated to impose on the civil air transport industry of the United Kingdom and on the services it provides for users of air transport services the minimum restrictions consistent with the performance by the CAA of its duties.'[57] The duties here are thus radically different from those applying to the utility regulators and discussed earlier in this book, reflecting the international environment of aviation licensing. The CAA is also required to take into account international obligations.[58]

The Regulatory Approach

More details of the CAA's general approach will become clear in discussing regulatory issues below. However, it should be stressed that it has shown a strong commitment to competitive markets in a field where they have been unusually difficult to establish due to the difficulties of intergovernmental negotiations.

It will be recalled that the system of policy guidance from government was replaced after the 'Skytrain' case by a duty for the CAA to publish a statement of its licensing policies; this is to be

---

[54] Civil Aviation Act 1982, s. 68(1).　　[55] Civil Aviation Act 1982, s. 68(3).
[56] Civil Aviation Act 1982, s. 68(2).　　[57] Civil Aviation Act 1982, s. 68(4).
[58] Civil Aviation Act 1982, s. 60.

issued after consultations with representatives of the UK civil air transport industry and with users of air transport services.[59] The most recent statement was published in May 1993 and, for reasons which will become apparent in discussing the scope of licensing later, concerns only routes outside the European Union.[60] The statement has been summarized by the Authority as having 'emphasised the CAA's commitment to licensing policies, which encourage competition, by removing barriers to entry and by preventing or remedying anti-competitive behaviour'; a more critical commentator has stated that '[a]s with all previous statements, the language of the 1993 statement is vague, perhaps inevitably so, but a lasting impression remains, namely, that the decisions and reasons of the CAA can always be framed in such a way as to demonstrate that all relevant criteria are satisfied and all but to exclude a successful appeal to the Secretary of State'.[61] The CAA also published in 1993 a wide-ranging report setting out its view of likely future developments in EU civil aviation and with policy recommendations aimed at maximizing the benefits of competition; this was further developed in the following year with a similar report on European long-haul routes.[62]

A further point needs to be made however; the CAA has been far more committed that other regulators described in this book to fair and open procedures. Apart from the publication of periodic policy statements after a consultation exercise, it has used public hearings in licensing decisions; both policies are now however of reduced importance due to EC liberalization. In examining regulatory issues in more detail, it will be more useful to deal with general competition issues, as these now set the framework for pricing decisions.

Regulation for Competition and Deregulation

It will already be apparent that the CAA has strongly supported moves towards the liberalization of civil aviation. It is in a particularly difficult position, however, as it depends on the activities of

---

[59] Civil Aviation Act 1982, s. 69, as amended by the Licensing of Air Carriers Regs. SI 2992/1992.
[60] CAA, *CAA Official Record Series, misc. no. 1082*, CAP 620 (1993).
[61] CAA, n. 14 above, 26; Shawcross and Beaumont, n. 1 above, para. IV(48).
[62] CAA, *Airline Competition in the Single European Market*, CAP 623 (1993); *Airline Competition in European Long Haul Routes*, CAP 639 (1994).

not just the UK Government but of other governments also in negotiating international agreements, and this has often proved very difficult to achieve. On a large scale, this is vividly illustrated by the long-running difficulties in negotiating a new 'open skies' agreement between the United Kingdom and the United States; this has become bogged down in inter-governmental disputes relating to airport access and industry structure. A recent illustration of the difficulties on a more local level was a case involving the Channel Islands. The CAA made proposals to bring air services between the United Kingdom, the Channel Islands, and the Isle of Man into line with the liberal arrangements applying within the EU, including the abolition of the distinction between scheduled and charter services and fares liberalization. After a hearing the Authority decided to implement the proposals and invited applications for licences to operate the relevant services with a further public hearing scheduled. This was opposed by the Channel Island authorities and the hearing was postponed at the direction of the Secretary of State to give the UK and Channel Islands Governments time to put in place arrangements under which newly constituted Channel Islands licensing authorities could refuse permission to air services licensed by the CAA. However the objections were withdrawn after progress in establishing the Channel Islands authorities' own systems and licences were then granted without the need for further hearings.[63]

The most important developments in liberalization have concerned routes within the EU. It has already been noted that regulations effective from 1993 replaced air-transport licensing within the EU with operating licensing; further regulations provided that, in general, Member States must allow community air carriers holding an operating licence to exercise traffic rights on any route within the EC, thereby removing the need to hold any further licence. There is a transitional period until 1 April 1997 for full cabotage rights, and public-service obligations may be imposed on thin routes which are important for the economic development of particular regions.[64] These latter have so far been used by Ireland, Sweden, France, and the United Kingdom; the process involves competitive tendering followed by access for only one carrier for up to three years; complaints that it is being used to restrict competition unduly may be

---

[63] CAA, n. 14 above, 27; *Annual Review 1995*, 23.
[64] Reg. 2408/92 [1992] OJ L240/8. Cabotage means the right of an airline from one country to provide *domestic* services in another.

made to the Commission. Substantial steps have thus been taken towards full liberalization within the Union whilst retaining some limited public-service obligations; a recent detailed CAA analysis of airline competition in Europe concluded that 'taken overall, liberalisation has been implemented with impressive success'. The most important problems involved restrictions imposed by the French Government on access to Paris (Orly), but these were successfully resolved after Commission intervention.[65] Progress has been much more difficult as regards other international services, given the need to renegotiate treaties with other governments; the CAA also has a strong record of working for deregulation in this context, for example in the pioneering liberalization of the charter market in the early 1970s.

The adoption of formal liberalizing rules however is not sufficient to create and maintain a competitive market with full benefits to the consumer.[66] One major difficulty has been that of concentration of airlines into a small number of dominant carriers. This had already posed problems in the United Kingdom at the time of the privatization of British Airways, before which the Government had commissioned the CAA to produce a report reviewing the implications of the sale for competition. The report recommended that before sale British Airways should be reduced in size through transfer of routes to British Caledonian and other British airlines. After massive lobbying by British Airways the Government rejected the bulk of the recommendations; soon after the privatization its major UK rival, British Caledonian, experienced serious financial difficulties and was taken over by BA.[67] There have been several other examples of takeovers and concentrations more recently and in its present form European Community law is of limited effectiveness in providing scrutiny and controls over the process, as the thresholds for Community control of mergers are too high to permit many mergers to be examined, and national competition law is not adequate to scrutinize trans-national agreements.[68] However, since

[65] CAA, *The Single European Aviation Market: Progress So Far*, CAP 654 (1995), vii, 29, 43–8.

[66] For a more detailed account of the remaining problems see Prosser, T., n. 52 above.

[67] CAA, *Airline Competition Policy*, CAP 500 (1984); Department of Transport, *Airline Competition Policy*, Cmnd. 9366 (1984).

[68] See *R.* v. *Secretary of State for Trade and Industry, ex parte Airlines of British Holdings plc*, *Independent*, 8 Dec. 1992.

1993 merger and takeover activity in Europe has declined considerably, with alliance activity concentrated on the long-haul markets, particularly to North America.[69]

Secondly, despite the tentative moves mentioned above to create common Community rules on the allocation of slots at airports, access to such slots remains a formidable problem, especially in the heavily congested airports such as Heathrow; a critical account of the problems by the CAA proposed that available slots should be concentrated to maximize competition in dense short-haul routes, although this would require substantial changes as part of the 1997 review of the EC regulation on airport slots mentioned above.[70] The conclusion which must be drawn is the familiar one that liberalization does not simply involve a withdrawal of the state through deregulation of licensing, but requires the active involvement of public authorities, in this case at a supra-national level, to create and maintain the conditions in which competition can be effective.

Regulation for Competition and Price Control

The most important characteristic of fares policy also has been liberalization, which has revealed the necessity of strong policing to ensure effective competition. As with route access, the CAA has long promoted liberal policies on fares. Fares on domestic flights have been automatically approved since 1985 and examined only to decide if they are anti-competitive or an abuse of monopoly power. From 1990 the CAA permitted any fare change to be implemented immediately on notification to permit short-run changes to be made quickly and a rapid reaction to be made to changes by other operators. This was conditional on the airline keeping the Authority supplied with up-to-date economic information; new expedited procedures were also implemented in that year for dealing with anti-competitive conduct. The CAA expressed its wish to implement such procedures for international fares, but this was not possible because of their being set in accordance with treaties; in particular, it could not secure that a fare once introduced be withdrawn. Nevertheless, the Authority refused to allow fare increases on many international routes (in 1989–90 rejecting more than ninety increases in fares to twenty-six different countries). Its policy was

[69] CAA, n. 65 above, 2–3, 51–2.
[70] CAA, *Slot Allocation: A Proposal for Europe's Airports*, CAP 644 (1995).

that it would not interfere with high quality, high priced products if there was also on the same route a 'basic' fare providing a reasonably priced option.[71]

Once more considerable liberalization has taken place within the EU, and this has created problems of institutional response. The third part of the package which came into effect at the beginning of 1993 introduced free pricing for scheduled services within the Union. Member States may require fares to be filed up to twenty-four hours in advance, but they come into immediate effect without requiring approval. There are two qualifications to this: a Member State may withdraw a basic fare which is excessively high in relation to costs and may also intervene in order to prevent a 'downward spiral' which leads to losses for all carriers on the route, though safeguards include the provision that these powers cannot be used if another Member State or if the Commission objects.[72] The implementing regulations provide that where a fare has been set at an excessively high or artificially low level the CAA must notify the Secretary of State who, if neither the European Commission nor any other Member State notifies disagreement within fourteen days, may require the fare to be withdrawn. In addition, the European Commission may itself investigate the level of a fare on the basis of a complaint from a party with a legitimate interest.[73]

In one respect, however, the scrutiny of anti-competitive fares at first became less effective with European liberalization. Previously the CAA had responsibility for preventing anti-competitive behaviour and had developed expedited procedures for dealing with such allegations. However, after an earlier stage in the EU liberalization process prior to the final package, large fare increases were introduced by a number of EU airlines; these could no longer be simply disapproved by the CAA but only referred to the Commission by the UK Government. Over thirty fares were referred in this way, but the Commission took almost a year to decide, by which time the fares had already expired. The CAA was not allowed an input into the investigation, and the eventual decision was devoid of reasons.[74] These fares had applied to the winter of 1990–1 (the

---

[71] CAA, *Annual Report 1989–90*, 41–2.   [72] Reg. 2409/92 [1992] OJ L240/15.
[73] The Air Fares Regs. 1992, SI 1992/2994.
[74] CAA, *Annual Report and Accounts 1991–2*, 21, and *Commission Decision*, 92/8/EEC [1992] OJ L5/26.

decision being given at the end of November 1991!); about sixty fares for the summer of 1991 were referred in April 1991. In this case a decision was given in early July 1992, accompanied by detailed reasons.[75] The 1993 package continues to give a discretion to national governments in blocking fare increases; an illustration of the remaining ministerial discretion in this process occurred in 1995, when the Secretary of State for Transport refused to require withdrawal of several British Airways business-class fare increases in Europe, despite objections from the CAA, which considered that they could not be justified by costs.[76] However, the earlier problems with the Commission have not been repeated, as in Europe as a whole it has not been asked to act against excessively high or low fares since 1993, though it has now threatened to act.[77] The CAA has concluded that 'the fares Regulation seems to have operated smoothly'.[78]

Regulatory Procedures

There have recently been a number of suggestions that utility regulators could operate more accountably and fairly if they adopted public hearings for key decisions. In fact, the CAA and its predecessors have operated such procedures for almost fifty years.[79] Subject to limitations as a result of EC liberalization to be discussed below, regulations provide that decisions relating to air-transport licensing not consented to by the licensed airline may be taken only by members of the Authority and not by its staff; this, together with its status as a tribunal under the supervision of the Council on Tribunals, highlights the quasi-judicial role of the CAA in performing licensing functions. Objections may be lodged to applications for licences, and a public hearing will then take place at which legal representation and cross-examination must be permitted; third parties such as users' groups may also be allowed to participate if they have lodged an objection. A record of the hearing is made available afterwards and reasons must be given for the decision,

---

[75] *Commission Decision* 92/398/EEC [1992] OJ L220/35.

[76] 'BA Told Business Class Fare Increases Can Stay', *Financial Times*, 24 Aug. 1995.

[77] 'Kinnock May Force Cut in EU Airfares', *Financial Times*, 25 Oct. 1996.

[78] CAA, n. 65 above, 48.

[79] For the history see Baldwin, n. 2 above, ch. 10. Current procedures are governed by The Civil Aviation Authority Regs. 1991, SI 1991/1672.

and in practice these are substantial; appeal lies to the Secretary of State, who is also obliged to give reasons for his decisions. Although only a small proportion of applications for licences involve an objection and hence a hearing, in practice this will be the case in most of the important ones. Moreover, similar procedures also apply in the case of licence revocation and variation of licences where objections have been made; since licence conditions have been extensively used to control fares and competition the hearing is of considerable importance in relation to those matters also.[80]

The use of such procedures appears to have been highly successful. Thus the authoritative account of CAA regulation concludes its discussion of their use by stating that 'for all its departures from the court paradigm, the public licensing hearing has one virtue perceived by all: even if tainted with vagueness it provides an opportunity for the applicants to air their case in public and it thereby increases confidence in the fairness, if not the efficiency, of the licensing system'.[81] The most important problem has been that of disclosure of information considered to be commercially sensitive (also a problem in airport charging regulation, as we saw above); here the Authority has encouraged as much disclosure as possible and has been prepared to undertake part of the hearing *in camera* to consider arguments relating to such information.[82] If the question of disclosure has not caused insuperable problems in the highly competitive airline industry, it is unlikely to be more difficult to handle in the case of utilities with a considerable degree of monopoly power.

It must be added, however, that the role of the licensing hearing has been considerably reduced owing to EC liberalization. It will be recalled that the key licence is now an operating licence which gives automatic access to most routes within the European Community. The conditions for the award of such licences are set out in the regulation and further specified in the domestic implementing regulations.[83] If the conditions are satisfied the operator is entitled to be granted the licence unconditionally. No provision is made for objections, and so public hearings are not held in relation to such applications, but only in relation to applications for route licences and air transport licences. Instead, a right of appeal lies to the

---

[80] For more details of the hearing procedure see Baldwin, n. 2 above, 143–59.
[81] *Ibid.* 159.   [82] *Ibid.* 154–8.
[83] Council Reg. 2407/92 of 23 July 1992 on Licensing of Air Carriers [1992] OJ L240/1; Licensing of Air Carriers Regs. 1992, SI 1992/2992.

European Commission, and the domestic regulations also provide for appeal to the Secretary of State. Given the unconditional nature of the operating licence no procedure exists for its amendment; revocation merely carries a right of appeal to the Secretary of State. Whilst the desire of the EC to prevent Member States erecting artificial procedural barriers to licence applications is understandable, the new system has led to a regrettable lessening of transparency. It should be noted that the conditions to be met by applicants are by no means such that their being met can be determined by a mechanical process; they include, for example, a test of the adequacy of the applicant's financial resources to be assessed through an examination of its business plan for the first two years. Since the liberalization package in effect dispensed with hearings in relation to European services, the use of hearings has declined from thirteen over eighteen days in 1989–90 to only two over two days in 1994; in 1995 once more only two hearings were held, both concerned with services to Beirut by British Airways and a new entrant.[84]

Conclusion

The CAA appears to have largely escaped the current criticisms of the way in which British regulatory bodies undertake their role, at least as regards its air-transport licensing functions. This is no doubt partly due to the considerable degree of liberalism of its policies; it has been firmly committed to the view that a multi-airline, competitive industry is in the best interests of users, and indeed has since the mid-1970s prefigured more general European developments by adopting a presumption in favour of granting licences unless there is a strong reason not to do so and by adopting particularly liberal policies on charters and domestic fares. Secondly, the procedures adopted by the Authority have provided a major source of its legitimacy, though here liberalization policies at an EC level seem to have underestimated the degree to which discretionary decision-making by public authorities will remain necessary for the maintenance of effective competition, and at first led to some decline in openness and effectiveness in relation to fares and policing of competition, although for the moment these problems seem to have been resolved.

[84] CAA, *Annual Review 1995*, 23.

In drawing lessons for other utility regulators, the key features are the role of hearings, the obligation to develop policies after a consultative process, and the former written policy guidance from government. If such hearings are possible in a highly competitive industry where rapid decision-making and confidentiality of costing information are seen as crucial by participants, the arguments against them in relation to the part-monopoly utilities seem to be seriously weakened. The process of policy-making has been useful in emphasizing the Authority's commitment to liberalization, and we have seen similar moves towards the statement of aims and objectives by other regulators, notably in telecommunications and in rail. Although the use of policy guidance fell foul of successful legal challenge of its misuse to direct the outcome of an individual case, the proper use of guidance to provide a framework for decision-making seems to have been broadly successful. This and the procedural lessons to be drawn from the Authority will be addressed more fully in Chapter 10 below.

9

The Regulation of Independent Broadcasting: Public Service, Codes, and Auctions

The final regulatory institution to be examined in this book is the Independent Television Commission (ITC). I shall consider only part of the regulation of broadcasting in the United Kingdom, and exclude the BBC, which is subject to very special forms of regulation under its Royal Charter and Agreement with the Secretary of State. I shall also exclude radio, which is regulated by a Radio Authority in many ways similar to the ITC. Nevertheless, by concentrating on the most important regulatory institution which also has the role closest to that of the other regulators described in this book some important lessons can be learned. In particular, the regulation of commercial broadcasting has a longer history than the forms of utility regulation discussed in earlier chapters, yet it now faces a rapidly changing environment in both technological and economic terms. In some senses the ITC's work concerned with avoiding concentration of ownership in the media can be seen as regulation for competition, yet is a type of regulation for competition radically different from any examples discussed earlier, and based on very different rationales. It also raises unavoidably the relationship between competition and public service discussed in earlier chapters; indeed, public-service broadcasting is a far more developed concept than the other forms of public-service obligation discussed above, and so we shall have the opportunity to examine an area of regulation in which public-service ideals are central to the regulator's work. A number of procedural issues are also raised by the experience of the ITC and its predecessor. Thus it makes extensive use of rule-making through issuing codes to clarify and implement public service and other obligations, a method which has been suggested for adoption by other regulators as a way of improving their accountability and predictability.[1] Secondly, the IBA's predecessor was subjected to even stronger (justified) criticisms of its lack of procedural fairness than have been the utility regulators. Some improvements were made, but the major innovation was the adoption of an auction procedure for the allocation of broadcasting licences in 1991. An assessment of this process will enable us to consider whether it is feasible to replace regulatory discretion with such a system, thereby bypassing problems of procedural legitimacy. Finally, the ITC has developed particularly strong mechanisms for monitoring the observance of licence conditions which may provide further lessons for general regulatory procedures.

The Institutions

The regulation of commercial, or independent, television has a fairly long history, dating back to the establishment of the Independent Television Authority (later the Independent Broadcasting Authority (IBA)) in 1954. The IBA allocated the authority to broadcast through the issue of 'franchises', a form of private-law contract; it administered statutory programming requirements, detailing them in codes of practice; it engaged in the prior inspection of programme schedules and of the programmes themselves, and used its transmission system for the broadcasting of programmes made by the independent television companies. The operation of the Authority was dogged by controversy; in particular its procedures came under sustained attack, especially in relation to the allocation of the franchises which gave, in effect, the right to broadcast.[2] This allocation took place through a highly secretive process, and there were very limited means of accountability to applicants or to a broader public, or even of challenging the decisions. In the case of the first reallocation of franchises in 1967 no warning had been given to the companies from which these valuable assets were removed, and during the brief interviews held by the IBA no detailed discussion of their performance took place. No

[1] See, e.g., Veljanovski, C., *The Future of Industry Regulation in the UK* (European Policy Forum, London, 1993), 85; Souter, D., 'A Stakeholder Approach to Regulation' in Corry D., Souter, D., and Waterson, M. (eds.), *Regulating Our Utilities* (Institute for Public Policy Research, London, 1994), 7–99, 81.
[2] See Lewis, N., 'IBA Programme Contract Awards' [1975] *Public Law*, 317–40.

criteria for decision-making were announced in advance, no reasons were given for the decisions, and the applications and franchise contracts were not made public, so it was not possible to compare publicly promise with performance. These defects were largely repeated in the second reallocation in 1980, although a greater degree of public consultation took place and the interviews were a little longer.[3]

The IBA also experienced difficulties in holding successful applicants to their promises; the only powers available to the Authority were to suspend or withdraw the franchise, powers far too extreme to permit effective supervision of promises. It should also be noted that the nature of the franchises as private-law contracts was interpreted by the Court of Appeal as precluding judicial review of decisions taken by virtue of their provisions; in the case in question the decision was to refuse permission for a shareholder to exercise more than 5 per cent of voting rights in the company, thereby blocking a proposed takeover.[4]

Discretionary regulation in this area had not, then, had a happy history by the 1980s, and broadcasting seemed a natural area for deregulation because many of the traditional grounds for regulation based on scarcity of frequencies were being rapidly overtaken by the development of other forms of delivery, notably by cable or satellite. Thus the prospect of a competitive market in broadcasting services seemed a more plausible possibility than when regulatory structures had been established. Together with an ideological preference for partial deregulation of economic aspects of broadcasting on the part of the Thatcher Governments, this led to attempts to regulate with 'a lighter touch'. The first expression of this philosophy came with the establishment of the Cable Authority in 1984 implementing more relaxed programming requirements and with a less interventionist style than that of the IBA.[5] The assumption became that the abuses of discretionary power allegedly

---

[3] See *ibid.*; Sendall, B., *Independent Television in Britain*, ii, *Expansion and Change, 1958–68* (Macmillan, London, 1983), chs. 36–7; Briggs, A., and Spicer, J., *The Franchise Affair* (London, 1986).

[4] *R. v. The Independent Broadcasting Authority, ex parte the Rank Organisation plc*, CA (Civ. D), 26 Mar. 1986, LEXIS. Cf. the decision of the Court of Appeal in *R. v. Panel on Takeovers and Mergers, ex parte Datafin* [1987] QB 815.

[5] See Veljanovski, C., 'Cable Television: Agency Franchising and Economics' in Baldwin, R., and McCrudden, C. (eds.), *Regulation and Public Law* (Weidenfeld and Nicolson, London, 1987), 267–97.

inherent in bureaucratic regulation could be replaced by the efficiency and accountability of the market-place. Deregulation was
accepted in part as Government policy in the White Paper on
broadcasting of 1988.[6] This contained an emphasis on the need to
replace existing regulation with a new system placing greater stress
on freedom of consumer choice. Nevertheless, important rules regulating programme content would remain in the form of 'consumer
protection requirements'. The IBA was to be replaced by an
Independent Television Commission without direct responsibility
for transmission and without the power to preview schedules and
programmes; it would apply 'lighter, more objective programme
requirements' with 'a less heavy-handed and discretionary
approach' than that of its predecessor.[7] The most controversial proposal was that the award of franchises was to be replaced by competitive bidding for licences, most importantly at first for the
regional licences of Channel 3 where they were to be awarded to
the highest bidder amongst those which had passed an initial 'quality threshold' to satisfy the ITC that they would be able to comply
with their programming requirements. The proposals were implemented in the Broadcasting Act 1990; as we shall see a number of
important changes were made during its passage through
Parliament, notably in the strengthening of the 'quality threshold'
and permitting the award to a bidder other than the highest in
'exceptional circumstances'.

As established by the 1990 Act, the ITC is a commission composed of a chairman, deputy chairman, and eight to ten other members; it has a number of different functions. First, as outlined
above, it licenses commercial television services in the United
Kingdom. This includes not just Channels 3 and 4 but Channel 5,
cable and domestic satellite services and some text and data services; an important later addition is digital terrestrial television.
The last major reallocation of licences was that in 1991 referred to
above; in the future takeovers are likely to become the most important means of reallocation, and as we shall see important takeovers
have already taken place. The licences last for ten years with provision for application to renew at the beginning of the seventh year,
but nevertheless we are not likely to see once more the wholesale

[6] Home Office, *Broadcasting in the '90s: Competition, Choice and Quality*, Cm 517
(1988).
[7] *Ibid.* para. 6.5.

administrative reallocations characteristic of the 1991 process and those under the IBA. This of course makes other types of regulation more important, in particular enforcement of quality standards and licence conditions. All licensees are subject to the ITC's programme code, and similar provision is made through codes on advertising and sponsorship. In addition to the content of the codes, other requirements are included in licence conditions, in particular positive programme requirements relating to Channel 3 which include minimum percentages of original programming, independent production, and European programmes. The various provisions are enforced through monitoring of programmes and of complaints, together with an annual performance review of companies; unlike its predecessors, the ITC has no power to preview programmes or schedules. Sanctions available include warnings, financial penalties, and shortening or revocation of a company's licence.

The ITC is also obliged to ensure enforcement of the rules on concentration of ownership which will be more fully described below. It should be added that the ITC possesses other powers more closely related to those of the utility regulators described in earlier chapters; thus, as we shall see, it is under a duty to ensure fair and effective competition in the provision of services, and has responsibility together with the Director General of Fair Trading for approving the networking arrangements for Channel 3, in some ways comparable to the interconnection matters so important in utility regulation.

Regulatory Complexity

The problem of regulatory complexity dealt with in discussions of the utilities is peculiarly acute here; so much so in fact that the National Heritage Select Committee has stated that '[t]he Committee is concerned that there is a plethora of bodies, with confused and overlapping terms of reference, responsible both for regulation of broadcasting and representation of the consumer interest.'[8] This remains the case even if one omits the BBC and radio as outside the scope of this Chapter.

If I take first matters within the ITC's own responsibilities, it is advised by a number of specialist committees with outside

[8] National Heritage Committee, *The Future of the BBC*, HC 77, 1993–4, para. 42.

membership: the Advertising Advisory Committee, the Medical Advisory Panel, the Central Religious Advisory Committee, the Schools Advisory Committee, and the Gaelic Television Committee. In its representation of the consumer interest, the Commission is assisted by ten Viewer Consultative Councils. However, apart from enforcement of programme standards by the ITC, two other bodies were established to perform essentially the same role: the Broadcasting Complaints Commission to handle complaints relating to such matters as accuracy, impartiality and protection of privacy, and the Broadcasting Standards Council (given a statutory basis for the first time by the 1990 Act) to prepare a code relating to broadcasting standards in relation to the portrayal of violence, of sexual conduct, and taste and decency; it also considers complaints on these matters.[9] The two latter bodies are however to be merged into a new Broadcasting Standards Commission from April 1997.[10]

As was the case with the utilities, government retains an important regulatory role. This is most striking in relation to renewal of the BBC's Charter, where the non-statutory form adopted removes the need even for Parliamentary debate of the provisions involved, though in the 1996 renewal such an opportunity was in fact given; it is supplemented by a new Agreement between the Secretary of State and the Corporation setting out how it will meet its objectives and including, for example, obligations on programme standards.[11] In independent broadcasting the Secretary of State also has some important powers. The most important of these is the making of the ownership rules which limit concentration and cross-media ownership; as we shall see, these have taken the form of a mixture of primary and secondary legislation and are perceived as having been rapidly overtaken by technological and economic change. Reaction has been limited initial change by government, followed by a review process resulting in clearer proposals for change implemented by new legislation.[12] Enforcement is for the ITC, though the Government had suggested in its consultative paper that this

---

[9] Broadcasting Act 1990, ss. 142–61.

[10] Broadcasting Act 1996, ss. 106–30.

[11] *BBC Royal Charter*, Cm 3248 (1996); *Agreement Between Her Majesty's Secretary of State for National Heritage and the British Broadcasting Corporation*, Cm 3152 (1996).

[12] *Media Ownership: The Government's Proposals*, Cm 2872 (1995); Broadcasting Act 1996, s. 73 and sched. 2.

might pass to another regulator such as the Director General of Fair Trading in the longer term; under the current arrangements the Commission is expected to take the advice of the Director General in implementing the public-interest test in cross-media ownership to be discussed below.

A further player of growing importance is the European Commission. The most important current legal instrument is the so-called *Television Without Frontiers* Directive.[13] Provisions in the Directive include a prohibition on the restriction of reception or re-transmission of broadcasts from other Member States, programme quotas for European material of 10 per cent 'where practicable', limitations on advertising content and amount, and rules relating to the protection of minors and right of reply. In addition to these programming controls, the Commission published in 1992 a Green Paper on concentration of media ownership, setting out various approaches for European regulation of this, followed by further consultation. Amendments to the Directive are being considered by the European Parliament.[14] The European Court of Justice has also had an important role in broadcasting matters.[15]

I mentioned above that the ITC is under a duty to secure fair and effective competition in the provision of television services. As we saw in the previous chapter, this involves a potential overlap of jurisdiction with the competition authorities and has raised questions of who will be lead regulator of ownership issues in the longer term; the Government suggested that this could probably be the Director General of Fair Trading, whilst the ITC supported the retention of its own regulatory role in relation to cross-media ownership.[16] The ITC is responsible for monitoring the quota of independent productions commissioned by Channels 3 and 4, though in the case of the BBC this is the responsibility of the Office

---

[13] Council Dir. 89/552/EC [1989] OJ L298/23.

[14] *Pluralism and Media Concentration in the Internal Market: An Assessment of the Need for Community Action*, COM(92)480 final; for details of developments since, see Beltrame, F., 'Harmonising Media Ownership Rules: Problems and Prospects' (1996) 7 *Utilities Law Review* 172–5; and Harcourt, A., 'Regulating for Media Concentration: The Emerging Policy of the European Union' (1996) 7 *Utilities Law Review* 202–10.

[15] See, e.g., C–222/94 *Commission* v. *UK* [1996] 3 CMLR 793.

[16] ITC, *Media Ownership: ITC Response to the Government's Proposals* (1995), paras. 50–1; cf. Borrie, G., 'One Regulator of More?' in Collins, R. (ed.), *Converging Media? Converging Regulation?* (Institute for Public Policy Research, London, 1996), 15–19.

of Fair Trading. The most complex issues arose with the Channel 3 networking arrangements by which the programmes of the regional companies and of independent producers are co-ordinated into a national network. The Act required the companies to draw up arrangements to be approved by the ITC and by the Director General of Fair Trading, the latter employing a test derived from European Community competition law.[17] If he was not satisfied with the proposed arrangements, he was obliged to specify modifications; the companies and the ITC could then refer the matter to the MMC. The original proposals made by the companies and the ITC were rejected by the Director General in terms which directly contradicted the ITC's interpretation of its statutory responsibilities, and a reference was made to the MMC by both the companies and the Commission, which produced a report differing in important respects from both the ITC proposals and those of the Director General but representing a compromise between the competition-oriented concerns of the Director General and the public-interest regulation of the ITC.[18] A more recent example of the ITC using its competition powers is its investigation into premium channel bundling in pay-TV at the retail level, the Office of Fair Trading having investigated it at the wholesale level.[19]

The most important regulatory complexity concerns, however, the regulation of new forms of delivery; commentators have identified at least fourteen statutory or self-regulatory bodies claiming jurisdiction over aspects of new media delivery in the United Kingdom alone.[20] In relation to cable delivery, for example, every cable and local delivery operator needs at least two different licences, one for the system itself under the Telecommunications Act issued by the Department of Trade and Industry and regulated by OFTEL, and one under the Broadcasting Act from the ITC for the provision of programming and a local delivery service; in the case of some services a third licence is needed from the Radio-

[17] Broadcasting Act 1990, s. 39; sched. 4, paras. 1-2.

[18] Monopolies and Mergers Commission, *Channel 3 Networking Arrangements: A Report on Whether the Arrangements Satisfy the Competition Test Contained in the Broadcasting Act 1990* (HMSO, London, 1993); see also Prosser, T., 'Channel 3 Networking Arrangement: The Monopolies and Mergers Commission Reports' (1993) 4 *Utilities Law Review* 127–30.

[19] ITC, *Consultation Document: Competition Investigation into Premium Channel Bundling in the Pay-TV Market* (London, 1996).

[20] Murroni, C., Collins, R., and Coote, A., *Converging Communications: Policies for the 21st Century* (Institute for Public Policy Research, London, 1996), 49.

communications Agency under the Wireless Telegraphy Act. As OFTEL has put it, 'broadcast services will become increasingly difficult to distinguish from other services with a telecommunication service component. Video-based services delivered over traditional telecommunications systems will increasingly look like broadcasting (eg cable television, video-on-demand) while those delivered over broadcasting systems may look like other services with a telecommunications component'.[21]

A further problem related to the convergence of different media and the digitalization of broadcasting has arisen in relation to the technology associated with subscription television, in particular the system for conditional access to such systems restricting such access to those who have paid for it.[22] The conditional-access technology for analogue broadcasting is dominated by a group of companies associated with News International; they are not licensed under the 1990 Act. Apart from the potential competition problems which might arise, the Government is required by a European Community directive to regulate conditional-access services.[23] The ITC is responsible for regulating conditional-access systems for analogue broadcasting under its general power to ensure fair and effective competition, and proposed that the provision of such conditional-access services should in itself become a licensable activity. The Government accepted this in its proposals for digital terrestrial broadcasting but proposed giving licensing responsibility for digital access systems to OFTEL, to which the ITC strongly objected.[24] The solution adopted was that class licences for conditional access in digital television will be issued by the Department of Trade and Industry and enforced by OFTEL, although both issue and enforcement will be 'in close co-operation' with the ITC.[25] This type of boundary dispute is likely to recur in other areas of

[21] OFTEL, *Beyond the Telephone, the Television and the PC* (1995), para. 1.4.4.
[22] For a detailed analysis of the important issues underlying these questions, see Graham, A., 'Exchange Rates and Gatekeepers' in Congden, T., *et al.* (eds.), *The Cross Media Revolution* (John Libby, London, 1995), 38–49.
[23] Dir. 95/47/EC [1995] OJ L281/51.
[24] *Digital Terrestrial Broadcasting*, Cm 2946, para. 4.17; ITC, *Media Ownership: ITC Response to the Government's Proposals* (1995), paras. 31–42.
[25] Department of Trade and Industry, *The Regulation of Conditional Access Services for Digital Television* (Department of Trade and Industry, London, 1996); *The Regulation of Conditional Access Services for Digital Television: Consultation Paper on Detailed Implementation Proposals* (Department of Trade and Industry, London, 1996).

regulation as media convergence develops further. It has been suggested that a more rational division of responsibilities in relation to the communications sector would be to separate economic regulation and content regulation, with economic regulation of broadcasting and of telecommunications concentrated within a single agency.[26] The Labour Party has proposed that an 'OFCOM' will regulate the whole communications infrastructure and ensure fair competition, whilst a revamped ITC will regulate content.[27]

This section of the Chapter commenced with a quotation from the National Heritage Committee on the extreme regulatory complexity facing consumers in complaining about broadcasting. It should now be clear that similar complexity exists in other areas of broadcasting regulation as well; indeed, this is the area of regulation with the greatest number of competing jurisdictions of all those examined in this book. The problem is particularly severe in relation to the rapidly developing forms of new technology which combine broadcasting and telecommunications technology, and is clearly likely to create serious problems unless some fundamental regulatory restructuring takes place.

The Legislation

As might be expected in an area with a strong history of public-interest regulation such as broadcasting, the statutory duties applying to the ITC are more extensive and more complex than in the other regulatory fields studied, and only a summary can be given here, concentrating on those relevant to Channel 3 as the most-viewed independent terrestrial channel. The first duty applying to the ITC is however more familiar; it is to discharge its functions in relation to the licensing of terrestrial services in the manner considered best calculated to ensure that a wide range of television programme services is available throughout the United Kingdom and to ensure fair competition in the provision of such services and in services connected to them.[28] Difference is quickly apparent how-

[26] Cave, M., 'Traffic Management on the Superhighway', in Collins, R., and Purnell, J. (eds.), *Managing the Information Society* (Institute for Public Policy Research, London, 1995), 19–29 at 26–7; see also Murroni, *et al.*, n. 20 above, ch. 5.

[27] Labour Party, *Communicating Britain's Future* (The Labour Party, London, 1995).

[28] Broadcasting Act 1990, s. 2(2)(a).

ever in the next duty which requires the members of the Commission:

to discharge their functions . . . as respects the licensing of television programme services in the manner in which they consider is best calculated to ensure the provision of such services which (taken as a whole) are of high quality and offer a wide range of programmes calculated to appeal to a variety of tastes and interests.[29]

Straight away, then, one finds the introduction of key elements of public-service broadcasting in the form of high quality of programmes and diversity so as to cater for a wide range of tastes, and this ensures that even the more competition-oriented goals are implemented in ways radically different from those of the other regulators. Public-service principles are developed in the general requirements relating to licensed services; these include the requirement to ensure that nothing is included in programmes which offends against good taste or decency or that is likely to encourage or incite to crime or lead to disorder or be offensive to public feeling; that news be presented with due accuracy and impartiality, and that such impartiality be preserved in relation to matters of political or industrial controversy or current public policy. Further duties apply to religious programmes and prohibit subliminal images.[30] Very importantly, the ITC is obliged to draw up a code giving guidance on impartiality, and it is also obliged to draw up a general programme code;[31] I shall return to its code-making functions below. Other duties relate to the control of advertising, again including a code-making duty.[32] Very detailed duties also apply to the licensing of Channel 3 services, including those requiring programming of high quality, with news and regional programmes, a proper proportion of European programmes, and programmes that appeal to a wide variety of tastes and interests; these public-service broadcasting requirements will be considered in more detail below.[33] More specific changes are also made by the Broadcasting Act 1996, including protection for public-service broadcasting in the new digital environment.[34]

[29] Broadcasting Act 1990, s. 2(2)(b).   [30] Broadcasting Act 1990, s. 6(1).
[31] Broadcasting Act 1990, ss. 6(3), 7.   [32] Broadcasting Act 1990, ss. 8–9.
[33] Broadcasting Act 1990, s. 16.   [34] Broadcasting Act 1996, ss. 28–32, 91.

The Regulatory Approach

It is difficult to summarize a distinctive regulatory approach of the ITC for a number of reasons. First, the degree of legal guidance is much greater than in the case of the other regulators, so the approach is more clearly determined by a distinctive body of legal material. Secondly, in the case of a commission it is always more difficult to establish a personal approach than in the case of a single Director General. It is nevertheless worth outlining an early view by the ITC Chief Executive; it can then be compared to the practice described below.[35] He considered that:

the case for regulation in broadcasting is no different in principle from the case for regulation in other public utilities. Regulation by statutory bodies set up for the purpose is intended to protect the public interest, prevent the abuse of monopoly power where monopoly exists, and to do so at arm's length from government in its day-to-day operations.[36]

Public-interest regulation includes universal service, in the sense both of making the service available to all who want to receive it and ensuring that it caters for a wide variety of tastes and interests, including minority interests. The IBA, as predecessor to the ITC, had been too closely involved in the system it regulated, taking a management and advocacy role, but the ITC intended to operate at arm's length from the licensees; '[t]o a considerable extent the system will be one of self-regulation by the licensees within a clear framework of obligations and codes of practice.'[37] It would also have a new role in ensuring effective competition within the system. In conclusion, however, 'its principal interest, and I hope that of its licensees, will be to see that programme services are of a high quality and do serve a wide range of tastes and interests. That will not come about if broadcasters are terrified to make the slightest move for fear of ITC sanctions cracking down on their heads.'[38] The particularly important role of ensuring diversity in programming as a form of universal service is thus very clear, as is the desire to avoid regulation that is too heavy-handed.

As was stressed above, the ITC is by no means the only actor in

---

[35] Glencross, D., 'Independent Television Commission: The Reform of Broadcasting Regulation' in Veljanovski, C. (ed.), *Regulators and the Market* (Institute of Economic Affairs, London, 1991), 141–51.
[36] *Ibid.* 142.   [37] *Ibid.* 145.   [38] *Ibid.* 150.

regulating broadcasting, and in the particularly important field of media ownership and diversity it is the Government which sets the rules. Government also has indicated that the media are different from other commodities and the application of competition principles is radically different here. As it put it in its 1995 proposals on media ownership:

[g]eneral competition legislation is mainly concerned with securing economic objectives, although it can also encompass other non-economic objectives. However, wider objectives are important so far as the media are concerned. A free and diverse media are an indispensable part of the democratic process. They provide the multiplicity of voices and opinions that informs the public, influences opinion, and engenders political debate. They promote the culture of dissent which any healthy democracy must have. In so doing, they contribute to the cultural fabric of the nation and help define our sense of identity and purpose. . . . Special media ownership rules, which exist in all major media markets, are needed therefore to provide the safeguards necessary to maintain diversity and plurality.[39]

This approach was strongly endorsed by the ITC.

It has been a constant theme of this book that social obligations exist for the utilities and other regulated industries as well; the area of commercial broadcasting is of particular interest, as the existence of such requirements is much more fully recognized and institutionalized here. How does this institutionalization take place? In the following sections I will examine the form of regulation related to regulation for competition discussed in earlier chapters, but here concerned with maintaining diversity, the role of public-service obligations for broadcasters, and finally the procedures used by the ITC in undertaking its various tasks.

Regulation for Diversity

In this section it will be possible to summarize only briefly the complex provision dealing with issues of media ownership; it must always be borne in mind that the aim of these controls is not simply maintaining fair competition but also maintaining diversity of information. The ordinary competition authorities retain a role; for example, the Office of Fair Trading has examined the relationship between BSkyB and the cable companies to which its sells packages

---

[39] Department of National Heritage, *Media Ownership: The Government's Proposals*, Cm 2872 (1995), para. 1.4.

of programmes, and it was noted above that the MMC was also involved in the Channel 3 networking arrangements; ordinary competition regulation has also set a limit of 25 per cent on concentration of airtime sales within ITV. As regards ownership matters, until the 1990s takeover and merger activity in commercial television was effectively banned. The 1990 Broadcasting Act did however permit it, subject to complex rules contained in both primary and secondary legislation attempting to limit concentration of ownership.[40] For example, when the first Channel 3 licences were allocated in 1991 it was not possible to control two licences if both were large or if they were contiguous. As regards cross-media ownership, national newspaper owners could control only up to 20 per cent of one licensee in terrestrial television, radio, or domestic satellite broadcasting.

The rules were quickly and progressively relaxed. After the award of the Channel 3 licences the ban on contiguous licences was lifted, and from the end of 1993 the ban on the holding of more than one large licence was also lifted (except for the London companies). A moratorium on takeovers and mergers without ITC consent also lapsed at the end of 1993, and substantial merger and takeover activity occurred, so that by mid-1995 four groups accounted for 82 per cent of total Channel 3 advertising revenue; the largest of the eight other licensees had only 6 per cent of revenue.[41] Strong pressure came from the companies for the rules to be relaxed further to allow the establishment of large multi-media groups able to compete effectively in the international markets; a consultation paper was issued in the summer of 1995, as noted above, and important changes were made in the Broadcasting Act 1996.[42] Once more the rules are too complex to permit more than a brief summary here, but they abolish the limit of two Channel 3 licences and replace it with a limit of 15 per cent of the total television audience; most newspapers will no longer be restricted in their ownership of broadcasting licences, although newspaper groups with 20 per cent or more of national circulation will continue to be restricted to 20 per cent holdings in Channel 3 licences, and other newspaper acquisitions in broadcast-

---

[40] See Broadcasting Act 1990, sched. 2, and the Broadcasting (Restriction on the Holding of Licences) Order, SI 1176/1991.

[41] ITC, *Media Ownership: ITC Response to the Government's Proposals* (1995), para. 7.

[42] Broadcasting Act 1996, s. 73 and sched. 2.

ing will be subject to a public-interest test based on issues of plurality of ownership, diversity of information sources, economic benefits and effects, and the proper operation of markets. The rules will be enforced by the ITC, which will also be responsible for undertaking the public-interest test. A new definition of control has also been introduced to permit greater discretion to the ITC and to prevent evasion of the existing test.[43]

Very special rules apply to broadcasting, then, which do not simply operate to protect open markets but have a strong social justification in ensuring diversity of programming and information sources; the continued existence of this type of regulation has been accepted by government even in a media world of rapid and far-reaching technological and economic change. In this case we see a type of merging of regulation for competition and social regulation; restrictions on media concentrations can be justified on both grounds.

Public-service Broadcasting and Auctioning Licences

It will already be evident from the description of the legislation above that elements of public-service broadcasting play an important role in the duties of the ITC.[44] The concept of public-service broadcasting is extremely difficult to define, having different meanings in different nations and being implemented in various ways including public ownership, restricted competition, regulation, and indeed through cultural expectations. The nearest thing to a definition came from the Home Affairs Select Committee in 1988; the principles underlying public-service broadcasting included universal service, freedom of broadcasters from direct governmental intervention, provision of a service which should inform and educate as well as entertain, and programmes which should cover a wide and balanced range of subject matter in order to meet all interests in the population (a different form of universal service).[45] Something was

---

[43] Broadcasting Act 1996, s. 78, and for the previous difficulties in the analogous area of radio regulation see *R.* v. *Radio Authority, ex parte Guardian Media Group plc.* [1995] 2 All ER 139.

[44] For a general account of public service broadcasting in the UK see Prosser, T., 'Public Service Broadcasting and Deregulation in the UK' (1992) 7 *European Journal of Communication* 173–93.

[45] Home Affairs Committee, *The Future of Broadcasting*, HC 262, 1987–8, paras. 11–16.

said already about the nature of the obligations of public-service broadcasting when the legislation was discussed above, and more will be said when the ITC's code-making is analysed below. Further examples of the protection of such broadcasting include ensuring the availability of certain key sporting events for terrestrial public-service broadcasters and the requirement that public-service broadcasters are given access to digital services.[46] One particularly interesting example of the implementation of public-service requirements occurred in the process of awarding Channel 3 licences by auction in 1991, and this will be analysed in more depth as it shows the interaction of market and social criteria most vividly; it will also provide an opportunity to ask whether administrative discretion can be replaced by a system of competitive bidding. Before discussing these questions directly, it is necessary to describe the background to the allocation.

As was described earlier, the plan set out in the 1988 White Paper was for the licences for Channel 3 to be auctioned to bidders who had passed a quality threshold satisfying the Commission that they would be able to comply with programming requirements; the initial assumption was that the market would be the main determinant of outcomes, with the quality threshold a residual device to exclude only particularly low-quality bids. This created considerable controversy and opposition, as it was felt that it would make the production of high-quality programmes impossible, because companies would spend the bulk of their resources in the cash bid so as to be sure of winning the licence, leaving little available for expensive programmes. In the face of these criticisms, the proposals were amended in a number of respects. First, rather than taking the form a simple cash bid, the payment was to consist of a proportion of revenue and index-linked annual cash payments. Secondly, the ITC was given financial sanctions against breaches of licence condition.[47] Most important, however, was the strengthening of the quality threshold and the inclusion of a power not to award a licence to the highest bidder in exceptional circumstances. Thus for Channel 3 the ITC was required to publish details of the quality threshold and to examine the applicant's business plan to ensure that it was adequate to support services which pass the threshold, and would continue to be adequate during the period of

---

[46] Broadcasting Act 1996, ss. 28–31 and 97–105.
[47] Broadcasting Act 1990, s. 41.

the licence. Statutory requirements to be incorporated in the threshold included the provision of high-quality news, current affairs, and other programmes, of regional programmes and of programmes calculated to appeal to a wide variety of tastes and interests, together with the inclusion of a proper proportion of material of European origin and the acquisition of not less than 25 per cent of programmes from independent producers; this is in addition to the general statutory requirements outlined above.[48] It was also provided that a licence might be awarded to other than the highest bidder 'where there are exceptional circumstances which make it appropriate' for such an award to be made; exceptional circumstances explicitly included a case where it appeared to the ITC that the quality of service proposed was exceptionally high, and substantially higher than that proposed by the highest bidder. The ITC was obliged to give reasons for the use of this last provision.[49]

In fact, the details published by the ITC suggested that the quality threshold would be considerably more demanding than that suggested by the statutory requirements; indeed, they explicitly stated that compliance with the statutory provisions alone would not be regarded as sufficient to pass the threshold, and imposed a number of other requirements. For example, at least 65 per cent of programming would be expected to be originally produced or commissioned; in addition 'the ITC will also wish to be satisfied so far as possible that the talents and abilities of the applicant's team are capable of supporting his aspirations for the service. Financial, engineering and general management will need to be taken into account, as well as the creative skills relevant to making and/or commissioning programmes'.[50] Very importantly, the ITC also made it clear that it would need to be convinced that financial resources would be adequate to support the quality service through out the period of the licence.[51]

It proved possible, then, to incorporate into the award of licences quite demanding quality requirements through a combination of statute and administrative policy-making; something similar also took place for Channel 5, though for this and for domestic satellite services the quality threshold is weaker, and for other satellite and

---

[48] Broadcasting Act 1990, s. 16.　　　　[49] Broadcasting Act 1990, s. 17.
[50] ITC, *Invitation to Apply for Regional Channel 3 Licences* (1991), paras. 80–1.
[51] This was in fact required by statute; Broadcasting Act 1990, s. 16(1)(a).

cable services no such threshold exists.[52] How were the quality requirements implemented in practice in the award of the licences?[53]

On the announcement of the results of the bidding process, two things were immediately apparent. The first was the extensive use of the quality threshold. In only half of the sixteen licensing decisions did the ITC in fact award the licence to the highest bidder. The others (including two existing franchise holders) were disqualified at the quality threshold stage; no use of the exceptional circumstances powers was made, and so no reasons had to be given for the decisions. Secondly, the amount of the successful bids was arbitrary. It is important to note that the bids were secret so the process did not take the form of a true auction, but of 'blind bidding' in which the size of offers made by competitors was unknown to each applicant. The highest bid was by TVS, a franchise holder which had experienced serious business and financing problems, and was for £59,728,000. This was disqualified through use of the quality threshold, but the highest successful bid was for £43,170,000 for the London weekday licence. By contrast, two of the existing franchise holders gambled correctly that their bids would be unopposed, and so put in very low offers of £2,000 per year, one of these being for Central, one of the most important licences. As there was no reserve price set, both of these bids were accepted. These arbitrary valuations of licences led to a report by stockbrokers on the process to describe it as 'possibly the most ludicrous in corporate history'.[54]

Any expectation that the auctioning process as employed here would replace administrative discretion with the formal rationality of the market proved to be ill-founded; the existence of the quality threshold proved of the utmost importance in the allocation of licences. Once more social aspects of regulation have proved to be more important than those which are essentially economic. Is this due to the peculiar circumstances of television, or of this allocation? It has been suggested that this is so:

it would be misleading to suppose that the same difficulties would inevitably occur in the allocation by tender of more easily definable licences

---

[52] Broadcasting Act 1990, ss. 29, 46, 47, 75.

[53] For an account of the auction process see Cave, M., and Williamson, P., 'The Reregulation of British Broadcasting' in Bishop, M., Kay, J., and Mayer, C. (eds.), *The Regulatory Challenge* (OUP, Oxford, 1995), 160–90, 170–87.

[54] 'Bids for TV Franchises Face Harsh Criteria', *Financial Times*, 12 Aug. 1991.

requiring less subsequent regulatory enforcement. For example, there is little reason to suppose that the difficulties attending the Channel 3 licence auction, which arose from an uneasy combination of competitive bidding and regulatory disqualification, would arise in the case of airport take-off slots or the radio spectrum.[55]

This may be the case in those two examples, but, as this book has shown, most of the regulatory areas covered involve, like television, a complex interaction of social and economic matters. The social principles may be more firmly embedded in legislation in the case of television, but are likely to arise in any of the other areas previously discussed; indeed, they have already done so in the franchising of rail services, the procedure closest to that for the allocation of Channel 3 licences, and I have already noted in Chapter 7 the problems concerning the rail minimum service levels. In television, the procedure was used again for Channel 5 with a weaker quality threshold, but the licence was not awarded to the sole applicant after it experienced financing difficulties. The process of bidding was then repeated and four bids received, the highest being of £36,261,158 and the joint second bids being of £22,002,000 each. The ITC awarded the licence to one of the second highest bidders, the highest being rejected on quality and diversity grounds. However, the plans for the allocation of licences for digital terrestrial television do not include sale to the highest bidder; instead the ITC is to assess applications on merit, with the overriding criterion being which bidder will do most to promote digital terrestrial broadcasting.[56] This must represent the final recognition that the auction process adopted in 1991 was deeply inappropriate.

Regulatory Procedures: Licensing

It should be clear that the attempt to move the emphasis from administrative discretion to market allocation in the 1991 licence allocation was unsuccessful; the process remained essentially one of discretion based on public-service requirements. This then makes it necessary to examine the procedures adopted for the allocation of the licences, both in terms of involvement of a broader public and of fairness to competing applicants. The ITC has engaged in a

[55] Cave and Williamson, n. 53 above, 186–7.
[56] Department of National Heritage, *Digital Terrestrial Broadcasting*, Cm 2946 (1995); Broadcasting Act 1996, Pt. I.

degree of public consultation. In the 1991 allocation of licences, the parts of the applications concerned with proposals for the service and the composition and identity of applicants were placed in 275 public libraries; the business plans of applicants remained confidential, however. Summaries of applications were made available by the ITC; 21,250 were requested, and comments were received from 2,278 individuals, companies, and organizations.[57] In the case of Channel 5, the reselection after the failure to attract a suitable bid involved the publication of similar details of each application; the size of the cash bid was made public, though not the business plan, and comments were invited; 353 were received. Reasons for the decision were also made publicly available.[58]

In examining fairness to competing applicants, it will be recalled that the procedures of the Commission's predecessor had been subjected to a barrage of criticism; indeed, the move to the auction system could be seen as a means of replacing the uncertainties and unpredictability of administrative allocation by the objective hand of the market-place, though this was not achieved and procedures remained crucial. In the licence allocation the lack of formal procedural protection was once more striking. Thus the duty to give reasons applied only to the use of the discretion to reject in exceptional circumstances the highest bid which had passed the quality threshold, and, as we saw, this power was not employed. Rejections at the quality threshold stage did not carry any such duty. Similarly, no provision was made for hearings before decisions were taken. Several of the rejected applicants attempted to challenge the procedures adopted by the ITC through judicial review, and one case reached the House of Lords.[59] The Commission had rejected the applicant's bid as it considered that it would be unable to support a quality service throughout the period of the licence. However, it refused to give reasons and refused to supply the applicant with the criteria to be used to judge financial viability; the Commission did, however, agree to grant an oral interview and, partly as a result of remarks made at the interview, judicial review proceedings were commenced. The Court of Appeal considered

[57] ITC, *Annual Report 1991*, 11.

[58] ITC, *New Channel 5 Licence: Your Chance to Comment* (1995) and *ITC Announces its Decision to Award Channel 5 Licence* (1995).

[59] *R.* v. *Independent Television Commission, ex parte TSW Broadcasting Ltd*, [1996] EMLR 291; see also Prosser, T., 'The House of Lords and Channel 3 Licences: The *TSW* Decision' (1992) 3 *Utilities Law Review* 47–50.

that reasons should be given to permit the court to review properly; the House of Lords also considered that reasons should have been given, at least to a franchise holder with reason to believe it was the highest bidder. The House stated clearly that the Commission is subject to the rules of natural justice, although, apart from invalidating decisions actuated by malice, it is unclear what the content of the rules would be in this context as no oral hearing was required, and indeed none had been given, before the decision had been made. On substantive grounds, however, the House did not accept that there were any grounds for granting judicial review and rejected the application. On the second award of the Channel 5 licence reasons were given, and all three unsuccessful applicants brought applications for judicial review against the Commission. Leave was granted to one on the ground that it was arguable that statutory requirements had been misapplied and that the successful bidder had been permitted to enhance its bid after the application had been made; the other two were permitted to be heard at the full hearing. However, the court rejected the application, stressing its reluctance to interfere with substantive decisions of the Commission;

we do not regard the Commission's judgment . . . as being in any sense 'readily reviewable' . . . Here, matters of judgment were entrusted to an expert body by Parliament. That body was also made responsible for finding the facts on which such judgment would be based, in circumstances where the level of the quality threshold was to be set by the Commission and no one else. Of its nature such an exercise is, as Mr Sumption submitted, judgmental in character and, therefore, one upon which opinions may readily differ. . . . It has to follow that a very heavy burden falls on the party seeking to upset a qualitative judgment of the nature described and arrived at by the qualified and experienced body which is the Commission.[60]

The case for review on substantive grounds did appear weak in all the cases, and what was more important, especially in the House of Lords decision, was the move towards requiring some degree of procedural protection by the court; this did indeed lead to reasons being given for the Channel 5 decisions. The issue will only arise in its strongest form for Channels 3 and 5 if it is proposed not to renew a licence in the future, takeovers rather than wholesale

---

[60] *R.* v. *Independent Television Commission, ex parte Virgin Television Ltd* [1996] EMLR 318.

licence reallocation having now become the means of reorganization in the industry, though similar considerations may come into play in the award of digital licences. At last the courts appear to have accepted that some procedural protections should be afforded while sensibly avoiding second-guessing the substantive decisions; in view of the analysis offered in earlier chapters, this could offer a model for judicial supervision of other types of regulation.

Regulatory Procedures: Licence Enforcement and Performance Review

Given the importance of the programming requirements and other obligations (including ownership restrictions) incorporated into the licences it is clearly of the utmost importance that the means exist for their enforcement, especially given that the possibility of takeover makes the licences effectively tradable. The ITC was given a range of sanctions, including for the first time financial penalties for breach of licence condition.[61] Where a takeover is proposed, the Commission, whilst not having a simple power of veto over it, must be satisfied that the new owner will be able to comply with licence conditions, and is able to include in a licence conditions enabling it to revoke the licence in the case of a change of control which would have led it not to grant a licence to the new owner, for example doubt about compliance with the quality threshold or about financial sustainability.[62] The first merger was the acquisition of Tyne Tees by Yorkshire; this was approved by the ITC after assurances had been given that licence conditions would continue to be met and that the programme services of both companies would be strengthened, particularly in relation to regional programmes. However, in the following year the Commission had to intervene when changes were contemplated in management which might have undermined Tyne Tees' position as the holder of a separate licence; after detailed discussions a reallocation of management responsibilities consistent with the licence was agreed.[63] After the Secretary of State had loosened ownership restrictions, three mergers in the following year were also approved after the ITC had received the assurances it had requested. The 1996 Act strengthens the ITC's

[61] Broadcasting Act 1990, s. 41.
[62] Broadcasting Act 1990, ss. 3(6)–(7), 5(5)–(7).
[63] ITC, *Annual Report 1992*, 5; *Annual Report 1993*, 4.

powers by requiring it to be given advance notice of proposals which might result in a change of control of a company; if it appears that this may be prejudicial to the quality or range of programmes offered, it shall vary the licence to provide new conditions preventing this.[64]

When I turn now to the more general use of financial sanctions outside the context of takeovers, the first example occurred in 1994 when Granada was fined £500,000 for repeated breach of the programme and sponsorship code requirements on undue product prominence and competitions after a formal warning. A further controversial issue in relation to which the potential use of enforcement powers was important was that of the timing of *News at Ten*. When changes to this timing were proposed, the ITC wrote to the companies pointing out that this would need ITC approval as it was in breach of commitments by at least some of the companies. The proposed change was strongly opposed by the National Heritage Committee of the House of Commons and indeed by the Prime Minister and was dropped, though it has shown signs of returning to the agenda.[65]

Much more important than the individual examples of enforcement have been the annual performance reviews carried out by the Commission from 1993. The reviews permit an overall view to be taken of the performance of the companies licensed by the ITC, rather than sporadic details becoming available relating to particular problems; they are drawn up with the assistance of audience research and of the viewer consultative committees and regional councils, and inform Commission annual assessments of licensee performance each year. Copies are sent to licensees in order that checking for factual errors can take place before publication. The first set of reviews covering 1993 dealt with the content of programme services, compliance, technical standards, subtitling for the deaf, training, and equal opportunities as well as including an assessment of the overall performance of the ITV network. It included the identification of specific deficiencies in the performance of two companies. The overall conclusion was that '[a]lthough many individual programmes and series displayed high quality production standards and creative ability the overall feel of the network schedule was cautious and predictable. There was little

---

[64] Broadcasting Act 1996, s. 67.
[65] National Heritage Committee, *News At Ten*, HC 799, 1992–3.

evidence of adventure or the surprise of one-off events.'[66] The 1994 review covered a similar range of matters, noting significant improvements in the performance of the companies criticized a year earlier and a generally more confident performance by ITV. A sufficiently wide range of programmes was offered to meet the requirement of diversity in the statute and licences, although lack of innovations and religious programmes remained areas for concern.[67] The review of performance in 1995 expressed some concerns about scheduling of regional programmes and levels of co-production in them, and observed a noticeable shift in the balance of programmes towards more entertainment-led programmes and away from documentary and arts output. A further criticism was a preoccupation with the work of the police and emergency services, both in drama and documentary programmes.[68] My brief summaries can give only a mere taste of the reviews, which cover the performance of each licensee in detail, including training, equal opportunities, provision for the deaf, and the handling of complaints. These regular and wide-ranging analyses permit a much more informed and developed assessment to be made of performance of the regulated industries than is the case for other areas of regulation, and could easily be adopted in them. It could be argued that they would be inappropriate where competition can perform a similar task; however, we have seen that, in the case of every utility, large areas remain where competition will not do this adequately and more information could effectively be made public in such a regular and developed form.

Regulatory Procedures: Code-Making

In examining civil aviation in the previous chapter we found that the CAA draws up and publishes a periodic statement of policies. This is far more developed in the case of the ITC. The provisions in the statute largely reflect those applying to its predecessor. Thus the Commission is required to draw up, and from time to time review, a code of guidance on the rules relating to the inclusion of violence in programmes, on the inclusion in programmes of appeals for donations, and on other matters it considers appropriate.[69] It is

[66] ITC, *1993 Performance Reviews* (1994), 2.
[67] ITC, *1994 Performance Reviews* (1995).
[68] ITC, *1995 Performance Reviews* (1996).   [69] Broadcasting Act 1990, s. 7.

also required to draw up and review a code relating to advertising and sponsorship, in this case after consulting licence holders and representatives of viewers, advertisers, and professional organizations.[70] Finally, it is obliged to draw up a code relating to the preservation of due impartiality in programming.[71] Enforcement of the codes is through their observance being required as a licence condition.

The code-making provisions have been used as the basis for extensive rule-making by the ITC. Thus the current version of the programme code is a lengthy and detailed document, including both very general principles ('material unsuitable for children must not be broadcast at times when large numbers of children are likely to be watching') and detailed rules ('[r]eports should not, even where the law does not prohibit it, identify living children under 16 who are involved in police enquiries or court proceedings concerning sexual offences, whether as victims or as witnesses or as defendants').[72] It both restates statutory requirements, including, for example, those relating to elections under the Representation of the People Act 1983, and indicates how the ITC will normally exercise its discretion; for example, in the context of recorded entertainment programmes, '[p]rogrammes not used immediately should be checked before transmission to ensure that any content is not rendered tasteless by intervening events, such as death, injury or other misfortune'.[73] The Code is periodically revised and updated to take account of changing circumstances. In addition there are similarly detailed codes on advertising and on sponsorship, again ranging from the statement of broad general principles ('[t]elevision advertising should be legal, decent, honest and truthful') to detail (full appendices are devoted to special rules relating to advertising and children, financial advertising, and advertising of medicines and treatments).[74] The use of code-making in this way to flesh out statutory obligations and to give an indication of how discretion is to be exercised is also something which could be adopted by other regulators. In particular, the issues dealt with in the codes, such as portrayal of violence or sex, impartiality, and advertising control, are

---

[70] Broadcasting Act 1990, s. 9.   [71] Broadcasting Act 1990, s. 6(3), (5)–(7).
[72] ITC, *The ITC Programme Code* (1995), paras. 1.5, 2.7.
[73] *Ibid.* sect. 4 and para. 1.4(iv).
[74] ITC, *The ITC Code of Advertising Standards and Practice* (1995); *The ITC Code of Programme Sponsorship* (1994).

inherently controversial and inspire strong judgements; yet it has proved perfectly possible to develop successful codes relating to them. It is hard to see why this would not be possible in relation to other regulatory areas, for example public-service requirements for the utilities. We have seen moves towards this with the issue of detailed consultative documents by OFTEL; the codes discussed here represent a statement of the outcome of such a process in a relatively detailed and accessible form.

Conclusion

The history of regulation of independent television in the United Kingdom has not been a happy one. The ITC's predecessor suffered much justified criticism because of its failures to observe fair procedures or to provide proper rational justification for its decisions; the auction process in 1991 proved a fiasco. The first lesson is indeed that it is impossible to reduce social obligations to such residual 'consumer protection obligations' as to make an auction a feasible replacement for administrative discretion; in both the allocation of Channel 3 licences and the more recent allocation of those for Channel 5 the outcome was determined more by discretionary decisions on quality matters than by bidding in the market-place. More important than the move to bidding in improving the transparency of the allocation process has been the role of the courts in requiring reasons to be given, though they have wisely adopted a relatively undemanding standard of substantive review. There are also a number of more positive lessons to be learned. The first is that it has proved perfectly possible to develop a set of statutory obligations implementing the norms of public-service television and that these can be developed in detail through code-making. This is despite the inherent controversy of norms in this area, and does not prevent the ITC from having an approach which is broadly supportive of increased competition. Secondly, the use of general performance reviews has offered a far more sophisticated way of assessing the performance of regulated enterprises than does sporadic enforcement action or complaint handling. We simply know much more about the activities of the regulated companies here than we do for any other industry analysed in this book.

The most important difficulty encountered here is that of regulatory complexity; there is no clear pattern to the distribution of responsibilities between a plethora of different regulatory bodies, and the changes made by the Broadcasting Act 1996 will affect only the margins of this. To a large extent, the regulatory structure is still technology based, distinguishing telecommunications, television, radio, and other forms of delivery. Yet, as the Director General of Telecommunications has stressed, regulation should be based on markets, not on technologies, and convergence of means of delivery results in our moving rapidly towards a single communications market subdivided in ways which do not correspond to existing regulatory distinctions.[75] This raises questions of regulatory structure which go far beyond those encountered earlier in this book.

---

[75] Cruikshank, D., 'Regulation for Convergence' in Collins, R. (ed.), *Converging Media? Converging Regulation?*, n. 16 above, 11–14. For a detailed account of the effects of convergence see Goldberg, D., Prosser, T., and Verhulst, S., *The Impact of New Communications Technologies on Media Concentrations and Pluralism* (Council of Europe, Strasbourg, 1977).

10

Alternatives and Conclusions

The preceding chapters have described the legal mandates of the British economic regulators and the ways in which they actually carry out their tasks. A central theme is that both the legal mandates and the operational practice suggest that regulation is a complex task, irreducible to a single goal of efficiency maximization. In particular, three different regulatory tasks should be recognized; regulating monopoly, regulation for competition, and social regulation, especially in the form of universal service. These different tasks may have contradictory policy implications; as a result it is necessary to conceive of regulators as 'governments in miniature' whose decisions cannot be predetermined by rules or by economic technique. This of course raises the problem of regulatory legitimacy. In this Chapter I shall assess possible alternatives to the present regulatory structure to see if they have the potential to resolve more successfully the legitimacy deficit which, as we saw in Chapter 2, has been identified by a number of commentators. First I shall ask whether we can simply dispense with the existing regulatory structures in favour of other controls. The second, and longest, section of the Chapter will attempt to learn from overseas experience, both in the United States and in Europe, something which was signally ignored when the regulators were established. Finally, I shall address more particular changes which have been proposed within the existing institutional structures.

Alternatives to Regulation: Nationalization

One possible solution which could be conceived as resolving the legitimacy problems would be to renationalize those enterprises which have been made subject to regulation, as well as, presumably, nationalizing those such as independent television which have always been regulated whilst in private hands. This is of course not on the political agenda in Britain and goes against current tendencies almost everywhere else, and so an easy way of dismissing this solution would be simply to suggest that it is outside the realms of practical politics. This may be true, but it may not always be so. It is thus essential to stress that, even should nationalization return to the political agenda, the regulatory problems described in this book will continue. As was briefly described in Chapter 2, earlier experience of nationalization (particularly in the United Kingdom) was dogged by uncertainty of purpose, lack of clarity in relations with government, and institutional structures far from any satisfactory model of public accountability.[1] Indeed, as is evident from discussion in the previous chapters, we know far more about the operation of the privatized but regulated industries than we did when they were under public ownership, and when, for example, pricing decisions were made in private negotiations between government and enterprise. To stress the point very simply, public ownership does not itself *in any way* create public accountability or responsiveness to consumers; it all depends on the institutional structures adopted. As a result, should nationalization return to the political agenda, it will not be to solve problems of regulation but adopted for other reasons, such as employment relations or support for strategic investment. This will mean that something resembling the present regulatory structures will have to be retained, and so legitimacy questions will continue to pose themselves. This is reinforced by experience with the largest remaining public enterprise in the United Kingdom, the Post Office, where relations with government have continued to pose serious problems and calls have been made for an independent regulator whether or not privatization should take place.[2] The recent Labour Party interest in regulation rather than nationalization is in this sense merely a recognition of the inevitable.[3]

---

[1] For further details see Prosser, T., *Nationalised Industries and Public Control* (Blackwell, Oxford, 1986) and National Economic Development Office, *A Study of UK Nationalised Industries* (HMSO, London, 1976).

[2] See the Trade and Industry Committee, *The Post Office*, HC 170, 1994–5, paras. 11, 22, supporting proposals put forward by consultants commissioned by unions and by the Post Office Users' National Council.

[3] See, e.g., The Labour Party, *The Road to the Manifesto: Competition and Trade* (The Labour Party, London, 1996), and Short, C., *The Future for Rail*, speech delivered at Swindon, 29 Mar. 1996 (The Labour Party, London, 1996).

Alternatives to Regulation: No Regulation or Self-regulation

A diametrically opposed solution sometimes proposed is that of simply doing without regulatory institutions and leaving matters to the market-place; an example sometimes suggested is that of New Zealand.[4] This suggestion can also be quickly disposed of. As we have seen, regulation is not an intrusion on a naturally self-regulating market-place, but is necessary to limit monopoly power and to create and police the conditions for effective competition; this is true even if one rejects social regulation as an appropriate goal. Regulation for competition is particularly important; even if monopoly is broken up (and this is unlikely to occur in several areas we have discussed, such as water, rail, electricity transmission, and gas transportation), continuing regulation is needed to maintain competitive conditions. The reference to New Zealand experience is misleading in several ways. First, it is not true that the absence of specialist regulators there means an absence of regulation. Most importantly, privatization has been accompanied by the creation of a 'kiwi share', similar in some respects to the 'golden shares' of the United Kingdom in giving the Government special powers over the enterprise. In the case of New Zealand Telecom, for example, this goes much further than the UK examples in requiring free local calls, imposing a price cap, and requiring service to continue to be available as widely as at the time of privatization.[5] In addition, legislation has given the minister power to control prices of goods and services in markets where competition is limited. It is unlikely that such powers will be used in the present climate, as a leading commentator has pointed out; however, the Privy Council has used the existence of the power as a reason for refusing to treat other legislative provisions as limiting monopoly rents.[6] Indeed, the latter case makes an important policy point

[4] There is already a considerable literature on the New Zealand experience: see, e.g., Duncan, I., and Bollard, A., *Corporatisation and Privatisation: Lessons from New Zealand* (OUP, Oxford, 1992).

[5] Articles of Association of Telecom Corporation of New Zealand Ltd, Art. 11.4.2; see Taggart, M., 'Corporatisation, Privatisation and Public Law' (1991) 2 *Public Law Review* 98–100.

[6] Commerce Act 1988, Pt. IV; see Taggart, M., 'Public Utilities and Public Law' in Joseph, P. A., *Essays on the Constitution* (Brooker's, Wellington, 1995), 214–64, 258–9; *Telecom Corporation of New Zealand* v. *Clear Communications Ltd* (PC), 19 Oct. 1994 (LEXIS).

through showing that, if regulatory structures are not created, disputes such as those concerning interconnection (with which the case was concerned) will inevitably end up in the courts for resolution. History suggests that the common law courts are the least suitable place for such issues to be determined; this was reinforced in the Privy Council decision itself, in which the Council noted that proceedings at first instance had lasted some thirty-seven days and 'would echo the sentiments of the courts below as to the sterility of these proceedings which, having been pursued right through the appeal procedure, still do not determine the terms' of interconnection.'[7]

A related claim is that the regulatory institutions described in this book can be replaced by some form of self-regulation. Indeed, a sophisticated and convincing case has been made for the development of 'enforced self-regulation' involving negotiation between the state and individual firms to establish appropriate standards and regulations, which can then be publicly enforced.[8] However, to propose self-regulation as an *alternative* to the sort of regulatory institutions described in this book is to miss the point. Self-regulation is a *technique*, not a prescription for overall institutional design. Enforced self-regulation is in fact one of the techniques used by the existing regulators through, for example, the delegation of the setting of service standards to the companies themselves and requiring them to establish grievance procedures considered satisfactory by the regulator. Similarly, moves towards supporting universal service through a fund from which contributions are awarded competitively is a solution with self-regulatory characteristics through minimizing direct regulatory interventions. However, in other respects self-regulatory techniques are likely to prove unsatisfactory because of the existence of strong public-interest elements in matters such as price control, and because of the existence of divergent interests on the part of different firms in relation to regulation for competition; thus the issues at stake are not suitable for delegation to the firm in the way in which, for example, the setting of health and safety standards may be.[9] In this respect, it is noteworthy that,

[7] *Telecom Corporation of New Zealand*, n. 6 above.

[8] Ayres, I., and Braithwaite, J., *Responsive Regulation: Transcending the Deregulation Debate* (OUP, Oxford, 1992). See also Michael, D. C., 'Federal Agency Use of Audited Self-regulation as a Regulatory Technique' (1995) 47 *Administrative Law Review* 171–253.

[9] Cf. Ayres and Braithwaite, n. 8 above, 102.

whilst regulators have adopted an increasingly participatory style, they have not been prepared to engage in unilateral negotiation with regulated firms; thus in the case of the periodic review of water and sewage charges, '[t]here were no negotiations with OFWAT. Following submission of the SBPs [Company Strategic Business Plans], each company had a single formal meeting with the DG in June/July 1994 to make representations on the draft Determination issued in May.'[10] A further point to be considered is that where an apparently self-regulatory style has been adopted in regulation of the UK financial services industry, it has moved rapidly closer to direct statutory regulation; as the Treasury and Civil Service Committee put it in its report on the regulation of financial services, '*[t]he evidence we have received from the regulators has . . . stressed that the term "self regulation" is a misnomer and fails to reflect their independence or the statutory basis of their authority.*'[11] My conclusion must then be that, although self-regulation as a set of techniques has much to offer in particular areas of regulation examined in this book, for example setting of quality standards and delivery of universal service, as a regulatory or institutional style it cannot be a replacement for the regulation we have examined. Indeed, this reinforces the argument made in Chapters 1 and 2 above for a plurality of regulatory styles and objectives.

Alternatives to Regulation: Leaving Regulation to Domestic Competition Law

An alternative approach would acknowledge the necessity for continuing regulation of a pro-competitive kind but would deny that this implies the retention of industry-specific or sector-specific regulators. Instead, it might be suggested that the existing body of domestic competition law could perform this task. In fact, this is closer to the experience in New Zealand than is the model discussed above as, when privatization took place there, the Commerce Commission was to be the institution ensuring fair competition.[12]

---

[10] Smith, J., 'Water Service 1994—A Watershed Year' in Centre for the Study of Regulated Industries, *Regulatory Review 1995* (Centre for the Study of Regulated Industries, London, 1995), 105–29, 109.

[11] Treasury and Civil Service Committee, *The Regulation of Financial Services in the UK*, HC 332, 1994–5, para. 25 (emphasis retained).

[12] Any confidence that the Commission could act as a watchdog in particular sectors in a way similar to an industry specific regulator was short-lived: see *Commerce*

There are however at least three good reasons why this would not work in the United Kingdom. First, experience in the one area in which no specific regulator has been created, that of bus services, suggests that the competition authorities are quite unsuited to the role, both by reason of lack of expertise and because of inadequate powers to provide rapid remedies to prevent anti-competitive practices. Indeed, as was documented in Chapter 7 above, both the Director General of Fair Trading and the MMC have themselves called for the creation of a specialist regulator for the bus industry.

Secondly, it has become clear above that regulation for competition is merely one of several types of regulation. Regulation of monopoly has required scrutiny of particular enterprises which is constant and close; any suggestion that it can be reduced to periodic reviews of a mechanistic pricing formula is manifestly false. The MMC has of course played an important role in the process where the pricing formulae and other licence modifications cannot be agreed, and this has included laying down guidelines for the future. Nevertheless, it has acted as a long stop in particular cases, rather than being involved in the detailed day-to-day monitoring of the industries which has increasingly had to be carried out by the regulators. It could be argued that this type of regulation is withering away with the growth of competition; however it is highly unlikely that we shall see such withering away in relation to water, or gas transportation, or the railways; in all these cases regulation of monopoly will continue for the foreseeable future. Moreover, if the argument of this book is accepted, social regulation has also played an important role, and it is unclear how well the competition authorities are placed to handle this.

Finally, even where it is desirable and feasible *in principle* to transfer responsibility to the competition authorities, there are such serious problems with their operation that it is unattractive as a practical option. This can only be underlined by the fact that the Director General of Telecommunications, in proposing a standard licence condition outlawing anti-competitive practices, chose to base it on European Union law rather than on domestic competition law. A flavour of recent criticism can be gathered from a report of the Trade and Industry Select Committee on monopolies policy:

Commission of New Zealand v. *Telecom Corporation of New Zealand Ltd* (1994) 5 NZBLC 103, 431; and Taggart (1995), n. 6 above, 258.

the effectiveness of current monopoly policy can be judged, among other ways, by the criteria set out in the Government's White Paper on competitiveness. It is impossible to conclude that the current situation would score highly on any of the four criteria of respected and trusted, lean, clear or consistently applied. It is understandable that those involved in controversial cases would have complaints against the system. We accept that MMC inquiries cause much debate by their very nature and that the outcome will not satisfy all parties. Nevertheless, the degree of resentment is alarming and many of the criticisms appear to be well-founded.[13]

The report concluded that '[o]ur inquiry into UK policy on monopolies has highlighted major weaknesses in both the procedures and the underlying approach to monopoly investigations' and recommended reforms in both substantive law and procedure.[14] These were however rejected so thoroughly by the Government that the Committee issued a report stating that:

[w]e do not consider that the Government's response adequately addresses our recommendations and the evidence and arguments on which they are based. . . . No answer is therefore given to the charges against the current system made by those who have undergone MMC investigations. Their deep discontent is ignored. The need for transparency and openness in particular has not been recognised.[15]

Instead, reforms were proposed for competition law which would have introduced a prohibition-based approach closer to that of Community law in relation to anti-competitive agreements; however, reform of the law relating to abuse of market power (far more of a problem in the utilities sector) was not to be implemented in the legislative package, though the Director General of Fair Trading was to be given power to impose interim measures in monopoly and anti-competitive practices cases, and this power was to be shared with the utility regulators where they have concurrent jurisdiction with him.[16] Even these reforms are in doubt, however, as the Bill was not included in the 1996 Queen's Speech. The avail-

---

[13] Trade and Industry Committee, *UK Policy on Monopolies*, HC 249, 1994–5, para. 81.

[14] *Ibid.* para. 148.

[15] Trade and Industry Committee, *Government Observations on the Fifth Report of the Trade and Industry Committee*, HC 748, 1994–5, paras. 2–3.

[16] Department of Trade and Industry, *Tackling Cartels and the Abuse of Market Power: Implementing the Government's Policy for Competition Law Reform* (Department of Trade and Industry, London, 1996); *Tackling Cartels and the Abuse of Market Power: A Draft Bill* (Department of Trade and Industry, London, 1996).

ability of the interim remedies would be helpful in the sorts of cases which have caused so many problems in the bus industry, but, even if enacted, the reforms would do nothing to create a more rational structure of competition law to deal with abuse of market power.

In the case of mergers there is also considerable discontent, which came to a head in relation to the bids in the electricity sector in spring 1996, during which neither the Monopolies and Mergers Commission nor the Secretary of State was seen as having anything resembling a coherent approach to the issues involved; as the *Financial Times* put it, 'the MMC would appear to have employed thoroughly incoherent arguments, derived from a profound misconception of the aims of competition policy' and on ministerial policy, 'deeper issues of policy towards mergers and competition have also been thoroughly muddied'.[17] This reinforces earlier, more general, complaints: '[a] criticism of the merger provisions is that it is impossible to divine a coherent philosophy in the MMC's reports. Given the nature of the Act, this is hardly surprising; however, it does mean that it can be difficult for those appearing before the MMC to know how to present their case.'[18]

In addition, ministerial powers are extensive here, especially in the question of which mergers to refer to the Commission. Once more, recent criticism relating to the utilities echoes other complaints; '[i]t is the Secretary of State who actually refers mergers to the MMC. A common cause of complaint is that it can be difficult to predict whether a merger will be selected for a reference'.[19] Given this lack of consistency and the width of ministerial discretion, it appears curious to suggest that adopting the existing arrangements for competition policy would be an advantage in utilities regulation. Competition policy does not in practice operate in a way which provides a predictable environment for enterprises; indeed, the current model of arm's-length industry-specific regulation is more likely to do so. I thus conclude that leaving regulation to competition law is inappropriate, would neglect important forms of regulation, and would not work in a way which would be more satisfactory even to regulated companies themselves.

---

[17] 'MMC Blows its Circuits', *Financial Times*, 15 Apr. 1996; 'Power Bids', *Financial Times*, 3 May 1996 (leaders).
[18] Whish, R., and Sufrin, B., *Competition Law* (3rd edn., Butterworths, London, 1993), 692.
[19] *Ibid.* 687.

Alternatives to Regulation: Leaving Regulation to Community Competition Law

This argument is in many ways similar to that just discussed. Given the substantial progress in European Union-inspired liberalization in telecommunications and civil aviation, and the apparent superiority of the Community Treaty's competition provisions as illustrated by their adoption by OFTEL as a model for future regulation, why bother to regulate at all? Could not matters simply be left to the Community with strong policing of competition by the European Commission?

A number of the arguments which have just been rehearsed are also relevant here; for example the fact that regulation has a number of purposes which include regulation of monopoly and social regulation. Indeed, in this respect it should be stressed that it is precisely this question of the relationship between the promotion of competition and the implementation of broader social goals either through monopoly or through regulatory norms which has inspired some of the most difficult and uncertain jurisprudence of all European law, especially that centring around the exception provided to the application of the competition rules by Article 90(2) of the Treaty where such application would obstruct the tasks of undertakings entrusted with the operation of services of general economic interest.[20] Again, if what is required is a reasonably coherent approach to the regulation of public utilities, the law of the European Union is not yet sufficiently developed to offer this.

There are also further institutional problems. Thus, as we saw in the case of civil aviation discussed in Chapter 8, the Commission had some serious problems at first as an enforcement authority and one for handling complaints; it was much slower than the existing regulators. In the context of civil aviation this appears to have been resolved by the liberalization process, at least for the moment, but such extended deregulation will not happen in other areas. Partly for this reason, in the field of telecommunications regulation has been delegated to national regulatory authorities. The development of such authorities has not been free from problems, but this makes

---

[20] For an account of the problems see, e.g., Smith, F., 'Deregulation of Public Utilities: The Scope of the Exemption in Article 90(2) of the EC Treaty' (1996) 7 *Utilities Law Review* 111–16.

the point very clearly that liberalization in Europe is not an alternative to national regulation but is dependent on the creation of effective national regulators.

It should finally be added that I have dealt with telecommunications, civil aviation, and broadcasting as examples of developed liberalization within the European Union. In other sectors liberalization is not only much less well advanced; it may not even come to pass at all in any recognizable form. Thus liberalization of energy has faced lengthy and formidable political problems. A compromise deal was reached in June 1996, but political obstacles have resulted in considerable delay and in very watered-down proposals. In the case of water it is unlikely that there will be Community competence at all, given that water is rarely traded between Member States and so interstate trade is unlikely to be affected. For all these reasons, then, despite the enormous importance of European Community law in regulatory matters, it is far-fetched to suggest that it can provide an acceptable substitute for the sort of regulators we have developed in the United Kingdom.

Learning from Overseas: US Proceduralism

It therefore seems that there is no obvious alternative to something resembling the regulatory regimes which have been created in the United Kingdom; they will continue to be necessary in one form or another, and we shall not see a 'withering away' of regulation across sectors, although, as we are already seeing in telecommunications, certain types of regulation may cease to be necessary. Later in this Chapter I shall discuss possible reforms to their operation. Before doing so, however, it is important to examine experience in other countries in order to suggest different ways of administering regulation. I shall first discuss the United States and then continental Europe.

Recent interest in US administrative law has emphasized in particular the procedures for rule-making; the rule making provisions of Federal law 'constitute the single most marketable commodity currently available for producing procedural means of accountability and participation'.[21] To summarize very briefly a hugely important

---

[21] Harden, I., and Lewis, N., *The Noble Lie: The British Constitution and the Rule of Law* (Hutchinson, London, 1986), 235. For a description of the rule-making process see *ibid.* 235–7, 246–8, 272–7; and Breyer, S., and Stewart, R.,

area of administrative law, section 553 of the Administrative Procedure Act requires that a federal agency before making a rule must (with certain exceptions) give a general notice in the Federal Register including details of the procedure to be followed, the legal authority under which the rule is proposed, and either the substance or the subject matter of the proposed rule. The notice of proposed rule-making may be a substantial document in itself; for example, that issued by the Federal Communications Commission relating to universal service under the provisions of the Telecommunications Act 1996 runs to seventy-one closely-typed pages setting out the issues to be considered during the rule-making process in very considerable detail.[22] Interested persons are then entitled to make written submissions and may be given an oral hearing. After consideration of the material presented, the agency must incorporate into the rules adopted a concise general statement of their basis or purpose; this is also likely to amount in practice to a detailed statement of reasons for adopting the rules. A person aggrieved by agency action may seek judicial review, and the courts have in some circumstances required further procedural protections. For example, during the 1970s there was a move towards transforming this 'notice and comment' rule-making into a more complex paper hearing procedure involving several rounds of notice and comment, and requiring agencies to disclose the evidentiary and analytical documentation relied on in proposing a rule in order to permit effective comment. This process was eventually restrained by a decision of the Supreme Court to the effect that it was for the agencies, not the courts, to determine when extra procedural devices were required.[23] Nevertheless, innovative procedural devices are still used in agency rule-making procedures, as we shall see below.

As I described in Chapter 3, the Director General of Telecommunications has moved towards this type of rule-making in recent decisions, and its adoption would seem to have clear potential advantages for the British agencies. Thus if we accept that

---

Administrative Law and Regulatory Policy (3rd edn., Little Brown & Co., Boston, Mass., 1992), 523–649.

[22] Federal Communications Commission, FCC 96–93, *Notice of Proposed Rulemaking and Order Establishing Joint Board* (Federal Communications Commission, Washington, DC, 1996); the process will be discussed in more detail below.

[23] *Vermont Yankee Nuclear Power Corp.* v. *Natural Resources Defense Council* (1978) 435 US 519.

the regulators are really 'governments in miniature' but potentially lack democratic legitimacy, the alternative of procedural participation would seem to offer an alternative form of such legitimacy; indeed, the search for legitimacy in this way lay behind the development of rule-making techniques in the United States.[24] The argument for learning from the US techniques would thus seem to have considerable power. Nevertheless, as we saw in Chapter 2, the British Government sought at all costs to avoid borrowing American regulatory techniques. This may have been due to a generalized distrust of American reliance on lawyers and courts to resolve economic disputes and fear of resulting litigiousness, stagnation, and delay. In fact these complaints are more appropriately directed towards the technique of adjudication through formal on-the-record hearings than towards rule-making. Yet even in the relatively simple procedure of rule-making there have been serious complaints of 'ossification', making it impossible for agencies to develop rules due to complex procedural requirements and far-reaching judicial review.[25] For example, it has been suggested that the agencies dealing with environmental protection and with occupational health and safety 'could not possibly perform their statutorily assigned missions through use of rulemaking in less than several centuries'.[26] However, when one comes to analyse the causes of this 'ossification' one finds that they cannot simply be assumed to be due to the procedure itself or to be likely to come into play in a British environment. As one of the most critical commentators has put it:

the ossification of the rulemaking process cannot be explained by the accretion of procedural requirements to the bare minimum of section 553, as very few additional procedures have in fact been added. Even when agencies provide for more procedure . . . very little of the time consumed in the rulemaking process can be attributed to time spent in hearings. We must therefore look elsewhere for the causes of ossification.[27]

---

[24] Stewart, R., 'The Reformation of American Administrative Law' (1975) 88 *Harvard Law Review* 1669–813; Freedman, J., *Crisis and Legitimacy* (Cambridge University Press, Cambridge, 1978).

[25] See, e.g., McGarity, T., 'Some Thoughts on "Deossifying" the Rulemaking Process' (1992) 41 *Duke Law Journal* 1385–462; Pierce, R., 'Seven Ways to Deossify Agency Rulemaking' (1995) 47 *Administrative Law Review* 59–95.

[26] Pierce, n. 25 above, 61.

[27] McGarity, n. 25 above, 1399 (footnote omitted).

The two most important causes of ossification have been identified as first extended substantive (rather than procedural) requirements imposed through judicial review which require extreme detail in the reasons and record of rule-making proceedings; '[a]lthough not especially burdensome in theory, these additional analytical requirements invite abuse by regulatees who hire consultants and lawyers to pick apart the agencies' preambles and background documents and launch blunderbuss attacks on every detail of the legal and technical bases for the agencies' rules.'[28] This extreme form of the 'hard look' doctrine has never been implemented by British courts, and the likelihood of their doing so is remote; as we saw in Chapters 2 and 9, they have generally been prepared to give a considerable margin of discretion to decision-makers in the field of economic regulation.[29] Even the interventionist attitude shown in the recent *Mercury* decision was concerned more with a regulator asking the wrong question through misinterpreting the law than with failure to analyse the factual matters before him in sufficient depth; it is also significant that it involved an individual dispute about interconnection terms rather than rule-making.[30] It is thus unlikely that the British courts would impose substantive requirements or demand an extended record in such a way as to create the problems encountered in US rule-making.

The second cause of regulatory ossification was the involvement of the executive branch through its detailed oversight of the regulatory process, beginning with the implementation of the celebrated Executive Order 12,291 requiring, amongst other things, cost-benefit analysis of proposed rules and their submission to the Office of Management and Budget for review. Apart from serious concerns about the fact that the executive review takes place behind closed doors and has been forcefully alleged to be a means of covert influence by regulated industries, 'OMB staffers not infrequently attempt to substitute their judgments in such highly technical areas as science, engineering, and economics for that of the agencies to which Congress has delegated decision-making responsibility.'[31]

---

[28] McGarity, n. 25 above, 1400, see also 1410–28; and Pierce, n. 25 above, 65.

[29] See, e.g., *R.* v. *Independent Television Commission, ex parte TSW Broadcasting Ltd*, [1996] EMLR 291 (HL).

[30] *Mercury Communications Ltd* v. *Director General of Telecommunications* [1996] 1 All ER 575 (HL).

[31] McGarity, n. 25 above, 1433; see generally 1405–10, 1428–36; Friedman, H., 'The Oversupply of Regulatory Reform: From Law to Politics in Administrative Rulemaking' (1992) 71 *Nebraska Law Review* 1169–93.

The requirements for regulatory oversight have now been substantially simplified under the Clinton Administration, and the new process seeks to overcome the problems of ossification in a number of ways, including the encouragement of negotiated rule-making within the context of the Administrative Procedure Act requirements.[32] Despite attempts at introducing regulatory impact-analysis procedures in the United Kingdom,[33] once more it is not conceivable that anything of the same kind will be introduced in relation to the economic regulators described here, especially in view of the importance of distancing them from government in order to retain their credibility as independent regulators. Where government guidance is required, I will suggest later a means by which this can take place without causing the difficulties encountered in the United States. We can thus conclude that the rejection of *all* US procedures in the creation of the British regulatory institutions was a serious mistake; in the words of a commentator on the current US problems:

I see the primary benefits of the notice and comment procedure as independent of judicial review. Agencies are more likely to make wise and well-informed policy decisions if they solicit, receive, and consider data and views from all citizens who are likely to be affected by a policy decision. Similarly, agencies are more likely to make policy decisions that are consistent with the views of the people and their elected representatives if they provide public notice of their intention to make a particular policy decision.[34]

United States Proceduralism in Practice

Having established these preliminary general considerations, how does US rule-making operate in practice in areas similar to those being examined in this book? The first important point to make is that some of the important issues I have covered are dealt with there as adjudication rather than rule-making, this requiring a full evidentiary public hearing with cross-examination and the keeping

[32] For a detailed analysis of the Clinton reforms see Pildes, R., and Sunstein, C., 'Reinventing the Regulatory State' (1995) 62 *University of Chicago Law Review* 3–129.
[33] For a good overview of these see Baldwin, R., *Rules and Government* (Clarendon Press, Oxford, 1995), ch. 7.
[34] Pierce, n. 25 above, 86.

of a full record as the basis for judicial review.[35] This will apply not just to adjudicative decisions such as interconnection between different companies and decisions about supply in an individual case, but also to many issues of price control. For example, the New York Public Service Law requires that in the case of any major change to a gas or electricity tariff, a hearing is to be held. The burden or proof to justify the rate lies on the utility.[36] The procedures involved will permit extensive hearing rights to a number of interests; for example, in New York tariff cases there will be 200–300 interested parties of whom about fifty will be active participants in the process.[37] Similarly, at federal level the Administrative Procedure Act imposes detailed hearing requirements for adjudication, and these have in turn spawned an extensive case law.[38] In addition the agencies will themselves be subject to more particular rules setting out procedural requirements in each case.[39]

For reasons already noted, these procedures have not been greatly admired in the United Kingdom and regulatory procedures here set out to avoid what were seen as their excesses. Yet the caricature of never-ending, lawyer-dominated proceedings is not entirely true, even in the case of formal adjudication. For example, the New York procedures referred to are subject to a time limit of eleven months from the filing of the notice by the utility; this compares with times of sixteen months' consultation plus at least six months for MMC investigation for TransCo prices and twenty months from the first consultation paper to implementation for BT prices in the most recent price reviews. Nor is judicial review necessarily the huge problem perceived from this side of the Atlantic. Thus review of Federal Communication Commission decisions lies directly to the US Courts of Appeals for the District of Columbia and thence to the US Supreme Court, avoiding the overcrowded District Courts and achieving a considerable degree of judicial spe-

---

[35] For the distinction between rule-making and adjudication, itself a highly complex issue, see Breyer and Stewart, n. 21 above, 524–59.

[36] New York State Consolidated Laws, Public Service, Art. 4, s. 66(12)(f), 66(12)(i).

[37] For details of the procedure including a case-study which still remains broadly applicable, see Henney, A., *Regulating Public and Privatised Monopolies: A Radical Approach* (Policy Journals, London, 1986), esp. annex 2.

[38] Administrative Procedure Act, ss. 554–7; for the case law see Breyer and Stewart, n. 21 above, 649–708.

[39] For the Federal Communications Commission, see Code of Federal Regulations, 47, Ch. 1, Pt. 1, 1.201–1.364.

cialization.[40] Even at the state level, judicial review may be relatively restricted in scope; for example, review of decisions of the California Public Utilities Commission lies direct to the state Supreme Court as the Commission has a direct source of authority in the state constitution; this severely limits the number of cases brought. Finally, it should be stressed that the formal adjudication process has advantages in providing a guaranteed forum for participation by public interest groups and, through the requirement of a record, they are able to gauge the degree to which their views are taken into account; for example, Toward Utility Rate Normalization (TURN), a small organization representing domestic and small-business consumers in California, in the year ending in June 1994 participated in thirteen telephone cases, thirteen electric cases, and ten gas cases, its proposals being accepted in 65 per cent.[41] Such groups perceive major disadvantages in moving towards a less formalized set of procedures as it will remove this guaranteed right.

Nevertheless, a number of regulatory bodies in the United States are developing procedures such as negotiated tariff-setting and rule-making rather than adjudication.[42] In addition, as Cosmo Graham has noted, 'I do not think that the American Administrative Procedure Act's division between rule-making and adjudication is likely to be suitable in British circumstances.'[43] An important difference is the lack of an equivalent to a formal record in UK regulatory proceedings; it is the requirement of a record which contains all the evidence upon which the agency can base its decision which has caused over-formality in US rate-making, and this in turn is based on the need to make possible US judicial review.[44] The effect of the requirement of such a record is that *all* evidence has to be part of it and that *ex parte* communications out-

---

[40] See Wald, P., 'Regulation at Risk: Are the Courts Part of the Solution or Most of the Problem?' (1994) 67 *Southern California Law Review* 621–57.

[41] TURN, *Annual Report 1993–4* (TURN, San Francisco, Cal., 1994), 2.

[42] See, e.g., Federal Communications Commission, *Improving Commission Processes*, FCC 96–50 (Federal Communications Commission, Washington, DC, 1996); California Public Utilities Commission, *Vision 2000: A Report on Our Progress Towards Change* (California Public Utilities Commission, San Francisco, Cal., 1996).

[43] Graham, C., *Is There a Crisis in Regulatory Accountability?* (Centre for the Study of Regulated Industries, London, 1996), 55.

[44] See Breyer and Stewart, n. 21 above, 534–59 and *United States* v. *Florida East Coast Railway* (1973) 410 US 224.

side the record are banned.[45] Moreover, the basic constitutional requirements of the due-process clause have done much to shape regulatory proceedings in the United States and have no British equivalent. It seems that, although the use of hearings has an important potential role in British regulation (as indeed has been shown by the experience of the CAA), we should not see an adjudicatory on-the-record hearing as appropriate means for taking decisions such as on price control; in particular, hearings may be an important part of the process, but should be only one means out of many for gathering information, and the strict *ex parte* rules applicable to on-the-record adjudication should not be adopted as a model for the United Kingdom. It will be most realistic, therefore, to concentrate on rule-making procedures.[46] I will therefore give at this point an example of an important US rule-making process to suggest some lessons which might be learned from it.

A good example is universal service rule-making under the provisions of the Telecommunications Act 1996; apart from its inherent importance, we saw earlier that both OFTEL and the European Commission have examined similar issues on this side of the Atlantic. Rather than using the ordinary notice and comment procedures of the Federal Communications Commission, as the issues involved state as well as federal regulators a federal–state joint board was convened and a notice of proposed rule-making issued on 8 March 1996; it was made available on the Internet as well as by more conventional means.[47] The notice ran to 151 paragraphs describing in detail the issues to be addressed in implementing the provisions of the Act; the most important ones were goals and principles of universal service support mechanisms, support for rural, insular, and high-cost areas and low-income consumers, support for schools, libraries, and health care providers, and enhancing access to advanced services for these latter institutions, other universal service support services, and the administration of support mechanisms. Interestingly, as well as being concerned with implementing the statutory provisions, the notice invited interested parties to propose additional principles. To give an example of more detailed content, the section on support for rural, insular, and high-

---

[45] Administrative Procedure Act, ss. 551(14), 556(d), 557(d); Breyer and Stewart, n. 21 above, 660–7.

[46] See also Harden and Lewis, n. 21 above, for a strong statement of this theme.

[47] FCC 96–93, n. 22 above.

cost areas included a subsection on which services to support, discussing in some detail the arguments for and against including voice-grade access to the public switched network, touch-tone, single party service, access to emergency services, and access to operator services, as well as asking for additional services to be identified by commentators.

The basic procedure was to be double notice and comment, as employed by OFTEL and discussed in Chapter 3 above. The first round of comments was to be filed by 8 April 1996; the second round of comments on these was to be completed by 3 May 1996. About 250 comments were received in this period, and after reviewing them the FCC at the request of the joint board issued a further list of seventy-two questions on 3 July; these concentrated on a number of issues of considerable complexity, including the definition of 'affordability' in universal service, the effects on competition of denial of support for universal service and support for schools, libraries, and health care providers. Comments on these further questions were required by 2 August 1996. The board also held a number of open meetings with panels of experts and, for example, with consumer groups and local government to discuss the issues arising. Public fora were organized, including two on educating the public on how to participate in FCC proceedings and how to find FCC information on the Internet; a Telecoms and Healthcare Advisory Committee was also established. The board was then to make recommendations to the FCC by 8 November 1996 and met this deadline; the Commission then commenced a public proceeding on universal service to be completed by 8 March 1997.

A matter of particular interest in view of developments in the United Kingdom is the treatment of *ex parte* submissions, in this context meaning those written comments not served on other parties to the proceedings and oral comments not subject to advance notice to parties with an opportunity for them to be present.[48] The status of the rule-making is 'non-restricted notice and comment'. The effect of this is that, rather than having the ban on *ex parte* submissions characteristic of on-the-record adjudication, such communications are permissible provided that copies are lodged immediately in the public record and so become openly accessible; oral

---

[48] For a discussion of the problem and summary of the US position see Harden and Lewis, n. 21 above, 246–9.

comments must be immediately summarized in this way in writing. General exemptions to the *ex parte* rules are extremely restricted and do not include, for example, commercially sensitive information; no *ex parte* submissions are permitted during the 'Sunshine Agenda' period of seven days before the matter is due to be determined by the Commission.[49] This compromise on *ex parte* communications should provide a way of ensuring that all information considered enters the public domain.

The lesson from this section is that the procedures adopted in the United States by regulatory agencies offer important lessons for UK regulators. Indeed, this seems already to have been appreciated, in that the procedural developments championed by Don Cruikshank at OFTEL are very close to the model of rule-making under the Administrative Procedure Act and the Telecommunications Act in the United States, for example in provision for the opportunity of a second round of notice and comment at each stage. Nor does there seem to be evidence that the effect of the procedures is to slow decisions down; the timetable for the Telecommunications Act universal service rule-making is remarkably tight, especially when one remembers that the Act required a number of other rule-making procedures to be carried out simultaneously, most importantly in relation to interconnection. One difference is, however, the greater rigour imposed by the structure of rules creating rule-making procedures, rules which have no formal legal counterpart in the United Kingdom. A striking example concerns *ex parte* communications, where, as we saw in Chapter 4, OFGAS faced criticism from the regulated firm through failing to provide access to its consultants' reports to the regulated company in price-control proceedings. Overall, the practice of rule-making as discussed here shows that it can be an effective technique for handling matters of wide impact, and that alleged ossification has not paralysed the administrative process in the areas of regulation discussed in this book, whatever may be the case in others, such as environment and safety regulation.

[49] The legal regime for *ex parte* communications to the FCC is set out in *Code of Federal Regulations* (Office of the Federal Register, Washington, DC, 1995), vol. 47, ch. 1, 1.1200–16.

Learning from Overseas: Service Public and Servizio Pubblico

Impressive and important as is the US experience, the discussion earlier in this volume suggests that regulatory legitimacy requires something more than procedural principles. The same point has been made neatly by an American author in concluding his examination of regulatory reform, 'Americans generally prefer to substitute procedures for the difficulties of substantive value choices. Until this tendency is overcome, little change can be expected. Value choices are neither easy nor popular. But they are critical to reestablishment of a rule of law in administrative rulemaking.'[50]

In one sense we have such principles already for two types of regulation discussed in this book. In relation to regulation of monopoly there is a very substantial body of economic literature dealing with how we can mimic competitive markets and increase allocative and productive efficiency. Of course, the principles are controversial and do not provide a single right answer to all the disputes which may arise; as we saw in earlier chapters, price control is as much an art as a science in important respects. Nevertheless, there is an accepted structure in which the debate can take place. Similarly, with regulation for competition there is a considerable body of economic principle concerned with anti-competitive practices and abuse of market power; and this body of principle is also reflected in the legal doctrines of competition law. Where such a body of principle seems to be lacking is in social regulation and, as we saw in Chapter 1, this has led to suggestions that social regulation is essentially arbitrary, and so not the proper province of the regulator; if it is to be tolerated at all, it should be implemented by elected representatives, as only they can claim democratic legitimacy for such policies.

In Chapter 1 I attempted to suggest that social regulation could be justified on the basis of provisions of statute, common, and European Community law applying to the regulators. Moreover, if one simply looks across the Channel to France (or, to a lesser extent, to Italy) one finds a well developed corpus of law dealing with *service public* or *servizio pubblico* which can provide a strong jurisprudential base for social regulation; this is worth further development here, as it has been paid little attention in the United

---

[50] Friedman, n. 31 above, 1193.

Kingdom though it has been an important influence on European Union policy.

In France, the concept of public service has a constitutional base; the Preamble to the 1946 Constitution, incorporated into the Constitution of the Fifth Republic by its Preamble, includes the provision that '[a]ll property and enterprises of which the running has, or acquires, the character of a national public service or an actual monopoly (*monopole de fait*) are to become public property'. There is considerable doubt about the meaning of this provision, and it has been interpreted extremely loosely by the Conseil Constitutionnel.[51] The concept of *service public* is much more fully developed in French administrative law.[52] What does this concept mean? A recent account has defined it as follows: 'in French public law, public service is an activity in the general interest, provided by a public or private actor and subject to a special legal regime (requiring equality of treatment, adaptation to changing needs and security of supply, etc.).'[53] The principle has been implemented in two ways; the first is the familiar one of public ownership, however the second is through the granting of public-service concessions to private concerns.[54] Similar concessions are used, in fact, for publicly owned enterprises also. Thus that for France Télécom includes provisions on interconnection, relations with consumers, accounting rules, tariff setting, etc. in a way very similar to the British Telecom licence.[55] Nevertheless, it is important to make the point that *service public* is in no way synonymous with public ownership, or indeed with the granting of monopoly rights, but may also be a means of incorporating certain social principles into the operation of private enterprises in the market-place.[56] It is also important to note that it is essentially non-economic and distributive in nature;

[51] See the *Privatisations* decision, no. 86–207, 25 and 26 June 1986 [1986] Rec. 61.

[52] For a detailed analysis see the Conseil d'Etat, *Etudes et Documents No 46, Rapport Public 1994* (La Documentation Française, Paris, 1995).

[53] Debène, M., and Raymundie, O., 'Sur le service universel: renouveau du service public ou nouvelle mystification?' (1996) 52:3 *AJDA* 183–91 at 186; my translation is a loose one in view of the difficulty of conveying the flavour of the concept in English.

[54] For details of public-service concessions see de Laubadère, A., Moderne, F., and Delvolvé, P., *Traité des Contrats Administratifs* (2nd edn., Librairie Générale de Droit et de Jurisprudence, Paris, 1983), i, paras. 224–48.

[55] Décret no. 90–1213, 29 Dec. 1990 [1990] *Journal Officiel* 16578.

[56] See Conseil d'Etat, n. 52 above, 26–29.

'it is the essence of *service public*, as a means of consolidation of the social contract and of social solidarity, that it contributes to some types of redistribution and of transfers between social groups'.[57] Thus regulatory principles which are in essence distributive are by no means innovative in France; on the contrary, *service public* has a long history and is supported by an extensive case law.

What are the implications of a regime of public service? This is complex and controversial, especially as rather complex disputes have arisen concerning its relation to principles of Community law, including universal service.[58] The basic principle is that of equality, requiring equal access to services and requiring that consumers be treated equally unless there is a good reason not to do so. Without getting into the complexities of the relationship between this and universal service, it is quite clear that the two principles share much in common, although advocates of *service public* have resisted limiting it to providing a minimum service to the most needy. The second and third principles are closely linked; they are continuity and adaptation, or security of supply, requiring that public services function in a manner which is assured, and that, if for any reason the concessionaire cannot continue to provide services, the concession can be transferred to another operator. Security of supply has been one of the key issues of debate in the attempts to liberalize European energy markets, and the principle of continuity is clearly related to the question of disconnection discussed in earlier chapters. Other aspects of public service include neutrality (in a different context, this of course plays a major part in broadcasting regulation in the United Kingdom[59]), participation of consumers in the administration or at least the regulation of the services, responsibility, and transparency, which may require independent regulation for its full realization,[60] and simplicity and accessibility in consumer relations.

This list of principles may appear vague and difficult to translate into detailed prescriptions. However, within them can be seen the seeds of many of the aspects of social regulation discussed in

---

[57] *Ibid.* 53.
[58] See Debène and Raymundie, n. 53 above; Conseil d'Etat, n. 52 above, 114–16; and Hancher, L., 'Utilities Policy and the European Union' in Centre for the Study of Regulated Industries, *Regulatory Review 1996* (Centre for the Study of Regulated Industries, London, 1996), 119–40, 136–8.
[59] Broadcasting Act 1990, s. 6(1)(b)–(c), (4).
[60] Conseil d'Etat, n. 52 above, 90.

earlier chapters. It is of course true to say that the concept of public service has been used politically to defend public ownership through allegedly requiring monopoly privileges; however, it has been used also to impose constraints on private enterprises. What it may do, of course, is to support policies such as cross-subsidy, given that, as mentioned earlier, the principles of *service public* are essentially based on principles of social solidarity. In this way they may support some of the actions of regulators discussed earlier which appear to be based on redistributive foundations. Moreover, as a result of the need to particularize more fully the principles, a French Public Service Charter was developed in 1992 attempting to specify the content in greater detail; this has in turn helped to inspire the pressure for a European Public Service Charter discussed in Chapter 1.

In examining public utilities, however, France is not the best nation to consider as the utilities remain (with the partial exception of water) in public hands and there has been little attempt to establish independent regulators of the kind discussed in this book. Italy may provide a better example, given that steps towards the privatization of the public utilities are much more fully advanced; it provides an illustration of how principles of public service can be made compatible with the independent regulation of private or part-private utilities. In this case there is a more flexible constitutional base which nevertheless refers to the concept of public service; it permits the state to acquire or reserve to itself enterprises providing essential public services; historically, as in France, this has been used as a justification for monopoly.[61] Public-service concessions have however been used extensively also, for both private and public operators. For example, that of ENEL, the electricity utility, includes a number of public-service obligations such as universal service, as well as provisions for accounting separation and price control; in this respect it resembles licences such as those issued in the United Kingdom under the Electricity Act, though there is a conceptual difference, as a concession is conceived as a delegation by the state of its reserved powers, whilst a licence is more a regulatory intervention in relation to powers essentially private.[62] In the mid-1990s, however, as part of the preparations for privatization

---

[61] See the Italian Constitution, Art. 43, and Cassese, S., *La Nuova Constituzione Economica*, (Editori Laterza, Rome, 1995), 71–8.

[62] Decreto ministeriale, 28 Dec. 1995, *Gazzetta Ufficiale* n. 39, 16. 2. 1996.

and as a result of a serious disenchantment with the efficiency and service quality of Italian utilities, a number of steps were made to create more specific protections. The first was the law of 1994 on the delivery of public services.[63] This sets out fundamental principles of public service very much on the French model; thus they are principles of equality, impartiality, continuity, choice for consumers, consumer participation, and efficiency. Following the British model, however, the implementation of the principle is to be by the adoption of standards (interestingly, the concept of service standards proved untranslatable into Italian, and they are referred to as *gli standard*) which include both general and individual standards, breach of the latter giving rise to a right to compensation. Effective grievance procedures are also to be established, and the standards and procedures are published in the form of a *Carta del servizio pubblico* for each industry; implementation is supervised by a specialist committee. This development marked an important advance in the development of accountable public services in Italy.[64] Nevertheless, some of the standards are as yet relatively unsophisticated; for example, that concerning disconnection of electricity simply provides for proper notice to be given and for disconnection not to take place if evidence is produced that the debt has been paid, protections much more limited than those in the United Kingdom.[65]

The final, and in many ways most interesting, stage occurred with the preparations for privatization and partial liberalization of telecommunications and energy markets. A law of November 1995 set out the general principles to be adopted in the creation of independent regulatory authorities for energy and telecommunications, and defined in detail the arrangements for the energy sector; the establishment of the telecommunications authority has been delayed by political infighting around the principle of privatization.[66] Once more, the adoption of UK experience was striking in the regulatory arrangements; unlike the case of France the regulators are to be placed outside government, with the members of the authorities appointed by the President of the Republic on the

---

[63] Direttiva del Presidente del Consiglio dei Ministri, 27 Jan. 1994, *Gazzetta Ufficiale* n.43, 22. 2. 1994.

[64] For background see Cassese, S., *The Difficult Profession of Minister of Public Administration* (European University Institute, Florence, 1995).

[65] ENEL, *Carta del servizio elettrico, gennaio 1996*, para. 3.3.3.

[66] Legge n. 481, 14 Nov. 1995, *Gazzetta Ufficiale* n. 270, 18. 11. 1995.

recommendation of the government and after hearings by the appropriate Parliamentary Committee; the latter must give two-thirds support for a nomination to go ahead. Contrary to UK practice, the new authorities take the form of commissions of three members with seven years' security of tenure. Their tasks are varied, but include advising the government on amending concessions, protecting principles of public service, and supervising the implementation of service standards, applying complex pricing formulae to limit price increases, and policing accounting separation.

This section has a simple message. The problems of utility regulation in the United Kingdom are not unique, but mirror much older problems elsewhere and experience overseas is important as a means of learning how to resolve the problems effectively. In particular, case law in other nations has dealt more explicitly with two particular problems; in the United States procedural questions have been dealt with much more coherently, and in continental Europe there has been a fuller recognition of the plurality of regulatory goals through the establishment of a relatively sophisticated case law dealing with the social requirements of public service, and suggesting that there is something different about basic services linked to citizenship. The Italian experience suggests that it is possible to implement this through institutions and procedures similar to those developed in the United Kingdom so far. Of course there must be some caution expressed here; the rhetoric of public service may conceal a lack of practical consumer safeguards or of institutions for consumer representation.[67] Nevertheless we do have some sort of framework in which issues of how to develop principles of public service can at least be debated. This leads us to the final section of the Chapter, which will examine some of the proposals for changes to the regulatory arrangements in Britain and will attempt to assess them from the viewpoint of the problems identified earlier and of the insight provided by experience elsewhere.

Government and Regulation

If we accept that there is a plurality of regulatory goals, the question has to be asked who is responsible for implementing them. As

[67] For a similar point in a Spanish context, see Garcìa Garcìa, L., and Villiers, C., 'Administrative Structure of the Water Industry and Consumer Representation: A Comparison of Spain and England and Wales' (1996) 7 *Utilities Law Review* 157–67.

regards social regulation and principles such as those of universal service, much implementation has been carried out by the regulators themselves with the development and enforcement of policies restricting disconnection, or the imposition of social obligations in electricity supply licences, for example. However, in the continental examples I have discussed, implementation of public-service obligations has been seen as primarily a task for government in framing and enforcing concessions setting out such obligations, although in Italy there is now a move towards entrusting this to independent authorities. In Britain government also played a fundamentally important role in the definition of the original obligations in the initial licences. Moreover, as we saw in Chapter 2 there has also been controversy about the role of government in continuing regulation; thus, for example, should it set an overall energy policy within which the regulators would operate, and so avoid the problems faced by, for example, the Electricity Regulator in relation to the purchasing decisions of the generating companies and their effect on the coal industry?

One thing which has been rather lost in the debate is that no one appears to support the proposition that government should have no role in regulation; this is evident from even a cursory reading of ministerial powers in the statutes setting up regulatory systems.[68] Moreover, government has a more informal role in regulatory decisions; for example it was revealed that civil servants sat in on meetings between the Gas Regulator and British Gas concerning the setting of the TransCo price formula, and a meeting with the energy minister was scheduled before the final proposals were announced. The FCC rules on *ex parte* communications in non-restricted proceedings described above would not affect this as they do not apply to communications from the Federal Government.[69]

Instead, it has been suggested that powers should be given to government to set out a clearer policy framework for regulators; for example one commentator has suggested that ministers should draw up guidelines for Parliamentary approval and that the regulators should be required to submit rolling plans which ministers would approve.[70] Another has suggested that '[i]n the context of the

---

[68] The powers are summarized in Graham, n. 43 above, 10–13.
[69] 'DTI Sits in on Gas Traffic Talks', *Financial Times*, 17–18 Aug. 1996; Code of Federal Regs., 47, para. 1.1204(b)(5).
[70] Hain, P., *Regulating for the Common Good* (GMB, London, 1994), 22.

public utilities, government objectives should normally be set out in the form of integrated sectoral policies for energy, communications, transport and water supply'.[71] The latter two writers are close to the Labour Party and, while Party policy is in favour of retaining the regulators in their present form, it does envisage greater powers of governmental intervention; to quote the then Labour Shadow Transport spokesperson:

[t]he most immediate area of influence over Railtrack will be through regulation, using the considerable powers given to the rail regulator in the Railways Act 1993 . . . a simple amendment to the Railways Act 1993 is all that would be needed for a Labour government to enhance his accountability to the transport secretary. . . . A Labour government would expect the regulator to make greater use of his powers to promote the public interest.[72]

It is also interesting to note that in other nations regulation has been exercised within a considerable framework of government involvement; thus in the United States I have already discussed the role of the executive branch in relation to rule-making, something which continues in a simplified form under the Clinton Administration. In France and Italy it has been government which has set out public-service requirements and other fundamental conditions such as those relating to pricing in the concessions which it has issued. The question is thus not whether there should be government involvement in the regulatory process, but how it should be structured to be as open as possible and to result in a clear division of responsibilities.

The answer seems to be the adoption of something resembling the powers which used to exist in civil aviation for government to issue policy guidance for regulators. We saw in Chapter 8 above that this ended after exercise of the power to overrule a substantive decision was held to be unlawful by the courts in the *Laker* episode. However, rather than suggesting that this power would be inappropriate, that episode provides a further argument in its favour though showing that it could be effectively limited to guidance rather than permitting government a general override power for regulatory decisions; if the latter were to be attempted, the courts

---

[71] Corry, D., Souter, D., and Waterson, M., *Regulating Our Utilities* (Institute for Public Policy Research, London, 1994), 80.

[72] Short, C., 'A Better Way to Run the Railway', *Financial Times*, 13–14 Apr. 1996.

would intervene. Interestingly, the foremost commentator on the history of civil-aviation regulation has recently supported the development of such guidance (although, ironically, civil aviation is now one of the fields where it would have the smallest role to play, given recent European liberalization); it has also found favour with the Confederation of British Industry.[73] A similar proposal has been made in relation to the electricity sector,[74] and precedents can be found in the temporary power of the Secretary of State to issue guidance to the Rail Regulator and in the duty of the ministers to issue published guidance to the Environment Agency.[75] Further development of powers to issue guidance by government would be a potential means of clarifying the context in which regulators operate and clarifying regulatory objectives; it is essential, of course, that this be done publicly.

Reforming the Regulators

More open arrangements for the statement of government policy relating to the regulators is not enough, however. We have seen that the regulators themselves inevitably have a wide degree of discretion in taking their key decisions. Even in price control this does not represent any straightforward application of economic rules; regulation for competition has also proved a highly complex task, and social regulation, though important in practice, has been notable for the lack of principles enunciated to guide the regulators in undertaking it. Nor is it possible that any of these tasks will prove unnecessary; important pockets of monopoly will remain, it is not appropriate to leave regulation for competition to the generalist competition regulators and, though government will have some role in setting the framework for social regulation, it is inconceivable that any government will take full responsibility for social aspects of regulation. It is thus necessary to discuss potential reforms to the operation of the regulators themselves.[76]

[73] Baldwin, R., *Regulation in Question: The Growing Agenda* (London School of Economics, London, 1995), 118–19; Confederation of British Industry, *Regulating the Regulators: A Discussion Paper* (Confederation of British Industry, London, 1996), 24–5.

[74] McHarg, A., 'Accountability in the Electricity Supply Industry' (1995) 6 *Utilities Law Review* 34–43.

[75] Railways Act 1993, s. 4(5); Environment Act 1995, s. 4(2)–(9).

[76] For a discussion of the potential reforms see Graham, n. 43 above.

A number of lessons can be drawn from the description of the regulators' work in the earlier chapters of this book; one of my aims has been to identify best practice in each case. To summarize examples of this, OFTEL has clearly taken the lead in consultation procedures and making information available as part of the consultation process. Particularly noteworthy aspects of this are its use of two rounds of notice and comment and its use of hearings as means of consultation; the reasons for its decisions are also comprehensive and of high quality, and are distributed most widely, including through use of the Internet. It may be possible to improve its practice further through taking lessons from the use of hearings by the CAA and in a different form by the Rail Regulator in determining issues relating to access agreements. In neither of these cases does this appear to have fossilized the decision-making process. US material is of use here also; though the restrictions of on-the-record adjudication are to be avoided, the use of less formal types of hearing in the rule-making process may provide a model for the United Kingdom. A further protection might be to adopt some form of *ex parte* rules, including restricting the role of communications from government. If the system of policy guidance suggested above is adopted, there will be no justification for less formal contacts between regulator and government to be permitted.

In the case of OFGAS, what has been most interesting is the way in which domestic competition has been effectively implemented in a difficult environment, yet in a way which retains important social obligations. Indeed, it is precisely the move to liberalization which has forced these social concerns to be addressed openly; we have seen something similar also in electricity, although the process of liberalization seems likely to be more delayed there. Both OFGAS and OFTEL (and indeed OFWAT) have achieved considerable success in limiting disconnection of supply. If then OFTEL gives us a model for regulatory procedures on the US pattern, the energy regulators have gone some way to enunciating the sorts of social concerns which have characterized *service public* in continental Europe. Whether the protection of social rights after domestic liberalization will prove adequate has yet to be seen.

OFWAT has offered other lessons. First, the requirement of independent monitoring of information through the use of external reporters could usefully be adopted by other regulators, as could the degree of openness shown through the publication of letters from the Director General to the companies. Secondly, the pattern of consumer representation in water did permit a closer involvement of consumer representatives in the price-control process, and it seems that this affected the outcome in important ways. At first sight the close relationship between the consumer representatives and the regulator might appear anomalous, given that the latter has to weigh consumer and other interests in his decisions; yet it has had clear procedural advantages. The consultation process in water price setting was criticized by some consumer groups, however, and the way to improve it seems to be a combination of the direct involvement of consumer representatives used in the periodic review with the sort of rule-making procedures developed by OFTEL.

The lessons to be drawn from the CAA have already been mentioned; thus the ill-fated policy guidance offers lessons for the creation of a more formal means of providing a framework of government guidance for regulators, and the successful use of public hearings in licensing decisions also offers lessons for other regulators, as does the use of hearings by the Rail Regulator. In the case of the ITC, the inevitable resort to judicial review to challenge its decisions has not led to disastrous second-guessing of substantive findings; in its own procedures, the thorough annual performance reviews of the regulated companies provide a rounded picture of company performance and regulatory achievement not available in other cases.

Apart from these particular issues, a number of more general structural problems have emerged in this study. The first is the question of regulatory complexity; it has been argued by some writers that we simply have too many regulators with overlapping jurisdictions.[77] The analysis in this book has suggested that this is an urgent problem in broadcasting, where the convergence of different types of delivery has led to serious problems of jurisdiction, and the limited rationalization under the Broadcasting Act 1996 has affected only the margins of this. The answer, as a number of commentators have suggested, will be to distinguish issues of economic and of content regulation, and to make these, rather than delivery technology, the basis for regulatory jurisdiction. With the liberalization of electricity

---

[77] See, e.g., Graham, n. 43 above, 40–2; Helm, D., 'British Utility Regulation: Theory, Practice, and Reform' (1994) 10 *Oxford Review of Economic Policy* 17–39, 33–4; Hain, P., n. 70 above, 23.

and gas there is a case for merger of the two energy regulators as the issues they deal with have converged in relation to all three types of regulation discussed here. There is also an urgent need for specialist regulation of the bus industry; this could take the form of a separate OFBUS or could be added to the responsibilities of the Rail Regulator now that the initially heavy burden of supervising the preparations for rail privatization has lessened somewhat. A note of caution for advocates of agency merger should be added, however, based on experience in the water industry. Here the separation of the economic regulator from the environmental regulator actually proved beneficial through forcing out into the open questions of the cost of quality. The recent merger of environmental regulators has itself been beneficial, but experience shows a strong case for maintaining a separate economic regulator and encouraging debate between them.

A related issue is that of communication between regulators and the adoption of a common set of financial rules and other principles; serious criticism has been levelled at them for the lack of such a common approach in the past.[78] As regards the financial rules, in particular those for valuing existing assets and estimating the cost of capital, there are signs of increasing debate and contact between the regulators, as illustrated in the exchanges between the gas and water regulators at the time of the setting of the TransCo price formula.[79] In addition, reports by the MMC provide a precedent for use in determining the correct approach, as has occurred with the report on Scottish Hydro-Electric in relation to the cost of capital. I shall in a moment make proposals which will limit the number of MMC references; however, these issues are precisely those best suited to general references to the MMC independent of proposals for licence amendment. Such references could be made by a number of regulators to ensure a common approach.[80] It may be useful also to develop common approaches to issues of social regulation, such as policy on disconnections and how to fund universal service; this would be appropriate for governmental policy guidance of the kind proposed in the previous section of this Chapter, or for agreement between the regulators themselves.

---

[78] Helm, n. 77 above, 28–9, 34–5.

[79] See OFGAS, *1997 Price Control Review: British Gas' Transportation and Storage: The Director General's Final Proposals* (1996), app. 7.

[80] Cf. Graham, n. 43 above, 48.

A further proposal has been the replacement of individual Directors General by regulatory commissions in order to avoid the problems of personalization which have been so criticized in the past.[81] One can understand the wish to have individual regulators able to push through increased competition against the wishes of the main regulated industries in the first phase of regulation. However, this phase has now passed, and that the use of commissions is practicable is illustrated by experience not only in North America but by that of the CAA and ITC; in none of these cases has the commission form impeded their work, and indeed the CAA was able to adopt a single-mindedly pro-competitive stance well before this developed elsewhere in civil aviation. The advantage of a commission is that it is an admission that regulation involves a plurality of approaches and of different skills, and membership should reflect it. What should not occur, however, is appointment of members of a commission to represent different interests, such as those of consumers, employees, and suppliers, as this would be a recipe both for regulatory paralysis and for conflicts which should be worked out in the open through consultation procedures being determined instead by closed bargaining within the commission.[82]

Another issue of importance is that of price-control mechanisms. We have seen consistently in this book both that price control has been far more complex than initially envisaged and that the regulators have been put in the difficult position of having to correct outrageously generous formulae set by government on privatization. It is also clear that, although in some cases the role of price controls has diminished with the development of competition, in others it seems likely to be permanent. It is also apparent that the expectation that a fixed formula will provide a long-term degree of security for the regulated firm is naïve; price controls are inevitably affected by the changing environment of political and social perceptions of distribution between utility shareholders, directors, and consumers. The procedural changes proposed above are intended among other things to improve the openness of the price-control process. Other proposals have concentrated on the substance of price control through suggesting that the existing RPI–X structure

---

[81] See *ibid.* 42–5; Hain, n. 70 above, 223; Souter, 'A Stakeholder Approach to Regulation' in Corry, Souter, and Waterson, n. 71 above, 7–99 at 84–6.

[82] Despite his strong support for a 'stakeholder' approach to regulation, Souter does not in fact advocate composition of commissions in this way; n. 81 above, 85.

be replaced by a form of profit-sharing derived from earlier methods of UK utility price control.[83] This book provides a number of arguments to support such a change; apart from the lack of simplicity and stability of RPI–X, it has become rapidly apparent that it involves investigation of all the issues associated with profit control elsewhere:

[a]ll regulators set price: the question is the basis upon which price is set. The key components are: the operating expenditure (OPEX); the capital expenditure (CAPEX); the asset valuation; and the cost of capital. In *all* regulatory systems, the regulators are required to adjudicate—implicitly or explicitly—on *all* of these items. The difference between the British price cap and the US rate-of-return regulation is not one of kind, but of degree. In this regard, price-cap regulation does not escape the informational problems of regulatory capture.[84]

Nevertheless, the proposed system of profit control does have problems of its own, notably through reducing (though not eliminating) the incentive for regulated industries to improve on efficiency targets, and in posing further informational problems for the regulator through the danger of excess profits being hidden to avoid the operation of profit control. It should also be stressed that the most serious problems of RPI–X have not been the result of the structure of the formula but of the over-generous content of the formulae set on privatization. Recent controls, notably for TransCo and electricity distribution, have been far tougher. The jury is still out, then, on the question of whether RPI–X is so discredited as to require replacement.

A further question also poses some serious difficulties; this is that of due process in the case of regulatory decisions. I have suggested earlier that there is much for us to learn from the participative procedures associated with US-style rule-making. However, the question remains whether other procedural rights should be offered to the regulated firm. The extent to which this can be achieved under existing legislation is limited; the best example is the establishment by OFTEL of an advisory panel on fair-trading matters to which disputes may be referred by either the regulator or the regulated firm, though the committee's findings could, formally at least, be

---

[83] Burns, P., Turvey, R., and Weyman-Jones, T., *Sliding Scale Regulation of Monopoly Enterprises* (Centre for the Study of Regulated Industries, London, 1995).
[84] Helm, n. 77 above, 21 (emphasis retained).

only advisory. Looking at matters more broadly, despite complaints of lack of regulatory due process by regulated enterprises, it is very apparent that regulatory firms and their shareholders were highly privileged over other interests in the procedures required under the utility privatization statutes. This reflected the view that regulation can be seen as a contract between government and the regulated firm, and is apparent in the fact that licences can be amended if the regulated firm agrees, irrespective of the views of others affected. Moreover, the most important procedural protection, that of a reference to the MMC, though made at the initiative of the regulator, is in practice made only where the regulated firm will not accept a proposed amendment, and not, for example, at the instance of a consumer group which objects to a change agreed between firm and regulator.

The regulatory contract approach has its advocates:

[g]iven the political nature of the sale and the attempt to entice shareholders who had little experience of the market there was a feeling that the prospectus would provide a binding commitment or bargain between Government and shareholders. . . . It was envisaged that it [regulation] would operate with a light touch, based on a number of simple and stable rules which would be revised at set intervals. . . . If one group develops legitimate expectations which are disappointed or there is continuing uncertainty about what are legitimate expectations then it becomes impossible for business to plan with confidence and regulators' actions amount to expropriation of shareholder wealth.[85]

It should by now be readily apparent that this vision is radically incompatible with the analysis in this book. Such a rule-based regime is unattainable in any of the types of regulation described, and, if regulation is an essentially pluralist activity with a variety of goals and interests affected, why should the shareholders be privileged over, say, consumers or even the workforce? All these will also have formed 'legitimate expectations' as a result of governmental statements at the time of privatization.

If my approach is accepted, it would suggest that the current system of licence amendment being subject to agreement with the regulated firm, or reference to the MMC if the firm does not accept it, needs to be replaced by a system which does not privilege the firm

---

[85] Veljanovski, C., *The Future of Industry Regulation in the UK* (European Policy Forum, London, 1993), 59–60.

over other participants in this way. Something of the sort has been recognized by Clare Spottiswoode, the Gas Regulator, with her suggestion that the Government should be able to call for an independent investigation by the MMC into important regulatory decisions.[86] To a large degree the system could be improved through the forms of participative mechanisms advocated earlier in this Chapter, but the question remains of how the discretion of the regulator is to be checked, both to ensure that the consultation process has taken place properly and that there is a proper evidential base for the decision. Currently checking is for the MMC, but apart from the problems of the privileging of the firm, it is doubtful whether it is well suited to this task. The time taken and the ability to open up a wide range of issues concerning the regulated firm means that there are strong incentives not to use this route; as Dieter Helm has argued, and as experience with the bus industry has underlined, the MMC is not really appropriate as an appellate body in individual cases, though it could play an important role in considering general references to set regulatory principles on such matters as how to approach evaluation of the asset base and of cost of capital.[87] The cumbersome nature of an MMC reference as part of licence amendment has indeed led to a greater use of less formal instruments such as codes to permit easier amendment, for example in electricity.

It is easier to suggest problems with the MMC than to design an alternative appeals mechanism, however. The current favourite suggestion is a modified procedure for appeal to the MMC, perhaps to a panel of members and perhaps limited to major issues; a model was afforded by the proposed tribunal to hear appeals from decisions of the Director General of Fair Trading in cases concerning anti-competitive agreements.[88] This however raises the questions of who can use this mechanism and of the scope of the appeal. In the case of the proposed tribunal, anyone with a sufficient interest or

---

[86] 'Watchdog Stirs Up a Storm Over Reform of Regulation', *Financial Times*, 18 Apr. 1995; Graham, n. 43 above, 38. A similar point about the need to avoid privileging the regulated firm is made by the Director General of Telecommunications in OFTEL, *Pricing of Telecommunications Services from 1997: OFTEL's Proposals for Price Control and Fair Trading* (1996), para. 3.25.

[87] Helm, D., 'Regulating in the Public Interest' in Corry, D. (ed.), *Profiting from the Utilities* (Institute for Public Policy Research, London, 1995), 10–22 at 21.

[88] See Graham, n. 43 above, 28–34, 46–7; Confederation of British Industry, n. 73 above; Department of Trade and Industry, n. 16 above, first item, ch. 5.

who represents persons with a sufficient interest would be able to apply to the tribunal, thereby giving wide rights of standing similar to those in judicial review; consumer groups would also be permitted to participate in the tribunal process and proceedings would normally be in public.[89] This is much more in line with the analysis presented in this book than are the current arrangements, but the question of the scope of appeal is more difficult. It would be near impossible to define a 'major' issue for appeal, and the proposed tribunal will be able to consider all except frivolous and or vexatious appeals. Moreover, if, as is proposed for the new tribunal, appeal is *de novo*, so that the appellate body can effectively retake the decision, this transfers the discretion of the regulator to the appellate body, although as the appeal is not to the minister it need not result in the use of appeals as a means of policy implementation, as occurred in the case of the CAA's predecessor discussed in Chapter 8. If appeal is limited to points of law or reasonableness, this on the other hand simply duplicates existing rights to seek judicial review or to apply to the court for its statutory equivalent.[90]

My conclusion is thus that, if the model of the proposed tribunal for anti-competitive agreement cases were to be adopted, it would be preferable to the existing arrangements by virtue of giving wider interests such as consumer groups the right to bring an appeal, but this may raise difficult questions of the scope of appeal. The alternative of judicial review is similarly open to a wider range of interests than at present in licence modification, but provides more limited grounds for overturning a decision. In the absence of any other obvious solution, either of these procedures seems to offer a better alternative means of checking the regulator's discretion than the current use of the MMC in individual licence modification cases. The rules on standing would mean that in either case other affected parties, not simply the regulated firm, will have access to a tribunal (if the same rules as those proposed were to be adopted) or to judicial review.[91] As we saw in our discussion of broadcasting regulation

[89] Department of Trade and Industry, *Tackling Cartels and the Abuse of Market Power: A Draft Bill*, n. 16 above, cls. 33(1) and *Explanatory Document*, n. 16 above, paras. 4.21, 4.25.
[90] Graham, n. 43 above, 46–7. For the statutory procedure available to the regulated firm in relation to enforcement action see, e.g., the Telecommunications Act 1984, s. 18.
[91] See, e.g., *R. v. Secretary of State for Foreign and Commonwealth Affairs, ex parte World Development Movement* [1995] 1 WLR 386.

in Chapter 9, where judicial review has been employed the courts seem to have successfully avoided second-guessing the substance of regulatory decisions. Finally, the *Mercury* case discussed in Chapters 2 and 3 suggests that legal challenge may increase anyway; recognizing it as the main means of checking regulatory discretion would not necessarily do more than to accept the inevitable.[92] Either of these solutions would remove the regulated firm's ability to force reference of licence amendments to the MMC, but compensation could be in the form of improved procedural protections at an earlier stage through developing the consultation process. The MMC would retain a role as a source of reports on general issues referred by the regulators; further openness could be developed by systematizing scrutiny of the regulators by Parliamentary committee.[93]

Conclusions

The conclusions to this book can be stated briefly. Regulation is not a simple process of mimicking market forces; it involves three very different functions, regulating monopoly, regulating for competition, and social regulation. None of them is straightforward; thus regulation of monopoly is now extremely similar to such regulation in the United States. The adoption of the RPI–X formula may have advantages in providing incentives for the firm to increase efficiency, but it does not necessarily simplify the process of price control; nor in practice has it been possible to restrict it to infrequent and fixed intervals. As a result we have a process which involves the same sort of decision-making as US utility regulation, but without the associated procedural protections. Nor will this type of regulation wither away, for important pockets of monopoly are likely to remain indefinitely. Regulation for competition is also more complex than was envisaged; the experience of leaving the bus industry to the general competition authorities has proved to be disastrous, and the opening up of domestic markets in the energy industries has required more regulatory activity, not less, both to secure fair competition between suppliers and to provide protections for less powerful consumers. Once more, this will not wither away, for both these tasks will continue into the policing of the

---

[92] *Mercury Communications Ltd* v. *Director General of Telecommunications* [1996] 1 All ER 575 (HL).

[93] For detailed proposals see Graham, n. 43 above.

markets once they have been established, and specialist regulators will have powerful advantages over the existing generalist competition authorities here as well.

Perhaps most surprisingly, important elements of social regulation have been identified amongst the regulatory initiatives discussed here. It has been suggested that this is not some arbitrary intervention in a regulatory regime properly devoted to the maximization of technical economic efficiency but at the heart of the regulatory task, a task which involves consideration of 'non-commodity values' as well as economic expertise.[94] Thus social concerns can be found in both the regulatory legislation and the common law; they are reinforced by European Community law and are powerfully developed in the concepts of *service public* characteristic of continental European administrative law. This means that it is incorrect to assume that regulators are necessarily carriers of a barren and socially-divisive consumerism, which 'is essentially an expression of the negative, one-dimensional view of citizenship favoured by adherents of New Right political theory', and that they neglect questions of access and entry rights to public services.[95] There has been much criticism of the regulators in this book, but it is certainly untrue to say that access issues have been ignored; indeed, issues of universal service have been much more openly addressed than under nationalization, and much firmer action has been taken to limit disconnections of service. What is needed is a clearer articulation and development of the social principles lying behind such action, and possible sources have been suggested earlier in this Chapter.[96]

My conclusion is, then, that the regulators are in a sense 'governments in miniature' and that their tasks cannot be reduced to any single logic. Their activity is essentially pluralist, both in the sense of there being a number of different regulatory rationales and in the sense that they need to respond to a number of interests, not

---

[94] See Stewart, R., 'Regulation in a Liberal State: The Role of Non-Commodity Values' (1983) 92 *Yale Law Journal* 1537–90.

[95] Ernst, J., *Whose Utility? The Social Impact of Public Utility Privatization and Regulation in Britain* (Open University Press, Buckingham, 1994), 192.

[96] For contributions to the debate about the relationship between consumerism and social rights intrinsic to citizenship see, e.g., Ranson, S., and Stewart, J., 'Citizenship and Government: The Challenge for Management in the Public Domain' (1989) XXXVII *Political Studies* 5–24; Plant, R., 'Citizenship, Rights and Welfare' in Coote, A. (ed.), *The Welfare of Citizens: Developing New Social Rights* (Institute for Public Policy Research, London, 1992), 15–29.

just that of the regulatory firm. This makes the concept of a 'regulatory contract' with the firm quite inappropriate. These considerations of course raise questions of accountability, and I have made suggestions for building on existing procedures to develop this, and also for the clearer articulation of principles of public service to emphasize that such principles do indeed fall within regulatory responsibilities.

Colin Scott has recently suggested that, in the context of the European Community:

[b]y the mid-1990s . . . it was arguable that Community utilities law and policy was entering a new phase in which concerns about integration of utilities markets through liberalization were being balanced by more co-ordinative and co-operative concerns, notably in respect of the protection and development of public service obligations and the co-ordination of trans-European networks.[97]

It may be that we shall witness something similar in relation to domestic regulation as well once the liberalization currently being planned has taken place. This book has suggested that there is nothing which puts such a role in principle beyond the capacities of the utilities regulators; indeed, their presence and policies have resulted in the availability of the necessary information for the first time which will make it possible to develop a more effective system of social protection, for all the criticisms made in this book. It is hoped that the suggested reforms of procedure and of substance proposed here could make the work of regulation both more publicly accountable and more able to grapple with a range of different approaches to the task, approaches both economic and social in inspiration.

---

[97] Scott, C., 'Changing Patterns of European Community Utilities Law and Policy: An Institutional Hypothesis' in Shaw, J., and More, G., *New Legal Dynamics of European Union* (Clarendon Press, Oxford, 1995), 193–215 at 193.

Index